Ireland and the United Kingdom: A Century of Relations (1921–2021)

STUDIES IN POLITICS, SECURITY AND SOCIETY
Edited by Stanisław Sulowski
Faculty of Political Science and International Studies
University of Warsaw

VOLUME 67

Szymon Bachrynowski

Ireland and the United Kingdom: A Century of Relations (1921–2021)

PETER LANG
Berlin · Bruxelles · Chennai · Lausanne · New York · Oxford

Bibliographic Information published by the Deutsche Nationalbibliothek
The Deutsche Nationalbibliothek lists this publication in the Deutsche Nationalbibliografie; detailed bibliographic data is available online at http://dnb.d-nb.de.

Library of Congress Cataloging-in-Publication Data
Names: Bachrynowski, Szymon, 1981- author
Title: Ireland and the United Kingdom: a century of relations (1921-2021) / Szymon Bachrynowski.
Description: Berlin; New York: Peter Lang, [2026] | Series: Studies in politics, security and society, 2199-028X ; vol. 67 | Includes bibliographical references and index.
Identifiers: LCCN 2026019698 (print) | LCCN 2026019699 (ebook) | ISBN 9783631947876 print | ISBN 9783631947883 epdf | ISBN 9783631950913 epub
Subjects: LCSH: Ireland--Relations--Great Britain | Great Britain--Relations--Ireland
Classification: LCC DA964.G7 B33 2026 (print) | LCC DA964.G7 (ebook)
LC record available at https://lccn.loc.gov/2026019698
LC ebook record available at https://lccn.loc.gov/2026019699

This publication was financially supported by Catholic Academy in Warsaw - Collegium Bobolanum.

Cover Image Source: Adobe Stock

ISSN 2199-028X
ISBN 978-3-631-94787-6 (Print)
ISBN 978-3-631-94788-3 (ePDF)
ISBN 978-3-631-95091-3 (ePUB)
DOI 10.3726/b23835

Published by Peter Lang GmbH, Berlin, Germany

info@peterlang.com

This publication has been peer reviewed.

www.peterlang.com

Contact for General Product Safety Regulation (GPSR): gpsr@peterlang.com

Contents

Special Ties Between Two British Isles—Britain and Ireland (Methodological Aspects, Hypotheses and Literature)

This monograph offers a comprehensive and historically grounded examination of British-Irish political relations, from the Anglo-Norman invasion of Ireland in 1169 to the post-Brexit environment of the early twenty-first century. While the historical scope of the study is extensive, particular analytical emphasis is placed on the modern and contemporary periods—specifically, from the Anglo-Irish Treaty of 1921 to the United Kingdom's withdrawal from the European Union between 2016 and 2020, and the subsequent political, legal, and diplomatic challenges that emerged between 2020 and 2025.

The core objective of the study is to trace the transformation of British-Irish political interactions within evolving frameworks of sovereignty, national identity, intergovernmental cooperation, and regional integration. At the heart of this analysis lies the argument that historical legacies remain central to shaping Anglo-Irish relations, yet contemporary shifts in international political architecture—most notably Brexit—have introduced new pressures and variables that fundamentally challenge the institutional resilience and diplomatic assumptions that had governed relations since the peace process of the late twentieth century.

The methodological approach adopted in this work is predominantly qualitative and historical-analytical. It is rooted in the systematic examination of a wide range of primary sources, including constitutional texts, parliamentary debates, intergovernmental treaties, legal judgments, official correspondence, and policy documents. These sources are interpreted through critical engagement with an interdisciplinary body of secondary literature encompassing political history, comparative politics, international relations, and legal scholarship. This interdisciplinary approach allows for a multifaceted understanding of the political evolution and institutional dynamics that have shaped the bilateral relationship between Ireland and the United Kingdom.

Particular attention is given to conceptual frameworks drawn from institutional theory, including path dependency and institutional evolution, which are vital for understanding the long-term consequences of political settlements such as the Good Friday Agreement. Constructivist approaches are also employed to examine how evolving conceptions of sovereignty and national identity have influenced political discourse and policymaking, especially in the context of competing unionist and nationalist narratives. In addition, this study uses comparative methods to analyze the divergent ways in which Ireland and the United Kingdom have responded to major geopolitical developments, such as European integration, the global financial crisis, and Brexit.

Of special significance is the role of the European Union, which since 1973 has served not only as an economic and political anchor but also as a structural framework within which British-Irish cooperation has taken place. The EU's influence in facilitating peaceful coexistence and shared regulation has been substantial, and its loss as a common framework following Brexit constitutes one of the most consequential changes to the bilateral relationship in recent history.

To guide the interpretive structure of this analysis, four interrelated scientific hypotheses are proposed.

(i) The first hypothesis posits that the United Kingdom's withdrawal from the European Union has significantly disrupted the institutional architecture of British-Irish relations, weakening key mechanisms of cooperation established under the Good Friday Agreement and contributing to greater political and constitutional instability in Northern Ireland.
(ii) The second hypothesis contends that despite the dislocations caused by Brexit, new opportunities for pragmatic engagement and diplomatic recalibration have emerged, particularly as both governments seek to preserve peace in Northern Ireland and safeguard economic stability across the islands.
(iii) The third hypothesis addresses the enduring influence of historical narratives and contested identities, arguing that these symbolic and

emotive dimensions continue to inform political decision-making and often obstruct technocratic or legalistic solutions, particularly in relation to the constitutional status of Northern Ireland.

(iv) The fourth hypothesis introduces the notion of growing asymmetry in diplomatic capacity and strategic positioning between Ireland and the United Kingdom in the post-Brexit period. While Ireland has increasingly relied on its EU membership and multilateral alliances to assert its influence and safeguard its interests, the UK's pursuit of unilateral policy paths has contributed to increased legal friction and institutional strain, as evidenced by the contentious passage of the Legacy and Reconciliation Bill and subsequent legal challenges initiated by the Irish government.

Although the book engages with developments from the medieval period through to the twenty-first century, its analytical focus lies primarily in the twentieth and twenty-first centuries. Historical overviews are included where necessary to illuminate structural continuities and ideological legacies, but the central lens remains political and diplomatic. The study is not intended to serve as an exhaustive chronological history, but rather as a thematically and analytically focused investigation into the evolution of bilateral relations and their intersection with broader questions of identity, sovereignty, and peacebuilding. Cultural and economic dimensions are considered where relevant, but they remain subordinate to the central concern with political architecture, legal frameworks, and intergovernmental diplomacy. The scope of the work is necessarily shaped by the unfolding nature of many of the processes under consideration—particularly Brexit and its aftershocks—which remain dynamic and, in some cases, unresolved. Nevertheless, by situating these recent developments within a deeper historical and theoretical context, the study contributes to a broader understanding of post-Brexit Europe, the future of divided societies, and the challenges of maintaining cooperative statecraft in an increasingly fragmented international system. The structure of the book's content is organized into four main chapters, along with an introduction and a conclusion.

Chapter One: *Anglo-Irish Relations Before Ireland's Independence (1169–1921)*

This foundational chapter provides a longue durée overview of the structural inequalities and political subjugation that defined early Anglo-Irish relations. Section 1.1 offers a two-phase analysis of Anglo-Irish relations from the Anglo-Norman invasion to the Act of Union, focusing on political domination, the Tudor conquest, and the imposition of religious uniformity under the Act of Supremacy. Section 1.2 examines Ireland's integration into the United Kingdom post-1801, with emphasis on Catholic emancipation, the rise of Irish nationalism, and the turbulent pathway to independence marked by the Easter Rising and the Anglo-Irish Treaty of 1921.

Chapter Two: Ireland and UK Political Relations from Anglo-Irish Treaty to EEC Accession (1921–1972)

This chapter addresses the evolving nature of bilateral diplomacy in the inter-war and post-war periods. Section 2.1 explores the contested legitimacy of the Treaty settlement, the rise of Fianna Fáil, Ireland's neutrality during WWII, and the long-term impact of constitutional change culminating in the Republic's proclamation in 1949. Section 2.2 assesses post-war economic and political interactions, emphasizing how both states transitioned from imperial legacies to modern sovereignty, and traces the early roots of European integration as a shared strategic goal.

Chapter Three: United Kingdom and Ireland, European Union, and Northern Ireland Peace Process (1973–2016)

This chapter focuses on the transformative influence of the European Community/EU and the overlapping trajectory of the Northern Ireland peace process. Sections 3.1 and 3.2 examine how EU membership fostered convergence and institutional dialogue. Sections 3.3 and 3.4 shift focus to the conflict in Northern Ireland, the multiparty negotiations of the 1990s, and the implementation of the Good Friday Agreement, underscoring the EU's role in facilitating cross-border cooperation, legal harmonization, and socio-political reconciliation.

Chapter Four: Brexit and British-Irish Political and Economic Relations after Brexit (2016–2025)

The final analytical chapter explores the deeply disruptive and still-evolving effects of Brexit. Section 4.1 analyses diverging public attitudes toward European integration in the UK and Ireland, while Section 4.2 investigates the complexities of the Brexit process itself, especially the Northern Ireland Protocol. Section 4.3 discusses the renewed constitutional debate around Irish unity and the political implications for Northern Ireland. Section 4.4 evaluates both the deterioration and redefinition of British-Irish diplomatic relations in the context of ongoing negotiations, border politics, and legal disputes.

An integral part of this study is a critical engagement with the relevant scholarly literature, which has profoundly informed the analytical framework and interpretive strategies of this monograph. The work of J. Bowyer Bell is particularly valuable in understanding the historical dimensions of political violence and the organizational dynamics of the Irish Republican movement. His in-depth studies of the IRA highlight the legacy of colonial subjugation and the emergence of militant nationalism as a response to institutional exclusion and cultural suppression. Tim Pat Coogan, one of the most prominent chroniclers of modern Irish history, provides a comprehensive narrative of Irish nationalism and the Northern Ireland conflict. His biographies and historical overviews, although occasionally marked by a nationalist perspective, offer significant insight into the ideological foundations of republican politics and the complexities of post-colonial state formation in Ireland, especially under the leadership of Éamon de Valera. Etain Tannam's contributions bring a vital theoretical dimension to the study of post-agreement British-Irish relations. Her work on intergovernmental cooperation and institutional design within the context of the Good Friday Agreement underscores the importance of structured, rules-based diplomacy in maintaining peace and stability. Tannam's analyses are particularly pertinent in assessing the institutional vulnerabilities exposed by Brexit and the declining capacity of pre-existing frameworks to manage cross-border disputes in its aftermath. Jon Tonge and Jennifer Todd provide essential perspectives on political identity, party transformation, and post-conflict governance in Northern Ireland. Tonge's research into the evolution of unionist and nationalist party platforms, especially within the Democratic Unionist Party (DUP) and Sinn Féin, offers a nuanced view of shifting political allegiances and the fragility of the power-sharing arrangements. Todd, by contrast, offers a more sociological and constructivist lens, exploring how symbolic boundaries, emotional attachments, and identity discourses shape conflict and reconciliation. Her work is instrumental in understanding the persistent cultural and ideological undercurrents that challenge technocratic and legalistic approaches to peacebuilding.

Together, these scholars and the others (e.g., Diarmuid Ferriter) form an interdisciplinary corpus that enriches the analysis of British-Irish relations by incorporating historical, political, legal, and sociological perspectives. Their research facilitates a deeper understanding of how the interplay of institutions, identities, and geopolitical shifts continues to shape one of Europe's most complex and historically charged bilateral relationships.[1] Context of history is introduced where necessary to clarify enduring structural patterns and ideological legacies, but the primary focus of the study remains political and diplomatic. Rather than offering a comprehensive chronological account, the analysis adopts a thematic and analytical approach to examine the evolution of bilateral relations and their intersection with broader issues of identity, sovereignty, and peacebuilding. Cultural and economic factors are addressed where they bear directly on these concerns, but they remain secondary to the core emphasis on political institutions, legal frameworks, and intergovernmental diplomacy. The scope of the study is inevitably shaped by the ongoing and unresolved nature of several key processes—most notably Brexit and its aftermath—which continue to evolve. By situating these contemporary developments within a deeper historical and theoretical framework, the study seeks to contribute to a wider understanding of post-Brexit Europe, the governance of divided societies, and the challenges of sustaining cooperative statecraft in an increasingly fragmented international order.

The concluding section synthesizes the study's findings in light of the four guiding hypotheses. It argues that the future of British-Irish relations will hinge on the capacity of both states to adapt institutional mechanisms and diplomatic practices to a post-Brexit order, while managing the historical weight of identity, sovereignty, and contested borders. In doing so, it underscores the need for continued engagement with supranational frameworks, legal cooperation, and peacebuilding paradigms.

---

1 Coogan, Tim Pat, *The IRA*. London: Fontana, 1970; Tannam, Etain, *Cross-Border Cooperation in Northern Ireland and the Republic of Ireland*. Basingstoke: Macmillan, 1999; Tonge, Jon, *The New Northern Irish Politics?* Basingstoke: Palgrave Macmillan, 2005; and *Northern Ireland*. Cambridge: Polity, 2006; Todd, Jennifer, with Joseph Ruane, *The Dynamics of Conflict in Northern Ireland: Power, Conflict and Emancipation*. Cambridge: Cambridge University Press, 1996; Ferriter, Diarmaid, *The Border: The Legacy of a Century of AngloIrish Politics*. London: Profile Books, 2019; and *The Revelation of Ireland: 1995–2020*. London: Profile Books, 2024.

Anglo-Irish Relations before Ireland's Independence (1169–1921)

1.1. Early Anglo-Irish relations: a political perspective (1169–1800)

1.1.1. Anglo-Irish relations after Anglo-Norman invasion until Act of Supremacy (1169–1534)

Foreign invaders have always highly regarded the island of Ireland. Throughout its history, Ireland has been conquered by a multitude of foreign powers (Vikings, Danes, Normans, Scots, Spaniards, Dutch, French, and last but not least—British).[2] First conquerors who have invaded the island were the Vikings. In the 700s, land scarcity in Scandinavia forced young Norsemen out to find fortune elsewhere. The first recorded Viking raid in Ireland occurred in 795, when a group of ferocious Norwegian warriors pillaged Lambay Island near modern-day Dublin. Over the next two hundred years, waves of Viking raiders plundered monasteries and towns throughout Ireland until they eventually settled. Between 914 and 922, Dublin, Cork, Waterford, Wexford and Limerick were all established. Exactly a century after the Normans had conquered England at the Battle of Hastings in 1066, the King of Leinster,

2 J. J. N. Gurk, *Ireland before the Norman Conquest*, "History Today," Volume 16, Issue 2, February 1966, "The Irish Post," https://www.irishpost.com/news/a-coveted-island-nine-times-ireland-has-been-invaded-conquered-and-occupied-104171; "CELT" database, *Nationality and Kingship in Pre-Norman Ireland*, https://celt.ucc.ie/nation_kingship.html [both accessed 20.05.2022]. See also: B. English, William the Conqueror and the Anglo-Norman Succession , "Historical Research," Vol. LXIV, No. 155, October 1991, pp. 221–236.

Diarmait Mac Murchada, was ousted by Ireland's high king—Ruaidrí Ua Conchobair.[3]

Nevertheless, the origins of centuries-old Anglo-Irish animosity can be traced to the historical events of the twelfth century. Then there was a conflict between England, controlled in 1066 by the Normans, and Celtic Ireland, which was also a feudal and Christian, but non-centralized state organism. The Anglo-Norman invasion of Ireland in 1169 was started by a multi-factor tangle of historical events.[4] The period between the end of Viking domination and the Anglo-Norman invasion of Ireland has received relatively small-scale scientific attention. Consequently, the twelfth century has long been seen as prologue to the conquest of Anglo-Norman knights and the arrival of the King of Anjou Henry II. The invasion of Ireland is often motivated by the fact that the Irish church was considered the outcast of the Christian community.[5]

The centuries-old separation of the Irish Catholic Church in Ireland from Western Christianity and the papacy indirectly influenced the invasion and its subsequent legitimation. The Irish Church was characterized by monasticism, secularization, decentralization and the rejection of episcopal authority. Ireland, although Christianized in the fifth century, remained isolated from the political, social and religious life of the early medieval Christian community. Essential that Pope Gregory VII (1073–1085) recognized the sovereignty of the papacy over Ireland, which was to be exercised by the bishops of the Archbishop of Canterbury.[6] This fact was preceded by the events of the 6th century, when

---

[3] See further: D. Ó Corráin, *Ireland before the Normans*, Dublin 1972; D. O Croinin, *Early Medieval Ireland, 400–1200 (Longman History of Ireland)*, Harlow 1995; R. Flechner, S. Meeder (eds.), *The Irish in Early Medieval Europe: Identity, Culture and Religion*, Montgomery 2016.

[4] C. Harper-Bill, E. van Houts (eds.), *A Companion to the Anglo-Norman World*, Suffolk 2003 pp. 19–42; K. L. Campbell, *Ireland's History: Prehistory to the Present*, Bloomsbury 2014, p. 59. Read more about Anglo-Normans and the times before the invasion: B. English, *William the Conqueror and Anglo-Norman Succession*, "Historical Research," Vol. LXIV, No. 155, October 1991, pp. 221–236.

[5] John A. Watt, *The Church in Medieval Ireland*, Dublin 1998; J. O'Beirne Ranelagh, *A Short History of Ireland*, Cambridge 2012, pp. 42–44. Further read: A. Cosgrove (ed.), *A New History of Ireland II: medieval Ireland*, Oxford 1987.

[6] Gregory VII, brother of Hildebrand (c. 1021–1085), pope, chaplain to the deposed Pope Gregory VI in 1046. For several years a monk at Cluny, abbot of St. Paul's Monastery in Rome, and later a cardinal. A supporter of the church reform camp, the de facto

Pope Gregory I appointed St. Augustine as the first Archbishop of Canterbury, extending his nominal authority over all the British Isles. In the second half of the twelfth century, the long-awaited reforms in the Irish Church took place. During the Synod of Kells in 1152,[7] a new organization of the church was approved. As a result, the Irish clergy recognized the sovereignty of the main archbishopric in Armagh, alienating Canterbury's sovereignty. The archbishops of Canterbury, unable to accept the loss of their influence on the events in Ireland, used the civil war for supremacy (for the title of *ard-ri*—high king) between the local Celtic rulers in the second half of the twelfth century, to strengthen their influence over the eastern part of the island, which hitherto recognized their sovereignty.[8]

The real lack of central political power in Ireland prompted the then pope—the only Englishman in the history of the papacy, Adrian IV, to surrender Ireland, under the bull Laudabiliter of 1155, to the jurisdiction of the King of England (from 1154) Henry II Plantagenet , Count of Anjou. Insomuch as Pope Adrian IV (Nicholas Breakspeare, 1154–1159) issued Papal Bull Laudabiliter of 1155, which granted Henry II permission to invade Ireland. While the validity of a papal bull is still a subject of debate among modern scholars, years after the invasion, Laudabiliter was often presented as a justification. This naturally led to another factor that influenced the Anglo-Norman conquest of Ireland, and the so-called papal legitimation of

---

head of papal policy since the pontificate of Nicholas II. Since then, the papal reform opposed the imperial reform of the church. In 1073 he was hailed by the clergy and the Roman people as pope. He sought to centralize the church under the absolute authority of the popes (*Dictatus Papae*). Known for his clash with German Emperor Henry IV (Canossa, 1077). Bound together monarchies threatened by German expansion: Poland, Hungary, Croatia and England, France and Spain. With the help of Gregory VII, the metropolis of Gniezno was rebuilt, and Boleslaw II the Bold obtained the royal crown from his legates. He was canonized in 1728. See more: W. Ullmann, *A Short History of the Papacy in the Middle Age*, London 2002, pp. 142–172.

7 More on synod of Kells: H. J. Lawlor, *A Fresh Authority for the Synod of Kells, 1152*, "Proceedings of the Royal Irish Academy: Archaeology, Culture, History, Literature," Vol. 36 (1921–1924), pp. 16–22; M. Holland, *The synod of Kells in ms BL, Add. 4783*, "Peritia," Volume 19, pp. 164–172.

8 See: S. Duffy, Ireland in the Middle Ages, London 1997; R. Frame, *Colonial Ireland, 1169–1369*, Dublin 1981; G. H. Orpen, *Ireland under the Normans, 1169–1333*, Dublin 1911; M. T. *Flanagan, Irish society, Anglo-Norman settlers, Angevin kingship*, Oxford 1989.

English rule over the island. In return for supporting the papal plans to subjugate the Irish Church, Henry II gained political power over their territory, despite doubts about the authenticity of Adrian IV's bull.

Initially, the ruler was not interested in ruling Ireland, but several years after the alleged bull was issued, Laudabiliter decided to claim the rights to jurisdiction over the island contained in it. Another principle of the conquest was the motive that led him to take action. This factor was the tense political situation in Ireland itself, that is, the aforementioned civil war between the local Celtic clans, and consequently—the lack of a central political power, but also the desire to conquer Irish lands by the Norman knights settled in England and Wales. Henry II only lacked a direct excuse to invade Ireland. This reason was provided by both the Irish and the Normans.[9]

By the twelfth century, Ireland had a shifting hierarchy of petty kingdoms and over-kingdoms. Few regional dynasties dominated the island, competing against each other for control. The Northern Uí Néill ruled the west and center of what is now Uladh (Ulster), with the east still controlled by the ancient Ulaid themselves. The kingsman of the Northern Uí Néill, the Southern Uí Néill, were Kings of Mide and Kings of Brega. The kingship of Laighean (Leinster) was by this time held by Uí Cheinnselaig dynasty, who had replaced the Uí Dúnlainge. A notable kingdom between Leinster and Munster was Osraige. Most of Munster was controlled by the Eóganachta and their principal royal sept the MacCarthy dynasty, with the remainder under the control of the Dál gCais or O'Brien dynasty of Thomond. North of Thomond and west of Ulster, Connacht's supreme rulers were the Uí Chonchobhair. Between Connacht and Ulster and Mide lay the Kingdom of Breifne. After losing the protection of Tír Eoghain (Tyrone) Chief, Muircheartach Mac Lochlainn, High King of Ireland, who died in 1166, Dermot MacMurrough (Irish: *Diarmaid Mac Murchada*), was forcibly exiled by a confederation of Irish forces under the new High King, Ruaidhrí Ó Conchobhair. Diarmaid fled first to Bristol and then to Normandy.[10]

---

9 F. X. Martin argued against using term "Norman invasion," he saw it rather as a "peaceful penetration." See: J. Maple, *Anglo-Norman Conquest of Ireland and the Irish Economy: Stagnation or Stimulation?*, "The Historian," Vol. 52, No. 1, November 1989, p. 61.

10 S. Duffy (ed.), *The World of the Galloglass: Kings, Warlords and Warriors in Ireland and Scotland 1200–1600*, Dublin 2007; "New World Encyclopedia," https://www.newworldencyclopedia.org/entry/Norman_Ireland [accessed 20.05.2022].

He sought and obtained permission from Henry II of England to use the latter's subjects to regain his kingdom. By 1167 MacMurrough had obtained the services of Maurice Fitz Gerald and later persuaded Rhŷs ap Gruffydd Prince of Deheubarth to release Maurice's half-brother Robert Fitz-Stephen from captivity to take part in the expedition. His greatest achievement was obtaining the support of Cambro-Norman Marcher Lord Richard de Clare, 2nd Earl of Pembroke, known as Strongbow. The first Norman knight to land in Ireland was Richard fitz Godbert de Roche in 1167, but it was not until 1169 that the main forces of Normans, along with their mercenaries which consisted of Welsh and Flemings landed in Loch Garman Wexford. Within a short time Leinster was regained, Port Láirge Waterford and *Baile Átha Cliath* (Dublin) were under Diarmaid's control, and he had Strongbow as a son-in-law, after offering his eldest daughter Aoife to him in marriage in 1170, and named him as heir to his kingdom. This latter development caused consternation to King Henry II of England, who feared the establishment of a rival Norman state in Ireland. Accordingly, he resolved to visit Leinster to establish his authority. Ireland eventually changed from acquiring lordship over men to colonizing it during the late twelfth and early thirteenth centuries.[11]

The Anglo-Norman invasion of the island (1167–1171) proceeded in three phases, and finally Henry II landed with a large army in Ireland in October 1171, while sealing his reign over Ireland by the Treaty of Windsor in 1175. The year 1175 marked the end of Celtic Ireland and the beginning of English rule over the island. English Governments in Ireland. In 1172, Pope Alexander III confirmed Henry's position as Lord of Ireland. On October 6, 1175, Henry II of England and High King Ruaidrí agreed to the Treaty of Windsor. The treaty divided Ireland into two spheres of influence: Henry was acknowledged as overlord of the Norman-held territory, and Ruaidrí was acknowledged as overlord of the rest of Ireland. Lordship of Ireland (Irish: *Tiarnas na hÉireann*), sometimes referred to retroactively as Norman Ireland, was the part of Ireland ruled by the King of England (styled as "Lord of Ireland") and controlled by loyal Anglo-Norman lords between 1177 and 1542. In 1169–1171, the Normans invaded Ireland and created the lordship.

[11] S. Duffy, *Medieval Ireland: An Encyclopedia*, Routledge, London 2005, pp. 776–777.

Lordship was a papal fief, granted to the Plantagenet kings of England by the Holy See, via Laudabiliter. As the Lord of Ireland was also the King of England, he was represented locally by a governor, variously known as the Justiciar, Lieutenant, Lord Lieutenant or Lord Deputy.[12] The treaty was viewed by Ruaidrí's side as a major achievement which might have seen the survival of Ireland as a distinct kingdom only loosely subordinate to England, but the new colonists in Ireland no doubt resented the compromise for this very reason. The Treaty was therefore soon breached, most dramatically by John de Courcy's spectacular conquest of the kingdom of Ulaid (east Ulster), beginning in February 1177. Within months Henry had abandoned any pretense of abiding by the Treaty of Windsor, and at the Council of Oxford later that year he granted away two more Irish provinces—Thomond and Desmond—to others of his barons, and appointed his own ten-year-old son John as Lord of Ireland. It would be another eight years before the latter visited Ireland, in 1185, by which time accommodation with the Irish had been abandoned and an all-out conquest was under way.[13]

Initially, the Normans controlled large parts of Ireland, including the entire east coast, from Waterford to eastern Ulster, as well as the west coast to Gaillimh (Galway) and Maigh Eo (Mayo). The most powerful forces in the land were the great Hiberno-Norman Earldoms such as the Geraldines, the Butlers and the de Burghs, who controlled vast territories which were almost independent of the governments in Dublin or London. The Lord of Ireland was King John, who, on his visits in 1185 and 1210, had helped secure the Norman areas from both the military and the administrative points of view, while at the same time ensuring that the many Irish kings were brought into his fealty; many, such as Cathal Crobhdearg Ua Conchobair, owed their thrones to him and his armies. The Normans also were fortunate to have leaders of the caliber of the Butler, Marshall, de Lyvet, de Burgh, de Lacy and de Braose families, as well as having the dynamic heads of the first families.

---

[12] P. Sposato, *The Perception of Anglo-Norman "modernity" and the Conquest of Ireland*, "In Comitatus: A Journal of Medieval and Renaissance Studies," vol. 40, 2009, pp. 25–44. See "Britannica" online: https://www.britannica.com/place/Ireland/The-14th-and-15th-centuries [accessed 20.05.2022].

[13] S. Duffy, *Narrative: 1169 and all that*, "History Ireland" Issue 3, May/June 2019, Volume 27.

Another factor was that after the loss of Normandy in 1204, John had much more time for Irish affairs, and he did so effectively even from a distance.[14]

A number of permanent changes were brought about by the Norman invasion and occupation of Ireland, including the establishment of walled borough towns, the construction of numerous castles and churches, the importation of tenants, and the expansion of agriculture and commerce. Normans changed Gaelic society with efficient land use, introducing feudalism to the existing native crop-sharing system. Feudalism never caught on in large parts of Ireland, but it was an attempt to introduce cash payments into farming, which was entirely based barter. Some Normans living further from Dublin and the east coast adopted the Irish language and customs and intermarried, and the Irish themselves also became irrevocably Normanized. The Hiberno-Normans then suffered from a series of events in the fourteenth century that slowed, and eventually ceased, the spread of their settlement and power. In the first place, Gaelic lords repeatedly attacked the English lordships in rebellious acts. For the Gaelic kings to defend their territories against Norman armored knights, they changed tactics after pitched battles with Norman knights. They started to rely on raids against resources, and surprise attacks. This stretched the resources of the Normans, reducing their number of trained knights, and often resulted in the chieftains regaining territory.[15]

Initially, the Anglo-Norman rule in Ireland did not significantly affect its Celtic people. The area of the actual rule of the Normandy feudal lords extended only to the so-called *Pale*.[16] Aside from this territory, English sovereignty over the Celtic people can only be described as nominal. There is a

---

14 See: C. Veach, "Conquest and Conquerors," in Brendan Smith (ed.), *Cambridge History of Ireland, Volume 1: Medieval Ireland, 650–1550*, Cambridge 2018, pp. 157–181; R. Roche, *The Norman Invasion of Ireland*, https://wiki.acervolima.com/norman-invasion-in-ireland [accessed 20.05.2022].

15 See: M. T. Flanagan, *Hiberno-Papal Relations in the Late Twelfth Century*, "Archivium Hibernicum," Vol. 34 (1977), pp. 55–70.

16 The Pale (Irish: *An Pháil*) or the English Pale (*An Pháil Shasanach* or *An Ghalltacht*) was the part of Ireland directly under the control of the English government in the Late Middle Ages. It had been reduced by the late fifteenth century to an area along the east coast stretching from Dalkey, south of Dublin, to the garrison town of Dundalk. The inland boundary went to Naas and Leixlip around the Earldom of Kildare, toward Trim and north toward Kells. In this district, many townlands have

consensus among researchers that it was not yet possible to speak of a cultural expansion by the invaders, the opposite was actually happening, namely the Celticization of the Anglo-Normans. In order to prevent this from happening, the English established in 1264 an Irish parliament, modeled on its own counterpart, which was to take care of the interests of the Anglo-Norman conquerors. However, this Parliament did not represent the majority of the Irish people. As a result of his actions, in 1366, anti-Irish in their overtone acts,[17] called the Statutes of Kilkenny, were passed. They were to prevent anarchy on the island. This state was a consequence of the Anglo-Scottish War in the first half of the fourteenth century, as well as the progressive *Celticization* of the influx of Anglo-Norman people. The last pre-reform act of the will of the English legislator was to limit the role of the Irish parliament in the form of the so-called Poynings' laws which occurred in 1485 during the reign of Henry VII Tudor.[18]

A series of events occurred during the fourteenth century that slowed, and eventually halted, the spread of the Anglo-Norman settlement and power on the island, and curtailed their legislative arbitrariness on the island by making the local Anglo-Norman feudal lords dependent on the king, which was still stronger and more independent. Firstly, numerous rebellious attacks were launched by Gaelic lords upon the English lordships. Having lost pitched battles to Norman knights, to defend their territory the Gaelic's now had to change tactics, and deal with the charging armored knights. In an effort to protect resources, they started relying on raids and surprise attacks. This

---

English or French names, the latter associated with Norman influence in England. See "Britannica" online: https://www.britannica.com/place/The-Pale [accessed 20.05.2022].

17 The authorities in Pale became so concerned about the *Gaelization* of Ireland that in 1367 the Parliament in Kilkenny passed a special law (known as the Kilkenny Statutes) prohibiting people of English descent from speaking Irish, wearing Irish clothes, or intermarrying with Irish people. See: P. W. Joyce, *Concise History of Ireland*, Dublin 1910, pp. 260–274;

18 See more: A. E. Crowley, *Law and the Irish Language / An dlí agus an Ghaeilge: ceachtanna staire. An tUltach*, Leeds 2014, pp. 1–6; https://www.parliament.uk/about/living-heritage/evolutionofparliament/legislativescrutiny/parliamentandireland/overview/poynings-law/ [accessed 20.05.2022].

stretched their sources of the Normans, reducing their number of trained knights, and often resulted in the chieftains regaining territory.[19]

The high point of the Norman lordship[20] was the creation of the Irish parliament in 1297, following the Lay Subsidy tax collection of 1292—the first Papal Taxation register was compiled in 1302–1307. The Lordship of Ireland was a period of feudal rule in Ireland beginning in 1171, during which time the King of England was automatically also "Lord of Ireland." Henry II arrived for a seven-month stay with a large army to assume control of the situation (Strongbow and the other Norman lords) and to set himself up in the role of the protector against the plundering Norman Barons. For the next century the Normans fought to establish themselves throughout Ireland, but they were never wholly successful because of the Irish resistance. Instead, many of the Normans who had succeeded in establishing themselves among the Irish had taken Irish wives and adapted to Irish culture so well that it seemed that they were "more Irish than the Irish themselves." In the late twelfth and early thirteenth centuries a change from acquiring lordship over men to colonizing land followed. By establishing borough towns, castles, and churches, importing tenants, and increasing agriculture and commerce, the Cambro-Normans brought about many changes.

In 1297 the British king set up the Irish Parliament,[21] based on Norman laws and English practices, in order to collect taxes from the Irish people. As the main "tax-payers" were the clergy, merchants and landowners, these were the people who could participate in the parliament. The parliament had the effect of lessening the power of Brehon Law and putting the power into the hands of those with money and ties to the British Crown. The Domesday Book was similar to the census and list of properties for the first time in Irish history. The Hiberno-Normans then suffered from a series of events in the

---

[19] See further: B. Smith (ed.), *Britain and Ireland, 900–1300: Insular Responses to Medieval European Change*, Cambridge 1999; A. Cosgrove (ed.), *A New History of Ireland: Volume II, Medieval Ireland 1169–1534*, Oxford 2008; B. Smith, T. Bartlett (eds.), *The Cambridge History of Ireland: Volume 1, 600–1550*, Cambridge 2018.

[20] See further: J. F. Lydon, *The Lordship of Ireland in the Middle Ages*, Toronto 1972, pp. 82–119; https://sites.google.com/site/sukirishculture/cli/normans [accessed 2.06.2022].

[21] See: R. Frame, *"Les Engleys Nées en Irlande": The English Political Identity in Medieval Ireland*, "Transactions of the Royal Historical Society," Vol. 3 (193), pp. 83–103; https://www.libraryireland.com/Atlas/XXVI-Anglo-Irish-Lords.php [accessed 2.06.2022].

1300s that slowed, and eventually ceased, the spread of their settlement and power. Firstly, numerous rebellious attacks were launched by Gaelic lords upon the English lordships. Having lost pitched battles to Norman knights, to defend their territory the Gaelic chieftains now had to change tactics, and deal with the charging armored knights. They started to rely on raids against resources, and surprise attacks. This stretched Norman resources, reduced the number of trained knights, and often led to the chieftains regaining territory. Additionally, the Norman colonists in Ireland were deprived of financial support from the English monarchy to a large extent because both Henry III and Edward I (who were more concerned with the events occurring in England, Wales, Scotland and the continental domains) lacked direction. Their ability to hold territory was limited as a result. Furthermore, the Normans' position deteriorated due to divisions within their own ranks. These caused outright war between leading Hiberno-Norman lords such as the de Burghs, FitzGeralds, Butlers and de Berminghams. Finally, the division of estates among heirs split Norman lordships into smaller, less formidable units—the most damaging being that of the Marshalls of Leinster, which split a large single lordship into five.[22]

Politics and events in Gaelic Ireland served to pull the settlers deeper into the orbit of the Irish. This at times resulted in allying them with one or more indigenous rulers against other Normans. Hiberno-Norman Ireland was heavily influenced by several events in the fourteenth century. Irish lords rallied against the English presence in Ireland in 1315 after Edward Bruce of Scotland invaded Ireland.[23] Although Bruce was eventually defeated by the Anglo-Irish forces in Ireland at the Battle of Faughart, near Dundalk, his troops caused a great deal of destruction, especially in the densely settled

---

[22] See further: I. Warntjes, *Regnal succession in early medieval Ireland*, "Journal of Medieval History," vol. 30, 2004, pp. 377–410.

[23] See: C. McNamee, *The Wars of the Bruces: Scotland, England and Ireland 1306–1328*, Edinburgh 1997; W. Johnston, *1300–1450: The Norman Decline*, https://www.wesley-johnston.com/users/ireland/past/history/12501450.html; P. Dryburgh, *The end of the Bruce Invasion of Ireland*, 1318, https://blog.nationalarchives.gov.uk/end-bruce-invasion-ireland-1318/ [both accessed 30.05.2022]. See also: B. Smith, *The Bruce Invasion and County Louth*, 1315–18, "Journal of the County Louth Archaeological and Historical Society," Vol. 22, No. 1 (1989), pp. 7–15; R. Frame *The Bruces in Ireland, 1315–18*, Irish Historical Studies, Vol. 19, No. 73 (March, 1974), pp. 3–37; J. Lydon, *The Impact of the Bruce Invasion, 1315–27*, in: Art Cosgrove (ed.), *A New History of Ireland: Volume II, Medieval Ireland 1169–1534*, Dublin 2008, pp. 275–302.

area around Dublin. The conflict of the previous three years had however led to a further weakening of central government control over Ireland. In this chaotic situation, local Irish lords won back large amounts of land that their families had lost since the conquest and held them after the war was over. A few English partisans like Gilbert de la Roche turned against the English king and sided with Bruce, largely because of personal quarrels with the English monarchy. The second was The European famine of 1315 to 1317, which also affected Ireland. The Irish ports were unable to import wheat and other crops, or other foods, as none were available to buy. As a result of the Bruce Invasion, there were widespread crop burnings.[24] The third was the murder of William Donn de Burgh, 3rd Earl of Ulster in June 1333. This resulted in his lands being split in three among his relations, with the ones in Connacht starting the Burke Civil War, rebelling against the Crown and becoming new Irish clans. This meant that virtually all of Ireland west of the Shannon was lost to the Dublin administration. It would be well over two hundred years before the McWilliam Burkes, as they were now called, were again allied with the Dublin administration. In Ulster the O'Neill dynasty accede and renamed Clandeboye in the earldom's lands in County Down, and in 1364 they assumed the title King of Ulster. The fourth was calamity for the medieval English presence in Ireland was the Black Death, which arrived in Ireland in 1348. Because most of the English and Norman inhabitants of Ireland lived in towns and villages, the plague hit them far harder than it did the native Irish, who lived in more dispersed rural settlements. A celebrated account from a monastery in Cill Chainnigh (Kilkenny) chronicles the plague as the beginning of the extinction of humanity and the end of the world. The plague was a catastrophe for the English habitations around the country and, after it had passed, Gaelic Irish language and customs came to dominate the country again. The English-controlled area shrank back to the Pale, a fortified area around Dublin. In the background the Hundred Years' War of 1337–1453 between the English and French dynasties drew off forces that could have protected the Lordship from attack by autonomous Gaelic and Norman lords.[25]

---

24 https://www.tcd.ie/medieval-history/assets/pdf/bruceinvasion.pdf [accessed 23.11.2022].

25 R. Kee, *Ireland: A History*, London 1982. See also: "CAIN" database, *A Chronology of Key Events in Irish History*, https://cain.ulster.ac.uk/othelem/chron/ch1169-1799.htm [accessed 2.06.2022].

Gaelic revival was also triggered by political and personal grievances against the Hiberno-Normans, particularly the impatience of procrastination and the atrocities caused by successive famines. When the Irish were displaced from fertile areas, they were forced to farm for their subsistence on marginal lands, leaving them without a safety net during years of poor harvest (such as 1271 and 1277) or years of famine (virtually all of 1311–1319). Outside of Pale, the Hiberno-Norman lords adopted Irish language and customs, gaining the title Old English, and, in words coined in later historiography, became "more Irish than Irish themselves." They sided with the indigenous Irish in political and military conflicts with England in the centuries following the Reformation, and generally remained Catholic afterward. However, since the government in Dublin had little real power, the Statutes had little effect. Throughout the fifteenth century, these trends progressed rapidly, and central power continued to decline. The English monarchy itself fell into turmoil in the last phase of the Hundred Years' War until 1453 and the Wars of the Roses (1460–1855), as a result of which the direct involvement of English people in Ireland was greatly reduced. Successive kings of England delegated their constitutional authority to the mighty counts of Fitzgerald of Kildare, who maintained a balance of power through military force and wide-ranging alliances with lords and clans. This in effect made the English Crown even more distant from the realities of Irish politics. At the same time, local Gaelic and Gaelic lords expanded their powers at Pale's expense, creating a policy completely alien to English methods, and which was not completely overthrown until the Tudor re-conquered Ireland.[26]

As a result of the Norman invasion of Ireland, the power and influence of the English crown in Ireland had fluctuated, but at no time could it be said to have exerted total control. Such a situation was however to witness a significant change with the succession of the Tudor dynasty to the throne of England. This new approach was to be based on the need to enlarge the power and influence of the crown throughout Ireland by means of a powerful and centrally controlled administration. Although at times various methods were to be adopted to achieve such an objective there remained

[26] B. Smith, *Disaster and Opportunity: 1320–1450*, in B. Smith, T. Bartlett (eds.), *op. cit.*, Cambridge 2018, pp. 244–271. D. Edwards, *Beyond Reform: Martial Law & the Tudor reconquest of Ireland*, "History Ireland," Issue 2, Summer 1997, Volume 5.

throughout a determination that in the future Ireland would be subject to strong government under the crown. The pursuit of this goal was however to have implications for those groups in Ireland who had previously benefited from the crown remaining weak. In particular there were those Anglo-Irish lords and Gaelic chiefs who, although nominally loyal to the English king, had retained a measure of independence that had allowed them to pursue their own objectives. If anything the picture in Ireland was then to become further complicated by the break down in relations between the Papacy and Henry VIII. Later as this chasm widened with the advent of the Protestant reformation in the sixteenth century, people in Ireland were increasingly faced with a choice whereby their political loyalty to the English crown was also measured in terms of their religious faith. Not surprisingly such developments were to impact on the future development of events in Ireland.[27]

1.1.2. Anglo-Irish relations after Act of Supremacy until Act of Union (1534–1801)

In political terms, law, later referred to as Poynings' Law was very important factor in Anglo-Irish relations in the early renaissance period. It was enacted by the Irish parliament in 1494–1495 and had far-reaching effects on subsequent Irish parliamentary history up to 1782. It was Poynings' Law that laid the foundation for a peculiar system of legislative procedure that prevented the Irish parliament from developing on a parallel line with the English parliament. It prescribed conditions to be observed by the Irish executive, with regard to the summoning and proceedings of the legislature, which were seldom satisfactory to both parties at the same time, and resulted in protracted attempts by each in turn to have the law altered in accordance with changes in their own character, circumstances and interests. The function and interpretation of the law passed through a number of distinct phases, and it was only in the later phases that it came to be regarded as a hated symbol of the subordination of the Irish parliament. Under the terms of Poynings' Law, all Irish Bills had to be submitted by the English chief governor in Ireland to the King and Privy Council, via the English Parliament. There they could be amended and approved, or rejected. Although delegates from the

27 "CAIN" database, *op. cit.*, https://cain.ulster.ac.uk/othelem/chron/ch1169-1799.htm [accessed 2.06.2022].

Irish Parliament could influence each proposal as it was debated in the Privy Council, the final form of each Bill was effectively decided in the English Parliament. Beginning with the 1536 Protestant Reformation, King Henry VIII went even further. Church legislation from the English Reformation Parliament was extended to Ireland, and in 1541 Henry upgraded it from a lordship to a full kingdom. The Irish parliament "most willingly and joyously" consented to a Bill conferring on him the title King of Ireland.[28] Poynings' Law stated that no legislative activity of the Irish parliament could have binding legal force without prior approval in England. Practically, it was an English weapon against any Irish independent legislative activity.[29]

In religious terms, the Reformation, initiated in England by Henry VIII Tudor with the Act of Supremacy of 1534 and commonly known as the Anglican Reformation or the emancipation of the Church of England from the jurisdiction of the Roman Church was crucial date in the history of the Anglo-Irish relations. For Ireland, a very important date became 1541,[30] when Henry VIII proclaimed himself its king. Firstly, a Protestant Church of Ireland was established, which, although a minority, was a very important institutional determinant of the future centuries-long Protestant hegemony. It was a situation where a nominally pro-Protestant minority, supported by the governments in London, exercised power over a lone Catholic majority. Secondly, already during the reign of Henry VIII, plans were set up for Protestant colonization on the island, which involved the eviction of their Catholic owners from their own lands. Thirdly, thanks to the two factors mentioned above, the Reformation in England and Scotland,[31] and the Protestant colonizing expansion that followed, a state of conflictual majority-minority

---

[28] See: R. Dudley Edwards, T. W. Moody, *The History of Poynings' Law : Part I, 1494–1615*, "Irish Historical Studies," Volume 2 , Issue 8 , September 1941 , pp. 415–424; https://www.parliament.uk/about/living-heritage/evolutionofparliament/legislativescrutiny/parliamentandireland/overview/poynings-law [accessed 2.02.2023].

[29] See: J. Kelly, *Poynings' law and the making of law in Ireland, 1660–1800*, Dublin 2006, passim.

[30] D. B. Quinn, *Henry VIII and Ireland, 1509–34*, "Irish Historical Studies," Vol. 12, No. 48 (Sep., 1961), pp. 318–344; "History" portal, https://www.history.com/news/henry-viii-divorce-reformation-catholic-church; https://www.rmg.co.uk/stories/topics/why-did-henry-viii-break-rome [accessed 13.01.2023].

[31] N. Davies, *The Isles. A History*, Oxford 1999, p. 559.

relations was created in Ireland and later, especially in the province of Ulster. The unification of the Protestant kingdoms of England and Scotland in 1707 strengthened the hegemonic position of the Protestant minority in Ireland.

Since England—Wales was incorporated into England in 1536—and Scotland were united by a real union, the Kingdom of Ireland remained connected to the emerging British monarchy only by a personal union. This situation lasted until 1801, when Ireland was incorporated into this union as the United Kingdom of Great Britain and Ireland.[32] Protestant domination was evidenced by the Banishment Act of 1697, which officially banned the Catholic Church from operating on the island. The Oaths Acts, on the other hand, prevented Catholics from holding any office.[33] Religious and legal discrimination was also followed by economic discrimination. Protestants owned most of the land. Depriving the agricultural population of Ireland of the right to own land was a state of mutual disadvantage, since it gave rise, in addition to religious resentment, to economic hatred. Henceforth, these two factors, denominational and economic, intensifying mutual prejudice between the two communities, remained correlated. The political monopoly in Ireland was held only by Protestants, including mainly large landowners and the senior clergy of the Protestant Anglican Church in Ireland (*Church of Ireland*). Among the Protestant minority, it was only a small group that held real power. Practically throughout the seventeenth century, various types of armed uprisings took place in Ireland, which were pacified by England,

---

32 Act of Union 1707: https://www.parliament.uk/about/living-heritage/evolutionofparliament/legislativescrutiny/act-of-union-1707; Act of Union 1800: https://www.parliament.uk/about/living-heritage/evolutionofparliament/legislativescrutiny/parliamentandireland/collections/ireland/act-of-union-1800

33 See: S. Bachrynowski, *Między angielskim lwem a Irlandzką harfą. Myśl polityczna Irlandzkiego Ruchu Republikańskiego* [*The Political Thought of IRM – Irish Republican Movement*], Kalisz 2009, pp. 24–25; W. Konarski, *Pragmatycy i idealiści. rodowód, typologia i ewolucja ugrupowań politycznych nacjonalizmu irlandzkiego w XX wieku* [*The origins, typology and evolution of the political parties of Irish nationalism in the 20th century*], Warszawa-Pułtusk, 2001, pp. 62–63. The details of the Tudor Revolution and the Reformation in the British Isles read in: G. R. Elton, *The Tudor Revolution in Government*, Cambridge 1953, passim. The Reformation was also adopted in Scotland in the form of Presbyterianism, as well as in Cornwall, while in Ireland it largely failed. A very detailed description of the course of the Reformation in Britain and Ireland was presented by F. Heal, *Reformation in Britain and Ireland*, Oxford 2005, passim.

these events were a prelude to future national liberation uprisings in the eighteenth and nineteenth centuries. There were several Irish rebellions against England in the seventeenth century, including The 1641 Rebellion: This rebellion began in October 1641,[34] when a group of Irish Catholics, led by Rory O'More, staged an uprising against English and Scottish settlers in Ireland. The rebellion was sparked by a fear that the English were planning to dispossess the Irish of their land. The rebellion quickly spread throughout the country, and by the following year, most of Ireland was in open revolt. On October 22, 1641, a rebellion in Ireland triggered the onset of a decade of civil war, invasion and conquest. The colonial authorities thwarted an attempt to seize Dublin Castle, but could not prevent Catholic insurgents from capturing strategic strongholds in Ulster. Over the winter of 1641 and spring of 1642, the rebellion spread to engulf the rest of the country. The rising was accompanied by incidents of extreme violence as Catholics attacked, robbed and murdered their Protestant neighbors. The Protestants retaliated with indiscriminate attacks on the Catholic civilian population during one of the most brutal periods of sectarian violence.

Second revolt was the Cromwellian Conquest: In 1649, Oliver Cromwell, the leader of the English Parliamentarian forces, invaded Ireland with the goal of crushing the rebellion. The Cromwellian Conquest was a brutal campaign that saw the Irish population suffer greatly. It resulted in the deaths of thousands of Irish people and the confiscation of their land. And the third revolt was The Williamite War: This war, which began in 1689, was fought between the forces of King William III of England and the forces of King James II, who had been deposed in the Glorious Revolution of 1688. The war was fought on Irish soil, and many Irish people fought on both sides. The war ended in 1691 with a victory for William III. These rebellions were all driven by a desire to resist English domination of Ireland, and to assert Irish autonomy and independence. They were also driven by religious

---

[34] See: J. Ohlmeyer et al., *Ireland: 1641: Contexts and reactions*, Manchester 2013, passim; E. Hoya, *Provocation, Premeditation, and Pandemonium: The Irish Rebellion of 1641*, published online: https://scholar.smu.edu/cgi/viewcontent.cgi?article=1003&context=weil_ura [accessed 10.03.2023].

differences, with Irish Catholics often fighting against Protestant English and Scottish settlers.[35]

English (British since the Act of 1707) rule in Ireland in the eighteenth century not only did not weaken the island's colonization impulse, but actually intensified it. Originally Henry VIII's decision to declare himself head of the Church in England was the real challenge to the Catholic identity of the Irish. As he and later English kings became increasingly assertive in demonstrating their control over Ireland, they insisted that the Irish adhere to the established church of the realm. While the plantation in the seventeenth century brought some English settlers who identified with the established Church in England, most Irish continued to identify with their Catholic faith. The plantation period was characterized by the arrival of many Protestant dissenters, anxious to avoid the necessity of conforming to the established church in England. Presbyterians from Scotland were the largest single group in Ireland, but Quakers and other dissenters also settled in Ireland. These dissenting groups kept their dissenting faiths while maintaining their political loyalties to Britain. Meanwhile, the indigenous Irish attempted to retain their Catholic faith in spite of the proselytizing efforts of many Protestants. Thus, a division of religious belief and identification coincided with differing political allegiances in the aftermath of the Plantation. This reality allowed the connection of Catholicism and Irishness in the nineteenth century when Irish nationalism began to mobilize in its modern form.[36]

As T. J. White writes, in the case of Ireland, political independence coincided with religious independence. Such authors as Irene Whelan even appraise the revival of Catholicism in the nineteenth century as a response to the religious revival among Protestants in the early nineteenth century.[37] Moreover, agreeing with the opinion of the aforementioned White and

---

[35] See further about XVII century conflicts within Ireland: J. J. Cronin, P. Lenihan, *Wars of Religion, 1641–1691*, in: J. Ohlmeyer (ed.), *Cambridge History of Ireland, Volume 1I: 1550–1730*, Cambridge 2018, pp. 246–272.

[36] See: T. J. White, *The Impact of British Colonialism on Irish Catholicism and National Identity: Repression, Reemergence, and Divergence*, "Études irlandaises," 35–1, 2010, pp. 21–37.

[37] I. Whelan, *The Bible War in Ireland: The Second "Reformation" and the Polarization of Protestant-Catholic Relations, 1800–1840*, University of Wisconsin Press, Madison 2005, passim.

Whelan, the author is willing to admit that the main factor in the emergence of the republican (or wider: nationalist) movement was meant be the British (more precisely: Norman-English, earlier or Anglo-Scots, later) colonial interference in Ireland and its consequences, and the direct impulse to undertake political and military actions by the republicans was paradoxically Great French Revolution and its secular ideas.[38] T. J. White continues that much of the era of colonization is characterized by the cultural domination by imperial powers over the subjugated people's beliefs and religious practices. The dominance of the colonies was based on a cultural predisposition or rationalization for subjugation, as several works have indicated. In spite of the fact that imperialism may have created colonies, it inevitably led to the creation of resistance to that dominance. Those who rebelled against colonization sought to end what they perceived as unjust and inhumane domination. Even if many attempted to conform to the new culture of the imperialist, they were rejected because of their race, status, or ethnic origin. The very logic of imperial domination engendered the response of resistance and, ultimately, the drive for national self-determination and an end to colonial rule. An attempt to reinvent a Gaelic culture, preserve a Catholic religious identity, and revitalize Catholic religious practice led to the development of Irish nationalism and the rebirth of Catholicism during the nineteenth century. These actions were influenced by the reaction against British imperialism and the revival of Catholicism. It is important to acknowledge that the development of Irish nationalism and the rebuilding of the Irish Church, both physically and spiritually, are highly interrelated processes. As in other colonial settings, the means by which nationalism emerged and engaged society was based on a desire to achieve independence.[39]

As a diocesan structure gradually evolved with bishops assuming increasing authority, the Church of Ireland traces its history to St. Patrick's early Irish Church, which was primarily monastic in nature. In 1534, the English Parliament declared King Henry VIII to be head of the Church of England in response to the refusal of the Pope to grant an annulment of his marriage to Catherine of Aragon. Two years later, the Irish Parliament declared him

---

[38] S. Bachrynowski, *Między angielskim lwem a Irlandzką harfą…* [*The Political Thought of IRM – Irish Republican Movement…*], op. cit, p. 11.

[39] T. J. White, op. cit., p. 4.

head of the Church of Ireland; Henry VIII was Lord of Ireland at that time and was subsequently styled King of Ireland from 1542 onwards. Initially the dispute was a jurisdictional one and while Henry desired independence from the Papacy, he was theologically catholic. King Edward VI (1547–1553) and Queen Elizabeth I (1558–1603), two of Henry VIII's successors, were more reform-minded and introduced Protestantism to both the Church of Ireland and the Church of England during their reigns. In 1536 Henry VIII had the Irish Parliament declare him head of the Irish Church. When the Church of England traveled in a more Protestant direction under Edward VI so too did the Church of Ireland. All but two of the Irish bishops accepted the Elizabethan Settlement and there is therefore continuity and Apostolic succession in the Church of Ireland, separate from that of the Church of England and the doubts raised by the consecration of Matthew Parker as Archbishop of Canterbury. The established church in Ireland underwent a period of more radical Calvinist doctrine than occurred in England.[40]

The Reformation split the Irish Church. The established Church of Ireland was Protestant, and state approved and supported. Although the Roman Catholic Church was regarded with hostility and suspicion by the authorities, it was nevertheless supported by the majority of people, particularly outside Dublin, where the crown's authority was weakest. Each Church maintained that it was the authentic successor of the pre–Reformation Irish Church. The Plantations of Ulster in 1610 saw the introduction of Presbyterianism to the island of Ireland. The fourth major Christian Church in Ireland today—the Methodist Church—dates from the first visit to Ireland by John Wesley in 1747. However, the delay in providing scripture and liturgy in the vernacular of the majority of the population, caused a rift between the English-speaking minority who mostly adhered to the reformed church or to Presbyterianism and the Irish-speaking majority who remained faithful to the Latin liturgy of Catholicism which thus remained the majority denomination in Ireland. As before the Reformation, some clergymen of the Church of Ireland sat as Lords Spiritual in the Irish House of Lords; under the provisions of the Act of Union 1800, one archbishop and the three bishops chosen by rotation

---

40 See earlier history of Church in Ireland: C. Ó Clabaigh, *The Church, 1050– 1460*, in: *The Cambridge History of Ireland*, op. cit., vol. 1, pp. 355–385 and https://www.cs.mcgill.ca/~rwest/wikispeedia/wpcd/wp/c/Church_of_Ireland.htm [accessed 10.02.2023].

would be Lords Spiritual in the newly united United Kingdom House of Lords in Westminster, joining the two archbishops (Canterbury and York) and the 24 bishops from the Church of England. Although a minority, the Church of Ireland remained the established Church until the UK Parliament's passage of the Irish Church Act 1869.[41]

The aforementioned Act disestablished the Church of Ireland and divided it from the Church of England. It also provided that the Church of Ireland would be self-governing and have no connection with the crown or the state. To provide for its own government, the Church of Ireland created a General Synod. In 1833 the British Government proposed the Irish Church Measure to reduce the 22 archbishops and bishops who oversaw the Anglican minority in Ireland to a total of 12 by amalgamating sees and to use the revenues saved for the use of parishes. This sparked the Tractarian movement and wider repercussions in the Anglican communion. Though the religion of a minority of Irish people at the time, it remained the official, established religion of Ireland, until its disestablishment by mentioned Act of Parliament from 1869, which came into effect in 1871. The Church of Ireland still exists today, and has around 345,000 members—219,000 in Northern Ireland and 126,000 in the Republic of Ireland (as year 2023).[42]

In addition to the Reformation and the establishment of the churches, England and Ireland, Anglo-Irish relations were influenced by the Protestant colonization of the northern part of Ireland, Ulster. A planned settlement of English and Scottish Protestant colonists was established in the northern province of Ulster in Ireland during the seventeenth century, known as the Ulster Plantation.[43] The plantation was initiated by King James I in 1609,

---

[41] See: *The Church of Ireland. Brief history*, https://www.irishchurches.org/members/church-of-ireland, Irish Church Act: https://www.legislation.gov.uk/ukpga/1869/42/contents/enacted [both accessed 10.02.2023].

[42] A. Knapp, *Church of Ireland Denomination*, https://study.com/academy/lesson/church-of-ireland-history-lesson-quiz.html and https://www.ireland.anglican.org/about/about-us [both accessed 10.02.2023].

[43] See: R. J. Hunter (ed.), *Plantations in Ulster, 1600–41, A Collection of Documents*, Belfast 2019, https://www.nidirect.gov.uk/publications/plantations-ulster-1600-1641 [accessed 02.03.2023]. See also: J. Bardon, *The plantation of Ulster: the British colonisation of the north of Ireland in the seventeenth century*, Dublin 2011; C. J. Stevens, *The Londonderry plantation, 1609–1914: the history, architecture and planning of the estates of the city of London and its livery companies in Ulster*, Chichester 1986; R. Gillespie, *Colonial Ulster:*

following a series of conflicts between the English and the native Irish population. Under the plantation, large tracts of land in Ulster were confiscated from native Irish landowners and redistributed to English and Scottish settlers. The settlers were required to be Protestant and loyal to the English crown. The aim of the plantation was to establish a loyal population in the region and to undermine the power of the native Irish. As a result of Ulster Plantation, Ulster has undergone significant changes in terms of its demographic, economic, and social makeup. The plantation created a Protestant-dominated region that remained loyal to the British Crown, in contrast to the rest of Ireland which was predominantly Catholic and opposed British rule. There were also significant cultural and political consequences of the plantation. The Scottish settlers brought with them their own Presbyterian religious traditions, which had a lasting impact on the religious landscape of Ulster. The plantation also contributed to tensions between the Catholic and Protestant communities in Ireland, which continue to be felt to this day.

There were several waves of Anglo-Scottish colonization in Ulster, primarily in the province of Ulster. It began during the reign of Elizabeth I Tudor (the Great), continued during the reign of the Stuart dynasty and intensified particularly after Oliver Cromwell's pacification of Ireland between 1649 and 1652 (by driving the Catholics into the barren Connacht). Its final wave followed William I of Orange's victory over James II at the Battle of the Boyne in 1690, and Protestant supremacy on the island was underlined by the union of England and Scotland (the creation of the Kingdom of Great Britain) in 1707. As a result of these events, the old Catholic nobility had to go into exile in two waves (the so-called departure of the earls—at the beginning of the seventeenth century and the so-called departure of the wild geese—at the beginning of the eighteenth century). This resulted in a significant emigration of the Catholic population, deprived of all their property and most of their rights. British colonial plans for Ireland were not a new development in the

---

the settlement of East Ulster, 1600–1641, Cork 1985; M. Perceval-Maxwell, *The Scottish migration to Ulster in the reign of James I*, London 1973; P. Robinson, *The plantation of Ulster: British settlement in an Irish landscape, 1600–1670*, Dublin 1984; W. J. Roulston, *Researching Scots-Irish ancestors, the essential genealogical guide to early modern Ulster, 1600–1800*, Belfast 2005, and M. Ó Siochrú E. Ciardha (eds.), *The plantation of Ulster: Ideology and practice* (Studies in Early Modern Irish History), Manchester 2012, passim.

early seventeenth century. However, the settlements then introduced into Ulster occupy a special place in Irish history. The "Ulster Plantation" itself can be seen as a belated response by the British authorities to their victory in the Irish War, which occupied the last decade of Elizabeth's reign. This plantation, the result of an elaborate exercise in government planning, covered the six counties of Armagh, Cavan, Donegal, Fermanagh, Londonderry and Tyrone, which had been confiscated after the "Flight of the Earls" in 1607.[44] However, Antrim and Down, coastal counties with traditional trade links to the neighboring island, also developed substantial colonies in a less regulated manner. Small settlements were also established in areas of Monaghan. However, government policy did not envisage large-scale settlement. These various plantations effectively opened Ulster to British influence for the first time. Although the sixteenth-century governments had to take account of Ulster. Various local plantation projects had been initiated, but without success. Only conquest could bring about colonization or any kind of decisive change.[45]

It is worth noting that although so-called "the Restoration" is now thought of as a period in Irish history from 1660 to 1691, it has never been the subject of a real critical historical study. Until recently it was a backwater in both Scottish and English culture. As a result, it has long been regarded as an anticlimactic interlude between more dramatic events, for the interpretation of the emergence of the Protestant ascendancy with the crucial Cromwellian[46] and Williamite episodes. In recent years it is better interpreted as the first phase of a historical era—the era of Protestant Ascendancy—which spans the 140 years from the resumption of the crown by Charles II (1660) to the establishment of the Anglo-Irish Union in 1800. This reorientation has not diminished the validity or integrity of the Restoration as a field of study of the Restoration as a field of study, but it has had the effect of forcing those who study the eighteenth century to take a greater interest in the events of the nineteenth century. eighteenth century to take a greater interest in events and

[44] See further: J. McCavitt, *The Flight of the Earls, 1607*, "Irish Historical Studies," Vol. 29, No. 114 (Nov., 1994), pp. 159–173.

[45] R. J. Hunter (ed.), *Plantations in Ulster, 1600–41, A Collection of Documents*, op. cit., p. 9.

[46] P. J. Corish, *The Cromwellian Regime, 1650–60*, in: T. W. Moody, F. X. Martin and F. J. Byrne (ed.), *A New History of Ireland*, Oxford 1976, vol. 3, p. 384.

developments prior to 1691, and to recognize their events and developments before 1691 and to recognize their continuing importance for our understanding of the economic and political world of the eighteenth century.[47]

Overall, "the Restoration" period (1660–1691) and the Ulster Plantation (whole XVII century) is seen as a significant event in Irish history, with far-reaching consequences for the political, cultural, and social development of the island. The legacy of the Ulster Plantation can still be seen in modern-day Northern Ireland. It remains a contentious issue, with some viewing it as a positive development that brought economic growth and modernization to the region, while others view it as a violent and unjust displacement of the native Irish population. It is worth noting that two factors, sectarian and economic, continued to reinforce the mutual prejudice between the two communities. The political monopoly in Ireland was held only by Protestants, including mainly large landowners and the senior clergy of the Protestant Anglican Church in Ireland. Among the Protestant minority, only a small group held real power. The British rule in Ireland in the eighteenth century not only did nothing to weaken the colonizing impulse on the island, it actually strengthened it. The problem of discrimination against the indigenous Catholic population and Ireland's excessive dependence on Britain had already become so entrenched that the Protestants themselves, influenced in part by Anglo-Saxon Enlightenment thought and the events of 1776 in North America, sought to reinterpret their supremacist position. The result of their efforts was the creation of a Protestant Irish Parliament in 1782, independent of Westminster.

It is worth emphasizing that the reign of the Hanoverian dynasties was a period of stability and prosperity in Britain until the 1770s.The perfect symbiosis between the Whig oligarchy and the Crown was the cause of the exceptional political stability.[48] However during the period of the Dublin

---

47 See: D. Dickson, *New Foundations: Ireland 1660–1800*, Dublin 1987, pp. 1–28; R. Gillespie, *Seventeenth-Century Ireland: Making Ireland Modern*, Dublin 2006, pp. 215–298; S. J. Connolly, Divided Kingdom: Ireland 1630–180), Oxford 2008), passim, and T. McCormick, *Restoration Ireland, 1660–1688*, in: A. Jackson (ed.), *The Oxford Handbook of Modern Irish History*, Oxford 2014, passim.

48 See: T. Tulejski, *Quo vadis Britannia? Davida Hume'a rozważania nad angielską konstytucją* [*Quo vadis Britannia? David Hume's consideration on the English constitution*], "Przegląd Sejmowy" [*The Sejm Review*], nr 4(171)/2022, pp. 163–187.

Parliament, Ireland was able to achieve relative legislative and economic autonomy from Britain. It should be emphasized that despite the important role played by the autonomous Irish Parliament between 1782 and 1800 (e.g., Grattan party), it was not entirely successful in establishing lasting independence of local government from the government in London. This was due in part to the fact that the founders of the legislative body failed to analyze the economic and legal situation of the Catholic majority in Ireland. They also lacked a vision for the emancipation of the island. This situation led to a radicalization of the socio-political sentiments of the indigenous Irish population, triggered by the outbreak of the Great French Revolution in 1789. The direct influence of French revolutionary ideas on the birth of Irish republicanism was undeniable. It is believed that the main idea of the French Revolution that resonated in Ireland was nationalism in its Jacobin version (Theobald Wolfe Tone, among others, was an exponent of this idea).[49] It is important in this case to analyze which ideas of the Revolution were grafted onto the Irish soil and how this was done.

It is also worth recalling earlier events that had an indirect impact on the radicalization of sentiment in eighteenth century Ireland. One such thing was the union of England with Scotland, which in prospect led to the creation of the United Kingdom, to which Ireland was co-opted (largely, against its will) in the early nineteenth century. As a result of the union of the Protestant kingdoms of England and Scotland in 1707, the Protestant minority in Ireland was strengthened in its hegemonic position. As a result of the second wave of emigration (primarily to the American colonies), the Catholic community's position was further weakened. Compared to the Irish diaspora of the nineteenth century, the seventeenth and eighteenth century diaspora was more complex. Because Irish emigration flowed in so many

---

[49] See view by: E O'Brien , *The Years of the French: The French Revolution as a Spatio-Temporal Event*, in: E. Maher and C. Maignant (eds.), *Peter Franco-Irish Connections in Space and Time: Peregrinations and Ruminations*, Oxford 2012, pp. 93–116. See also: T. Murtagh, *Hibernian Sans-Culottes? Dublin's Artisans and Radical Politics 1790–1798*, "La Révolution française," Number 11, 2016, pp. 1–19. On Wolfe Tone ideology see: K. Lucas, *Developments in the Political Thought of Theobald Wolfe Tone*, Ph.D. thesis The Open University 2020, p. 258, published online: http://oro.open.ac.uk/71421/1/PhD%20-%20Developments%20in%20the%20Political%20Thought%20of%20Theobald%20Wolfe%20Tone%20July%202020%20K%20Lucas.pdf [accessed 02.03.2023].

different directions during these two centuries, it was particularly complex. It becomes evident that this is true when one considers the Irish settlements in the Amazon basin, North America, the West Indies, and Europe. English and French East India Companies had strong Protestant and Catholic presences, respectively. There are a number of factors contributing to the complex phenomenon of Irish mobility of the Irish diaspora, including dynamism, persecution, and poverty.[50]

Ireland was greatly impacted by the eighteenth century union of England and Scotland. The union of England and Scotland created the United Kingdom of Great Britain in 1707. Ireland remained a separate country, but was directly affected by the changes in the British political landscape. One significant effect of the union was the strengthening of the Protestant Ascendancy in Ireland. The Protestant Ascendancy[51] was a minority group of wealthy Protestants who held political and economic power in Ireland. Union with Scotland gave them a greater platform from which to assert their power and influence, further marginalizing the Irish Catholic population. Another important effect was the consolidation of British power in Ireland. The British government sought to extend its control over Ireland by implementing a series of laws known as the Penal Laws. These laws were designed to restrict the rights of Catholics and other non-Protestant groups, further consolidating British power over the country. The union with Scotland also created a sense of national identity for the people of Great Britain. This sense of identity was based on Protestantism, the English language and culture, and imperial ambitions. As a result, the British government began to see Ireland as a backward and inferior country that needed to be civilized and brought

---

[50] See: L. M. Cullen, The Irish Diaspora of the Seventeenth and Eighteenth Centuries, in: N. Canny (ed.), *Europeans on the Move: Studies on European Migration 1500–1800*, Oxford 1994, pp. 113–150.

[51] The Protestant Ascendancy, also known simply as the Ascendancy, was the political, economic and social domination of Ireland between the seventeenth century and the early twentieth century by a minority of landowners, Protestant clergy and members of the professions, all members of the Established Church (Anglican; Church of Ireland or Church of England). The Ascendancy excluded other groups from politics and the elite. The most numerous of these were Roman Catholics, but also members of Presbyterian and other Protestant denominations, as well as non-Christians such as Jews, until the Reform Acts (1832–1928). See further: D. George Boyce, *Nationalism in Ireland*, Routledge, London, p. 309.

under British rule. This attitude led to increased British control over Ireland and further marginalization of the Irish people.[52]

The impact of England's union with Scotland on Ireland in the eighteenth century was significant. It strengthened the power of the Protestant Ascendancy.[53] It consolidated British control over Ireland and further marginalized the Irish Catholic population. It also created a sense of British national identity that led to increased British control and oppression of Ireland. The Union also had a significant impact on Irish culture and identity. The English and Scottish Protestant elites sought to impose their cultural norms and values on Ireland. This led to the suppression of the Irish language, customs and traditions. This in turn fueled the growth of Irish nationalism and resistance to British rule. In conclusion, the union between England and Scotland had a significant impact on Ireland in the eighteenth century. It weakened Irish political power, led to economic decline and sparked cultural repression. These factors contributed to the growth of Irish nationalism and resistance to British rule, culminating in the Irish War of Independence in the early twentieth century. Before the French Revolution in the eighteenth century, the relationship between Britain and Ireland was complex and fraught with tension. Throughout centuries, Ireland has been governed by the English, first by conquest and then by the implementation of laws and policies that were designed to integrate the Irish into the English system. This process had led to a long history of English domination and exploitation of the Irish, which had resulted in a deep resentment among many Irish people. Tensions between the English and Irish remained simmering in the eighteenth century, with many Irish seeking greater autonomy and independence from English rule. This led to a series of uprisings and rebellions, most notably the 1798 Irish Rebellion, which sought to overthrow British rule in Ireland and establish an independent Irish republic. Furthermore, there were also those in Ireland who worked within the British system in order to improve their

---

52 See: J. Kelly, *The Politics of Protestant Ascendancy, 1730–1790*, in: T. Bartlett (ed.), *Cambridge History of Ireland, Volume III: 1730–1880*, pp. 48–73.

53 See further on this topic: S. J. Connolly, *Religion, law and power: the making of Protestant Ireland 1660–1760*, Oxford 1993; T. C. Barnard, *A new anatomy of Ireland: the Irish Protestants 1649–1770*, New Haven 2003; T. C. Barnard, *The kingdom of Ireland, 1641–1760*, Basingstoke 2004, passim.

lot. This included figures such as Edmund Burke, an Anglo-Irish statesman who championed the cause of Catholic emancipation and opposed British oppression of the Irish.[54]

There were many facets to Anglo-Irish relations in the eighteenth century, including cooperation, conflict and competition. Ireland was a colony of Britain, and the relationship between the two countries was largely defined by Britain's economic and political dominance over Ireland. The first half of the eighteenth century was marked by a period of relative stability in the relationship between Britain and Ireland. The Penal Laws, which discriminated against Irish Catholics, had been introduced in the late seventeenth century and, although they remained in force, they were not actively enforced. The Irish economy was growing and many Irish merchants and landowners had close links with Britain. However, tensions began to emerge in the mid-eighteenth century as the Irish economy became more dependent on trade with Britain, and Irish politicians began to demand greater political autonomy. In 1760, the Irish Parliament passed the "Declaration of Rights," which asserted the right of the Irish Parliament to make laws without interference from the British Parliament. The American Revolution also had a major impact on Anglo-Irish relations. Many Irish Catholics supported the American colonists who were fighting for their own independence from Britain. The British government responded by tightening its control over Ireland and suppressing dissent. The French Revolution in 1789 further complicated Anglo-Irish relations. The French government offered support to Irish nationalists and the United Irishmen, a revolutionary group, was formed in Ireland in 1791. The British government responded with harsh repression, including the suspension of civil liberties and the use of military force to suppress dissent.[55]

In 1782, a Protestant Irish Parliament, independent of Westminster, was established. During the period of the Dublin Parliament, Ireland succeeded in gaining relative legislative and economic autonomy from Britain. It should be emphasized that, despite the major role played by the autonomous Irish Parliament between 1782 and 1800, it was not entirely successful

[54] See further: T. McDonough, T. (ed.), *Was Ireland a colony? Economics, politics and culture in nineteenth-century Ireland*, Dublin 2005, passim.

[55] See: T. Bartlett, *Ireland during the Revolutionary and Napoleonic Wars, 1791–1815*, in: T. Bartlett (ed.), *Cambridge History of Ireland, vol. III...*, op. cit., pp. 74–95.

in establishing lasting independence of local powers from the government in London. This state of affairs was due, among other things, to the total disregard of the analysis of the economic and legal situation of the Catholic majority in Ireland by the creators of the legislative body and the absence of the idea of emancipation of the island. This type of situation consequently led to a radicalization of socio-political sentiment among the indigenous Irish population, triggered by the outbreak of the Great French Revolution in 1789.

In 1791, in response to events in France between 1789 and 1791, the Society of United Irishmen was formed in Belfast and Dublin, among other places, with the aim of uniting both Catholic and Protestant residents against "British tyranny." Initially, both the Committee and the Society were merely secondary to plans for parliamentary reform and a relaxation of the anti-Catholic nature of English law. However, under the influence of events in France, their members gradually began to radicalize their political activities. The British, fearing an outbreak of rebellion in Ireland, abolished a small number of anti-Catholic laws in 1793, allowing wealthy Catholics to vote in local elections and relaxing education laws (the Catholic Relief Act). One of the co-founders of the republican movement, Theobald Wolfe Tone, was a Protestant. He was critical of British attitudes toward Ireland. In his view the main aims of the movement were: "To overthrow the tyranny of our hated government, to break the connection with England, the ever-beating source of our political troubles, and to win independence for my country." Tone's criticism of the British laws of 1793 was eerily reminiscent of the Jacobin rejection of the French constitution of 1791. Both Wolfe Tone[56] and Maximilian Robespierre sought to seriously reduce the extreme economic inequalities in their countries and to fight what they saw as the eternal enemies of the republic, by analogy the British and French monarchies. In addition to Robespierre and Antonio Saint-Just, the nascent republican movement in Ireland was influenced by another Anglo-Irish thinker, Thomas Paine. His work The Rights of Man became a model for Irish revolutionaries.[57]

The influence of Enlightenment republicanism on the emergence of the nascent Irish republican movement in the late eighteenth century cannot

---

[56] See: F. Mac Dermot, *Theobald Wolfe Tone and His Times*, Dublin 1969, passim.

[57] See: A. Thomson, *Thomas Paine and the United Irishmen*, "Etudes irlandaises," Année 1991, no 16–1, pp. 109–119.

be overstated. Many radical, egalitarian and republican slogans were recycled in Ireland thanks to the political thought of the French Revolution and especially during the Jacobin dictatorship. It was thanks to them that the Irish were prepared, for the first time in their history, to fight for a free Ireland which would become a republic in its legal and constitutional form. The immediate reason for Irish republicans to take political action was the French Revolution. It is worth adding to the political factor another, perhaps from our perspective the most important, namely the military. It is widely, if simplistically, seen as a constitutive feature of Irish republicanism from the late eighteenth century onwards. It was and is associated with the "ideologically motivated use of violence." Henceforth, the political and the military were inextricably linked in the Irish republican movement. The military face of Jacobin republicanism in Ireland first emerged in the events of the 1798 Rising. This was preceded by an utterly unsuccessful attempt to overthrow British rule in Ireland militarily in 1796 with the help of revolutionary France, whereas the 1798 uprising prepared by the United Irishmen—again with the help of the French—was the largest Irish uprising for independence against English oppression since the Spanish Grand Armada, Cromwell's Pacification of Ireland or James II Stuart's battles in the late seventeenth century.

1.2. Ireland under British rule: political history of the Union (1801–1921)

1.2.1. Catholic Emancipation and Home Rule (1801–1914)

The Irish Rising of 1798,[58] which proved to be a failure, had many negative consequences for Ireland. The first of these was the forced Actual Union of Great Britain and Ireland in 1801. Secondly, the complete abolition of the autonomy of 1782–1800 and the consequent merger of the two Parliaments, that is, real government from London, and thirdly, the lack of willingness on the part of the British to improve the lot of the oppressed Catholics. In contrast, the events of 1791–1803 constituted the Irish republican movement and laid the foundations of modern Irish nationalism, which over the next two hundred years became the civil and military expression of the idea of a

[58] See: M. Hewitt, *1798. The Year of Revolution*, Dublin 1998, pp. 1–18.

free Ireland as a sovereign and indivisible republic. It should be emphasized that without the previous Anglo-Norman, English, Anglo-Scottish and British colonial interference on the island, the Irish republican movement would not have come into being. This interference, with all its consequences, was compounded by a factor as important as the Reformation. However, one has to stress that the immediate cause of the movement was the events surrounding the creation of the United States of America and the Great French Revolution. Overall, the relationship between Britain and Ireland in the eighteenth century was marked by a complex mix of cooperation, conflict, and competition, driven by economic, political, and social factors. The French Revolution in the late eighteenth century further complicated the relationship and set the stage for further conflict in the nineteenth century. Wawrzyniec Konarski argues that the French Revolution first awakened in Irish Catholics: "[…] a mass commitment to the realization of the idea of an independent, indivisible and republican Ireland, and […] without the participation of many Protestants and the interaction between the two religious groups, this form of extra-parliamentary nationalism would never have come into being."[59]

Ireland entered the nineteenth century still reeling from the aftermath of the Irish rebellion of 1798. Prisoners were still being deported to Australia and sporadic violence continued in County Wicklow. There was another unsuccessful rebellion in 1803 under the leadership of Robert Emmet.[60] The Acts of Union, which constitutionally made Ireland part of the British state, can largely be seen as an attempt to address some of the grievances behind the 1798 rebellion and to prevent it from destabilizing Britain or providing a base for foreign invasion. In 1800, the Irish and British parliaments each passed an Act of Union abolishing the Irish legislature and merging the Kingdom of Ireland and the Kingdom of Great Britain into the United Kingdom of Great Britain and Ireland from January 1, 1801. After a failed attempt, the Act was finally passed by the Irish Parliament, albeit, as with the Acts of Union of 1707 that united Scotland and England, with mass bribery of members of both houses, who received British peerages and other "encouragements." During this period, the administration of Ireland

---

[59] W. Konarski, [Pragmatycy i idealiści...], p. 101. In a similar vein, N. Davies wrote, op. cit., p. 562.

[60] See: R. O'Donnell, *Robert Emmet and the Rising of 1803*, Dublin 2003, passim.

consisted of authorities appointed by the British central government. These were the Lord Lieutenant of Ireland, representing the King, and the British Prime Minister's Chief Secretary for Ireland. Almost as important was the Under-Secretary for Ireland, who headed the civil service in Ireland. During the century, the British Parliament became increasingly involved in both administration and legislation. For this reason the Chief Secretary became more important in Ireland than the Lord Lieutenant, who became more symbolic than real. After the abolition of the Irish Parliament, Irish MPs were elected to the British House of Commons in Westminster.

It is worth returning to the characteristics of the peculiarities of the Union of the United Kingdom with Ireland, how Ireland was legally bound to Great Britain. It is important to note that Ireland was an integral part of the British Empire throughout the nineteenth century. For the first time in history, the Act of Union of the Kingdom of Great Britain and Ireland of 1801 brought together the British Isles under the jurisdiction of one central authority. The Union of the United Kingdom with Ireland was established in 1801, following years of political and social unrest in Ireland. The so-called Act of Union united the Kingdom of Ireland and the Kingdom of Britain to form the United Kingdom of Britain and Ireland. Under the terms of the Act of Union, Ireland was legally bound to Great Britain and the Irish Parliament was abolished. Irish members of parliament were allowed to sit in the Westminster Parliament, but the majority of decisions affecting Ireland were taken by the British government. The Union was intended to bring greater political and economic stability to Ireland, but it was opposed by many Irish nationalists who saw it as a betrayal of their country's independence. In the decades that followed, Ireland experienced a series of political and social upheavals. These included the Great Famine of the 1840s and the Easter Rising of 1916. Despite these challenges, Ireland remained an integral part of the British Empire throughout the nineteenth century. However, growing calls for Irish independence eventually led to the Irish Free State becoming established in 1922 and becoming a fully independent Republic in 1949.[61]

---

[61] See article from "Guardian," April 8, 2020, R. Nelsson, *The day Ireland became a republic – archive, April 1949*, available online: https://www.theguardian.com/world/from-the-archive-blog/2020/apr/08/ireland-becomes-a-republic-april-1949 [accessed 18.04.2023].

Ireland's first half of the nineteenth century was dominated by the unresolved issue of Catholic emancipation. Part of the attraction of the Union for many Irish Catholics and Dissenters was the promised repeal of the then existing Penal Laws (which discriminated against them) and granting Catholic Emancipation. However, King George III blocked emancipation, believing that to grant it would be to break his coronation oath to defend the Anglican Church. A campaign led by the Irish Catholic lawyer and politician Daniel O'Connell and the Catholic Association led to renewed agitation to repeal the Test Act.[62] Arthur Wellesley, the Anglo-Irish soldier and statesman and First Duke of Wellington, was at the height of his enormous prestige as victor of the Napoleonic Wars. As Prime Minister, he used his considerable political power and influence to steer the enabling legislation through the British Parliament. He then persuaded King George IV to sign it into law under threat of resignation.

The Roman Catholic Relief Act of 1829 allowed British and Irish Catholics to sit in Parliament. Daniel O'Connell became the first Catholic MP since 1689. As leader of the Repeal Association, O'Connell campaigned unsuccessfully for the repeal of the Act of Union and the restoration of Irish Home Rule. O'Connell's tactics were largely peaceful, using mass rallies to demonstrate popular support for his campaign. While O'Connell failed to achieve the repeal of the Act of Union, his efforts led to reforms in areas such as local government and the Poor Laws. Despite O'Connell's peaceful methods, there was also a good deal of sporadic violence and rural unrest in the country during the first half of the nineteenth century. In Ulster there were repeated outbreaks of sectarian violence, such as the Dolly's Brae riots,

---

[62] The Test Acts were a series of English penal laws that served as a religious test for public office and imposed various civil disabilities on Roman Catholics and Nonconformists. The underlying principle was that only those taking Communion in the established Church of England were eligible to hold public office, and the severe penalties imposed on recusants, whether Catholic or Nonconformist, were designed to enforce this principle. Similar legislation was introduced in Scotland in respect of the Presbyterian Church of Scotland. See: H. Chisholm, (ed.), *Test Acts*, "*Encyclopædia Britannica*," Vol. 26 (11th ed.) Cambridge University Press 1911, pp. 665–666; E. Neville Williams, *The Eighteenth-Century Constitution, 1688–1815: Documents and Commentary* Cambridge University Press, 1965, pp. 341–343.

between Catholics and the nascent Orange Order.[63] Elsewhere, much agrarian violence and social unrest was caused by tensions between the rapidly growing rural population on the one hand and their landlords and the state on the other.[64] Encouraged by London's initial concessions, the founder of the Catholic Association set an important goal, namely the revocation of the union of Great Britain and Ireland. O'Connell's peaceful methods, however, were unsuccessful. The British threatened to use force against Irish opponents of the Union.[65] The result of his efforts was only half a success. On the one hand he won the emancipation of the Catholics, but on the other he failed to break the Union by bloodless means.

In the mid-nineteenth century, the situation in Ireland became radicalized for several reasons: firstly, the famine of 1845–1848 (1852, the Great Hunger);[66] secondly, Ireland's great dependence on the United Kingdom; and thirdly, the radicalization of attitudes within the ranks of the independence movement itself on the island, especially in the second half of the nineteenth

---

63 Secret peasant societies such as the Whiteboys and the Ribbonmen used sabotage and violence to intimidate landlords into better treatment of their tenants. The most sustained outbreak of violence was the Tithe War of the 1830s, over the obligation of the mostly Catholic peasantry to pay tithes to the Protestant Church of Ireland. The Royal Irish Constabulary (RIC) was set up to police rural areas in response to this violence. See: S. McGraw, K. Whelan, *Daniel O'Connell in Comparative Perspective, 1800–50*, "Éire-Ireland; a journal of Irish studies," Number 40, 1 and 2(1), January 2005, pp. 60–89.

64 In 1823, Daniel O'Connell formed the Catholic Association in order to represent the interests of this religious group. Essentially it was a nationalist social movement based on peace and democracy, which aimed to advance the rights of the island's Catholic majority, which had been discriminated against up until that time. In 1829, O'Connell achieved political success when the Emancipation of Catholics Act was passed in Westminster. See: P. M. Geoghegan, *The Impact of O'Connell, 1815– 1850*, in: T. Bartlett (ed.), *Cambridge History of Ireland, vol. III...*, op. cit., pp. 102–127.

65 A. Jackson, *Home Rule: An Irish History 1800–2000*, London 2003, pp. 10–14.

66 Between 1845–1852 Ireland suffered a period of starvation, disease and emigration that became known as the Great Famine. The main cause was a disease which affected the potato crop, upon which a third of Ireland's population was dependent for food. See more: Ch. Kinealy, *A Death-Dealing Famine: The Great Hunger in Ireland*, London 1997, p. 200.

century.[67] Brian Girvin concludes that by the 1830s the majority of Catholics had become nationalist. The majority of Protestants had become unionist in the sense that they believed that the political and institutional arrangements should be maintained by the British state.[68] It is worth noting, as Alvin Jackson rightly points out, the United Kingdom (as a union of England, Scotland and Ireland) has always been a pragmatic union, characterized by functionality; it has not had any particular idea that has guided it.[69] In a sense, O'Connell's fight for the emancipation of Catholics (largely Irish nationalists) also, as it were, cemented the union of Britain for years to come, particularly during the reign of Queen Victoria (1838–1901).

To sum up Daniel O'Connell's impact on Irish history, it is worth mentioning that he was a prominent Irish political leader who had a profound impact on Ireland in the nineteenth century. Daniel O'Connell's impact on Ireland was profound and far-reaching. His legacy of championing civil rights, democracy and peaceful protest continues to inspire people around the world. There are at least four categories of O'Connell's achievements that are relevant to the starting point of British-Irish relations and the situation of both Catholics and other native inhabitants on the island:

1) Catholic Emancipation: O'Connell is best known for leading the campaign for Catholic Emancipation, which allowed Catholics to sit in Parliament and hold public office. This was a major victory for Irish Catholics and an important step toward greater political and social equality, achieved in 1829 with the passing of the Catholic Relief Act;
2) Repeal of the Union: O'Connell also campaigned for the repeal of the Act of Union (1800), which had united Ireland and Britain into a single political entity. He believed that Ireland should have its own parliament and government and worked tirelessly to achieve this. Although he was not successful in achieving the repeal of the Act, his efforts did help

---

[67] See: E. Curtis, *A History of Ireland: From Earliest Times to 1922*, London 2002, s. 318; L. O Broin, *Revolutionary Underground: The Story of the Irish Republican Brotherhood 1858–1924*, Dublin 1976, passim.

[68] See B. Girvin, *Nationalism and the Continuation of Political Conflict in Ireland*, in: B. Girvin (ed.), *Ireland North and South: Perspectives from Social Science*. Dublin 1999, p. 372.

[69] A. Jackson, *The two Unions: Ireland, Scotland and the survival of the United Kingdom, 1707– 2007*, Oxford 2015, p. 4.

to lay the foundations for the eventual establishment of the Irish Free State in 1922;

3) Land reform: O'Connell was a strong advocate of land reform in Ireland, which was a key issue in his time. He believed that tenant farmers should have greater rights and protection and worked to improve their conditions through legislation and political pressure;
4) Peaceful resistance: O'Connell believed in peaceful resistance and non-violent protest and encouraged those who followed him to use these tactics as they struggled for political and social change. His commitment to peaceful activism was a major influence on later leaders such as Mahatma Gandhi and Martin Luther King Jr.[70] It is worth adding that these principles were also sometimes referred to by the Republican hunger strikers in Maze Prison in 1981.[71]

O'Connell's greatest achievement was the successful campaign for Catholic Emancipation, which resulted in the passage of the Catholic Relief Act in 1829. He also played a pivotal role in the formation of the Repeal Association, which garnered significant support but ultimately fell short of achieving its objectives. Nevertheless, O'Connell's methods of peaceful agitation and mass mobilization laid the groundwork for future nationalist movements.

During the nineteenth century, as we know, Ireland was part of the British Empire and, as such, subject to British rule. However, Ireland's relationship with the Empire was complex and marked by a series of political and social struggles. One of the most significant events in Ireland's relationship with the Empire during this period was the Great Famine of the 1840s. The famine, caused by a potato blight, led to the deaths of around one million people and forced many others to emigrate to other parts of the Empire, particularly the United States. The British government's response to the famine was criticized for being inadequate and slow, which led to increased tensions between Ireland and Britain. The young Queen Victoria was impressed by the charms

70 See also: K. T. Hoppen, Riding a Tiger: Daniel O'Connell, Reform, and. Popular Politics in Ireland, 1800–1847, in: T. Blanning and P. Wende (eds.), "Proceedings of British Academy," 1999, pp. 121–143.

71 See: https://writingthetroublesweb.wordpress.com/2020/12/01/bobby-sands-mp-whose-idea-was-it. [accessed 26.04.2023].

of Ireland and holidays were often spent in Killarney, County Kerry, which led to the town becoming a popular holiday resort for the British upper class in the nineteenth century. In 1845 the potato blight wiped out the potato crop throughout Ireland. A famine then fell upon the country famine (the potato disease itself did not cause the famine, but the Irish had to sell the grain they grew to be able to high rents and this was the cause of the famine), which lasted until 1851. one million people died of famine at that time, and a second as many left Ireland. During the disaster, the Queen donated £5,000 sterling from her own casket for the starving Irish.[72]

In the late nineteenth century there was a growing movement for Irish independence, and in 1858 the Irish Republican Brotherhood[73] was formed to fight for a free and independent Ireland. However, despite these efforts, Ireland remained part of the British Empire until the early twentieth century. Ireland's relationship with the Empire was also marked by cultural and social struggles. The Irish language, which had been spoken for centuries, was suppressed by the British authorities in an attempt to Anglicize the Irish population. This led to a revival of Irish language and culture in the late nineteenth and early twentieth centuries, which came to be seen as an important part of fighting for Irish independence. Overall, Ireland's relationship with the Empire in the nineteenth century was characterized by conflict and struggle as the Irish people fought for greater autonomy and independence from British rule.

It is worth adding in the context of Queen Victoria's relationship to the British government's inept policy toward the Irish famine problem that Prime Minister Russell's policies were often criticized for failing to help Ireland during the famine. Against this backdrop, the Queen's actions were favorable, and she gained considerable popularity on the Emerald Isle. The Queen often sided with the Irish, supporting the Maynooth Grant, for example, and even visited a seminary during her visit to Ireland. The Queen's first official visit to Ireland took place in 1849, and was arranged by the then Lord Governor Earl of Clarendon. In this way, he wanted to divert public attention from the

---

[72] See more C. Algernon Cecil, Queen Victoria and Her Prime Ministers, Eyre and Spottiswode, 1953.

[73] See on the rising of IRB in: G. Dillon, *The Irish Republican Brotherhood*, "University Review," Vol. 2, No. 8 (Winter, 1961), pp. 25–33.

famine, as well as draw the attention of the British government to the presence of the Queen at the scene of the crisis. The visit did not change opinion of the queen in Ireland, where even nationalists ended party meetings by singing God Save the Queen.

In the 1870s and 1880s, however, the monarch's image deteriorated in the eyes of many Irish people. Victoria, for example, refused to visit Ireland, arguing that the Corporation of Dublin had refused to congratulate the Prince of Wales on his marriage to Alexandra of Denmark and the birth of the couple's eldest son, Albert Victor. Victoria has also consistently refused successive Prime Ministers and Lord Governors, and even members of her own family, to establish a permanent royal residence in Ireland. Lord Midleton, former chairman of the Irish Unionists, recorded in his memoirs in 1830 that this was one of those decisions that undermined the prestige of the British monarchy in Ireland. The Queen's last visit to Ireland was in 1900, when she made an appeal to the Irish to join the British army during the ongoing Second Boer War. In response to her visit, Irish nationalist leader Arthur Griffith formed the Cumann na nGaedheal organization to unite the opposition. Five years later, Griffith used his acquaintances from that period to form a new political movement that would weigh heavily on the fate of Ireland, the Sinn Féin party.[74]

Behind the idea of Home Rule, that is, Irish self-government with Great Britain and the entire impact on nineteenth-century Ireland, apart from the above-mentioned Catholic Daniel O'Connell, was a Protestant—Charles Stewart Parnell. He was born into a Protestant landowning family of English descent. His grandfather on his mother's side was a prominent U.S. naval commander. Charles Stewart Parnell graduated from Magdalene College in Cambridge and in 1875 became a member of Parliament from County Meath as an advocate of Irish autonomy. In 1877 he became chairman of the movement for Irish autonomy—taking over this position from its founder, Isaac Butt (1813–1879). He immediately undertook the use of parliamentary obstructionism in the House of Commons to draw attention to Irish

---

[74] See: B. Feeney, *Sinn Féin. One hundred turbulent years*, Dublin 2002, passim. See also: S. Bachrynowski, *Od konfrontacji do koncyliacji – historia irlandzkiej partii Sinn Féin* [*From confrontation to conciliation – the history of the Irish Sinn Féin party*], Kalisz 2010, passim.

problems. He was elected to the British Parliament in 1875 as a member of the Irish Parliamentary Party, which sought to secure greater autonomy for Ireland within the United Kingdom. Parnell quickly emerged as a charismatic and effective politician, and he soon became the leader of the party.

From 1878 he led an agitation among farmers, inciting them against demoralized landowners. From 1879 he held the office of president of the Irish National Land League. In October 1881, he was arrested as an instigator of rebellion, but during his imprisonment in Kilmainham the chaos in the countryside took a violent turn, causing Prime Minister William Ewart Gladstone to order his release in May 1882. This was intended to bring economic terror under control. Parnell himself exerted enormous influence in the House of Commons; the Irish party had 86 MPs in the House, making it so strong that in February 1886 it brought the Conservative government, which opposed Irish autonomy, out of power. It did so by voting with the liberal opposition. In March 1886 Gladstone agreed to introduce autonomy for Ireland. Parnell supported the prime minister in this, but after Joseph Chamberlain left the government, their plans were scuttled, and the Conservatives again formed a government that remained in power even after Parnell's death. The latter, in turn, won a lawsuit in November 1889 against The Times newspaper, which had published fabricated letters according to which Parnell allegedly supported terrorists. Winning the trial earned him sympathy. In 1890, however, he was involved in a divorce case that gained publicity. Captain O'Shea (a former hussar officer) divorced his wife Katherine known as "Kitty." She had been Parnell's mistress since 1881 and the mother of his three daughters. He married her in June 1891, but the affair caused a moral scandal that ended his political career. He was unable to rebuild his previous authority. He died at his home after struggling with acute rheumatism. One of the most important figures in Ireland and Britain in the nineteenth century. William Ewart Gladstone described him as one of the most significant people he had ever met. Future Prime Minister Herbert Henry Asquith claimed he was one of the three greatest figures of his time. Lord Richard Haldane thought he was the best politician in the House of Commons in 150 years.

Parnell's most significant achievement was his successful campaign for Home Rule. The aim was to establish a separate Irish parliament within the United Kingdom. He worked closely with British Prime Minister William

Gladstone to draft the Home Rule Bill, which was introduced in 1886 but ultimately defeated. Parnell's influence extended beyond Ireland and Britain. He was a key figure in the international movement for Irish independence and played a leading role in promoting the cause of Irish nationalism in the United States. However, Parnell's career was ultimately as mentioned before cut short by a moral scandal with "Kitty" O'Shea. The scandal caused a rift within the Irish Parliamentary Party and Parnell was forced to resign as its leader in 1891. Despite this setback, Parnell's legacy lived on. His skill as a politician and strategist is still studied and admired today, and his advocacy of Home Rule has inspired generations of Irish nationalists.[75] Parnell's most notable achievement was his leadership of the Irish Parliamentary Party, which became a powerful force in British politics. He successfully advocated for the Land Act of 1881, which aimed to improve the conditions of Irish tenant farmers. Parnell's efforts brought the issue of Irish self-rule to the forefront of British politics and inspired future generations of nationalists. However, his career was tarnished by a personal scandal (Parnell's involvement in an extramarital affair), leading to his political downfall and a temporary setback for the Irish nationalist movement.[76]

Overall, Charles Stewart Parnell's influence on Ireland and Great Britain in the nineteenth century was profound. His leadership, advocacy for land reform, parliamentary tactics, and role in the Home Rule movement significantly shaped the trajectory of Irish nationalism and the fight for self-determination. Charles Stewart Parnell's influence on both Ireland and Great Britain was significant, as he played a central role in the Irish nationalist movement and the fight for Irish Home Rule. Here are some key aspects of Parnell's influence:

1) Irish Nationalism: Parnell is considered one of the most important figures in the history of Irish nationalism. He led the Irish Parliamentary Party (IPP) and advocated for the rights and interests of the Irish people. Parnell's leadership and ability to organize and mobilize support were instrumental in shaping the nationalist movement during this period;

---

[75] On Parnell see both: C. Cruise O'Brien, *Parnell and His Party, 1880–1890*, Oxford 1964; F. S. L. Lyons, *Charles Stewart Parnell*, Dublin 1977, passim.

[76] See: B. O'Brien, *The Life of Charles S. Parnell, Vol. I 1846–1891*, London 1898, p. 236.

2) Land Reform: Parnell recognized that land ownership and tenant rights were crucial issues in Ireland. He championed the cause of land reform, advocating for fairer treatment of Irish tenant farmers and fighting against oppressive British landlordism. Parnell's efforts contributed to the eventual passage of the Irish Land Act in 1881, which aimed to address some of the grievances of tenant farmers;
3) Home Rule: Parnell's ultimate goal was to secure self-government, known as Home Rule, for Ireland within the British Empire. He led the Irish Home Rule movement, demanding a devolved Irish parliament and greater autonomy for Ireland. Parnell's influence and political maneuvering helped elevate the Home Rule cause to a prominent position on the political agenda in both Ireland and Great Britain;
4) Parliamentary Tactics: Parnell's political tactics in the British Parliament were unconventional yet effective. He employed obstructionist strategies, including filibustering and other delaying tactics, to draw attention to the Irish cause and gain concessions from the British government. Parnell's skillful use of parliamentary procedure and his ability to rally support within and outside of Parliament made him a formidable force in British politics;
5) Split in the Irish Nationalist Movement: Parnell's influence and leadership within the Irish nationalist movement led to a significant split among Irish nationalists. Following his involvement in a scandalous affair, Parnell's personal and political reputation suffered. This led to a bitter division within the movement, with factions emerging both in support and opposition to Parnell's leadership. The split had long-lasting effects on Irish politics and delayed the achievement of Home Rule;
6) Legacy: Parnell's impact on Ireland and Great Britain cannot be overstated. Although his personal and political career were cut short by his untimely death in 1891, his influence on Irish nationalism and the fight for self-government continued to resonate. Parnell's legacy inspired future generations of Irish nationalists, and the pursuit of Home Rule remained a central issue until the establishment of the independent Irish Free State in 1922.[77]

[77] See: E. Curtis, *A History of Ireland: From Earliest Times to 1922*, London 2002, p. 318.

Daniel O'Connell and Charles Stewart Parnell were both prominent Irish political leaders who played significant roles in the struggle for Irish independence from Britain. However, there are also some differences between the two figures. Daniel O'Connell, known as "The Liberator" and was a lawyer and politician. He was a prominent campaigner for Catholic emancipation and played a major role in securing the passage of the Catholic Emancipation Act of 1829, which allowed Catholics to hold public office and sit in Parliament. O'Connell was also a leading advocate for Irish independence and was a strong supporter of nonviolent resistance. Charles Stewart Parnell was an Irish nationalist politician and land reformer. He is perhaps best known for his leadership of the Irish Parliamentary Party, which aimed to secure Irish Home Rule. Parnell was a skilled orator and a masterful political organizer, and he was able to build a broad coalition of Irish nationalists and others who supported Home Rule.

One of the key differences between O'Connell and Parnell was their approach to achieving Irish independence. O'Connell was committed to achieving independence through peaceful and nonviolent means, while Parnell was willing to use more radical tactics, such as boycotts and land seizures, to achieve his goals. Another key difference was their focus: O'Connell was primarily concerned with securing Catholic emancipation and independence for Ireland, while Parnell focused more on land reform and Home Rule. Despite these differences, both O'Connell and Parnell played important roles in the struggle for Irish independence, and their legacies continue to be celebrated in Ireland today. In summary, both Daniel O'Connell and Charles Stewart Parnell were influential figures in Irish politics who fought for the rights and autonomy of the Irish people. O'Connell focused on Catholic emancipation and the repeal of the Act of Union, while Parnell shifted the emphasis to Irish Home Rule. They employed different strategies: O'Connell relied on peaceful mobilization and oratory, while Parnell employed a more confrontational approach in the British Parliament.

The parliamentary activities of Parnell (as well as O'Connells earlier) were important, not least the radicalization among large parts of the Irish national movement was becoming an increasing problem in Anglo-Irish relations. The emergence of radical Irish nationalism in the late nineteenth century was a response to the failure of earlier attempts to achieve Irish independence through constitutional means. The dominant position of British interests in

Irish politics, economics and society was largely responsible for this failure. The emergence of radical Irish nationalism in the late nineteenth century was a complex and multifaceted phenomenon, reflecting a variety of social, economic, political and cultural factors. The emergence of radical nationalism was also a product of wider political and social changes taking place in Europe at the time. These changes included the rise of socialism, the spread of nationalist movements across Europe and the growth of the middle class. In Ireland, the emergence of radical nationalism was marked by the formation of the Irish Republican Brotherhood (IRB) in 1858, which sought to achieve Irish independence by revolutionary means. The IRB was later replaced by the Irish Republican Army (IRA) in the early twentieth century. The IRA played a key role in the Irish War of Independence (1919–1921), which eventually led to the establishment of the Irish Free State. Radical nationalism in Ireland was also influenced by the cultural revival of the late nineteenth century, which sought to promote Irish language, literature and traditions as a means of asserting Irish identity and challenging British cultural dominance.[78]

It is also worth mentioning on this occasion another figure who was indirectly associated with the two attempts to establish Home Rule. William Ewart Gladstone, as four-time British Prime Minister in the late nineteenth century, was particularly associated with the issue of Irish Home Rule, which was a highly controversial and divisive issue in British politics at the time. Home Rule for Ireland referred to the idea of granting the Irish people a degree of self-government, with their own parliament or assembly, within the United Kingdom. It was seen by many Irish nationalists as a way of achieving greater autonomy and equality for Ireland, which had been ruled directly from London since the Act of Union in 1800. Gladstone initially opposed Home Rule for Ireland, but began to change his position in the 1870s. Gladstone had, before the 1885 election, already decided that some degree of home rule in Ireland was inevitable. Initially, he wanted to proceed on a cross-party basis but when that proved impossible the Prime Minister presented what was to be his first Home Rule Bill to Parliament on April 8, 1886. This granted Ireland limited self-rule within the British Empire, with the UK Parliament maintaining sovereignty over an Irish parliament and

---

[78] See: F. S. L. Lyons, *Ireland since the Famine*, London 1981, pp. 255–256.

executive based in Dublin. Irish representation in the Westminster Parliament would end. In 1886 he introduced the first Irish Home Rule Bill in the House of Commons, which proposed a separate Irish parliament with limited powers over domestic affairs. The bill was defeated in the House of Commons, largely due to opposition from the Conservative Party and some members of Gladstone's own Liberal Party. Gladstone tried again in 1893 with a second Irish Home Rule Bill, which was also defeated. However, this time he was opposed mainly by the House of Lords, who were empowered to block legislation passed by the House of Commons.[79]

The second half of the nineteenth century in Ireland was characterized also by a kind of two-pronged political struggle for the island's independence from Britain. There was the growing importance of Irish MPs in Westminster, who fought for the return of Parliament in Dublin, a form of self-government (devolution) within the United Kingdom—so-called Home Rule. This form of Irish nationalism can be described as constitutional or parliamentary. Thanks to the above radicalization of attitudes within the nationalist movement itself, there has been a revival of a republicanism that had been forgotten for several decades—known as integralist republicanism. The revival of republicanism took place chronologically before the formation of the Irish group in the British Parliament which fought for the autonomy of the island. A secret conspiratorial organization called the Irish Republican Brotherhood was formed in Dublin in 1858, linked to the Fenian Brotherhood founded by Irish dissidents in New York. So-called The Fenian movement made an unsuccessful attempt in 1867 to foment another Irish uprising.[80]

The defeat of this insurrection had two consequences for the Irish republican movement. Firstly, the Irish stopped believing in the sense of armed struggle for independence for a long time. Secondly, the republicans came under severe criticism from the Roman Catholic hierarchy both in Ireland and the Holy See. In line with the doctrine of ultramontanism, Pope Pius IX officially condemned—with all the consequences this entailed—the activities of both Brotherhoods. For the Fenians, most of whom were devout Catholics,

---

[79] See: E. F. Biagini, *Home Rule for Ireland (1874–1914): the Great Missed Opportunity?*, "Études anglaises," 2018/3, Vol. 71, pp. 259–275.

[80] See: S. Mcconville, *Irish Political Offenders, 1848–1922: Theatres of War*, New York 2002, pp. 107–213.

this was a situation they could not accept. It is noteworthy that the conflict then initiated between the Republican movement and the Roman Catholic hierarchy led, in effect, to the gradual "secularization" of the former entity. Irish Republicans, despite being predominantly Catholic and representing mainly this religious group, advocated the neutrality of the Church in matters of politics. Nevertheless, they could not underestimate the institution's influence on the socio-political life of the island's predominantly Catholic population. The turn of the nineteenth and twentieth centuries in Ireland was dominated by the public debate on autonomy. At this time, within Irish nationalism, its successive democratic representatives at Westminster, Charles Stewart Parnell, John Redmond and John Dillon, led the way among Irish republicans, two camps emerged. One led by John Devoy allowed cooperation with Parnell's constitutional nationalists, while the other centered around Charles Kickham rejected it altogether.

The response of the Unionist supporters to the Irish faction's autonomy aspirations was the formation of an opposition in the British Parliament in 1886 in the form of the Unionist Party. It also saw the revival of the Ulster Order of Orange, a loyalist grouping that had existed since 1795 and was committed to maintaining Protestant supremacy in Ireland. Finally, on May 25, 1914, the supporters of Home Rule succeeded when the British House of Commons passed the so-called Third Home Rule Act (Parnell had made two unsuccessful attempts in 1886 and 1892). In 1886, the Liberal Party Prime Minister of the United Kingdom, William Gladstone, decided that something had to be done to end the problems in Ireland. He felt that giving Ireland back its local parliament, which had been removed by the Act of Union in 1800, would solve the problem. So in 1886 Gladstone introduced the first Home Rule Bill. However, it was defeated in the London Parliament because others, particularly the Conservative Party, were against Home Rule, which they felt would weaken the United Kingdom. In 1886 the anti-Home Rule Conservatives came to power. Their policy was to introduce new and fairer laws for Ireland. These laws were called the Plan of Campaign. They gave tenant farmers more rights and helped them to become much better off financially. The purpose of this policy was to show the Irish, through kindness, that Home Rule was unnecessary. It worked well and between 1885 and 1905 most of Ireland's land changed hands from landlords to tenants. In 1892 the Liberals returned to power. Despite threats from the Unionists at their 1892 conference, William Gladstone introduced the Second Home Rule Bill in 1893. It was passed by the House of Commons in a victorious vote. But in the House of Lords, where Conservatives outnumbered Liberals, it was defeated. A bill can't become law in the UK unless both houses pass it (so-called: bicameral law legislation).[81]

In the aftermath of this attempt to introduce Home Rule, the Irish unionists formed an organization called the "Irish Unionist Alliance" to fight against Home Rule. This organization was very influential, although small in numbers, and received large donations from rich businessmen in Dublin, Cork and Belfast. These were the people who had the most to lose from Home Rule. The IUA also gained the support of the opposition in the British Parliament (the Conservatives) because they felt that if Ireland broke away from Britain, other parts of the British Empire would try to do the same. These people were called "British Unionists." This meant that the two sides in the London Parliament were opposed to each other when it came to the issue of Home Rule. After the first Home Rule Bill failed, the Conservative leader came to Ulster where Irish Unionism was much stronger than anywhere else. He told unionists that they could count on British unionists to help them resist Home Rule. He famously said "Ulster will fight and Ulster will be right." In 1892 the Unionists began to use the slogan "Erin go bragh," which is Irish for "Ireland for ever," to show their commitment to maintaining Ireland's position as part of the United Kingdom. In addition, sporadic riots broke out in Belfast because Ulster Unionism was being seen as anti-Catholic. This was a charge they didn't face in the rest of Ireland, where there was less trouble. In 1886 alone, 50 people were killed in the city of Belfast.[82]

Charles S. Parnell (and later John Dillon's), and William E. Gladstone's advocacy of Irish home rule could be perceived as a one of the major factors in the rise of Irish nationalism (except Gaelic revival and Sinn Féin creation,[83] and IPP home rule failure), and it helped to fuel the growing demands for

---

81 J. Szymanek, *Druga izba we współczesnym parlamencie. Analiza porównawcza na przykładzie europejskich państw unitarnych* [*The second chamber in the modern parliament. Comparative analysis on the example of European unitary states*], Warszawa 2005, p. 539.

82 See: A. Jackson, op. cit., p. 21.

83 Compare: B. Feeney, op. cit., M. Laffan, *Resurrection of Ireland: The Sinn Féin Party 1916–23*, Cambridge 1999, pp. 3–40.

Irish independence that would culminate in the Easter Rising of 1916 and the establishment of the Irish Free State in 1922. It is worth adding that The third bill had to wait for another Liberal ministry (the Conservatives had tried to "kill Home Rule by kindness," to undermine its programme with moderate reforms); its introduction in 1912 inflamed militant opposition from both unionists (led by Edward Carson) and republicans in Ireland. The Act was enacted on September 18, 1914, but was inoperative for the duration of World War I. After years of conflict, a system similar to Home Rule was established in the six counties of Ulster (Northern Ireland) by the Government of Ireland Act (1920). The Anglo-Irish Treaty (1921) gave dominion status to the remaining 26 counties in the south; the nominal link with the British Commonwealth was further eroded in 1937 and severed in 1949.[84]

However nationalism in Ireland is one of the oldest political traditions in the country, a tradition which acquired a new degree of effectiveness and influence at the end of the nineteenth century. Between 1874 and 1914, British and Irish politicians drew up and debated various plans for constitutional reform to transform the unitary parliamentary state into either a federation or a union with a special devolved parliament for the whole of Ireland. The latter came to be known as Home Rule, because it involved giving the Irish control over their internal affairs without ending the 1800 Union with Britain. Home Rule fell far short of independence or even what came to be known as dominion status. But it bitterly divided British and Irish political opinion for two generations and brought the country to the brink of civil war in 1912. Passed in 1914 but not implemented (due to strong Ulster opposition), Home Rule was then revised and passed again by the British Parliament in 1920. By this time, however, it was "too little, too late" for the nationalists who demanded full independence and were prepared to fight for it (in the War of Independence of 1919–1921 and the Civil War of 1922–1923). On the other hand, the most important event for Irish nationalism at the turn of the nineteenth and twentieth centuries was the so-called National Awakening or Celtic Revival. This was a response to the process of Anglicization of the island. The Gaelic Athletic Association (GAA) was founded in 1884 and the Gaelic League was established in 1893.

---

[84] See also D. Ferriter, *The Border: The Legacy of a Century of Anglo-Irish Politics*, London 2019, passim.

In 1884 Irish nationalists began the first phase of forging a unified Irish national identity. This started with the Gaelic Athletic Association (GAA) to promote Irish sports. In 1893, the Gaelic League was founded by two (Nationalist) Protestants. Its purpose was to promote the Irish language. The Irish language was mainly of Celtic origin with some Scottish influence. Both organizations were extremely successful, attracting thousands of members. Together, they instituted what is now referred to as the "Gaelic Revival" in Ireland. The organizations aimed to strengthen the internal national, cultural and ethnic identity of the Irish people.

The institutionalized effect of these activities was the creation, in 1908, of a political party called Sinn Féin. The emergence of Sinn Féin as a political party is disputed by scholars. The consensus is that it must have been between 1904 and 1908, as the movement's process of institutionalization was in stages. Around 1905 the existing nationalist forum, the National Council, adopted a Sinn Féin policy, and in 1907 the Sinn Féin League was formed, bringing together the Republican Clubs of Dungannon (the legal platform of the IRB) and the National Council, while from 1908 it was possible to speak of a political party under the name of Sinn Féin.[85] Its original purpose was to promote Irish nationalism and independence from British rule. The name Sinn Féin means "ourselves alone" in Irish Gaelic, reflecting the party's focus on Irish self-determination. At its inception, Sinn Féin was a small political party with limited support.

The party's roots can be traced back to the founding of the Irish Republican Brotherhood (IRB) in 1858. The IRB was a secret society dedicated to the establishment of an independent Irish republic. In 1905, Arthur Griffith, an Irish nationalist and journalist, established a new political movement called Sinn Féin, which means "Ourselves Alone" in Irish. Griffith sought to create a political party that would work toward Irish independence by promoting Irish nationalism and self-governance. Sinn Féin's founding principles were outlined in Griffith's book called "The Resurrection of Hungary," which advocated for the establishment of dual monarchy in Ireland, similar to the arrangement between Austria and Hungary. This concept aimed to achieve

---

[85] See: M. Laffan, op. cit.

Irish independence by forming a political union with Britain while maintaining a separate Irish parliament and government.[86]

It can be argued that Sinn Féin in this period, although it did not achieve the status of a mass grouping, was an interesting alternative organizational and substantive proposition to the dominant Irish nationalism of the time—the constitutional nationalism of the Irish faction led by Redmond. It is worth noting here that, from the perspective of twentieth-century Irish republicanism, one conception of Sinn Féin political action conceived by Griffith proved incredibly useful and remarkably durable. It turned out to be abstentionism. Abstentionism, the refusal of elected Irish representatives to participate in any deemed non-Irish (i.e., British) legislative and executive bodies, became one of the most important principles to which Irish republicans adhered in the twentieth century. In the nineteenth century, violent and constitutional campaigns for autonomy or independence culminated in an election in 1918 in which almost 70 % of the seats went to newly revived Sinn Féin, which declared Irish independence from Britain and set up a parliament in Dublin. A war of independence followed, which ended with the Anglo-Irish Treaty of 1921. This partitioned Ireland into the Irish Free State, which was given dominion status within the British Empire, and a devolved administration in Northern Ireland, which remained part of the United Kingdom. In 1937, Ireland declared itself fully independent of the United Kingdom, and in 1949 Ireland (Éire) withdrew from the Commonwealth of Nations.[87] To resume, it is worth quoting to underscore the importance of British-Irish relations during the Victorian period Dr. Gemma Clark: "The Empire was both a chain and a key for the Irish. Thus, the diversity and ambiguity of the British Empire is evident even at its heart, in the complex relationship between Britain and its closest neighbour, Ireland."[88]

---

[86] See: T. M. Kettle, *A Note on Sinn Fein in Ireland*, "The North American Review," Vol. 187, No. 626, January 1908, pp. 46–59.

[87] See: L. J. McCaffrey, *The Irish Question: 1800–1922*, London 1968, pp. 161–184.

[88] G. Clark, *Britain and Ireland: ambiguities of Empire*, University of Exeter, https://ugc.futurelearn.com/uploads/files/2b/80/2b80cfb1-f3b9-420d-b692-c11ab6bbcdd4/Wk1_Britain_and_Ireland.pdf [accessed 9.05.2023].

1.2.2. Toward independence, Easter Rising and Anglo-Irish Treaty (1914–1921)

Between 1912 and 1914, there was a debate in the British Parliament on the subject of future Irish autonomy, in which John Redmond's Irish parliamentary faction played an important role. John Redmond was an Irish politician who succeeded Charles Parnell as leader of the Irish Parliamentary Party (IPP) in 1900. Redmond was born in County Wexford in 1856 and became a lawyer before entering politics. He was first elected to the House of Commons in 1881 and became leader of the IPP in 1900 after a period of turmoil in the party following the fall of Parnell. Under Redmond's leadership, the IPP continued to pursue the goal of Irish Home Rule, which had been championed by Parnell. Redmond was a skilled orator and was able to win support for his cause in both Ireland and Britain. In 1910, the IPP became the largest party in the House of Commons, and Redmond believed that Home Rule was within reach. However, the outbreak of World War I in 1914 changed the political landscape in Ireland. Redmond supported the British war effort and encouraged Irish men to enlist in the British Army, but this led to divisions within the IPP and among Irish nationalists more broadly. Some nationalists saw the war as an opportunity to press for Irish independence, while others saw it as a chance to prove their loyalty to Britain and to win concessions for Ireland. Redmond's support for the war effort proved controversial, and he was increasingly criticized by more radical nationalists such as Sinn Féin, who advocated for complete Irish independence. Redmond died in 1918, just before the end of the war, and his vision of Irish Home Rule was ultimately overshadowed by the Easter Rising of 1916 and the subsequent War of Independence.[89] As Daniel Mulhall, former Ambassador of Ireland to the United States, and to the UK, writes: "by the time of John Redmond's death in 1918, Home Rule was on the statute book but with its implementation deferred until the end of the war. For his part, Redmond had offered wholehearted support to the war effort and had urged his followers to enlist for military service although he had opposed conscription."[90] As a curiosity, it is very common to add one

---

[89] See: J. Bruton, *The Redmond Family in Parliamentary Politics*, "An Irish Quarterly Review," Vol. 107, No. 426, Summer 2018, pp. 176–184.

[90] D. Mulhall, *Three great Irish parliamentarians: O'Connell, Parnell and Redmond*, published online: https://www.dfa.ie/irish-embassy/great-britain/about-us/ambassador/

of the architects of the Good Friday Agreement, John Hume, to these three figures from Irish history (O'Connell, Parnell, Redmond).[91]

The importance of constitutional nationalism increased further after the outbreak of the First World War. In contrast, Sinn Féin's position radically weakened. A factor in this weakening was the massive infiltration of its structures by the Republican Clubs of Dungannon, which provided a legitimate platform for action for the post-revival Irish Republican Brotherhood (IRB). Republican infiltration of Sinn Féin came to an end around 1911, when most members left the party along with Bulmer Hobson (the IRB's chief ideologue). A generating factor in the strife within Sinn Féin was Griffith's conservatism, that is, adherence to the abstentionist principle and opposition to armed struggle. To members of the party associated with the new, more radical version of republicanism—represented by the IRB—the chairman's views seemed all too anachronistic. On the eve of the First World War, the Irish republican movement was gaining more and more adherents among the younger generation of Irish nationalists. Conflict between supporters of Irish independence and their Unionist opponents then seemed inevitable. In response to the radicalization of the Unionist camp, the Irish Volunteers was formed in November 1913, with Eoin MacNeill as chief of staff. In October 1914, 11,000 people out of a membership of nearly 200,000 walked out of the organization, along with the chief of staff, in a gesture of protest against the use of the Volunteers on the war fronts on the British side. The organization's secessionists became known as the Sinn Féin Volunteers. The period between November 1913 and October 1914 was virtually the only time in the twentieth century that the entire nationalist movement in Ireland maintained unity. In 1915, the constitutional nationalists of Redmond's Irish party seemed satisfied with the project of autonomy promised after the end of World War I, while a new po-collection of radical republican activists, mainly members of the reactivated IRB, were thinking about seizing power

ambassador-blog-2017/february2017/three-great-irish-parliamentarians/ [accessed 28.04.2023].

91 "The Irish Times" 4th August 2020, published online: https://www.irishtimes.com/news/ireland/irish-news/john-hume-has-place-in-pantheon-of-irish-nationalist-leaders-such-as-o-connell-parnell-and-redmond-1.4321156 [accessed 28.04.2023].

in Ireland by armed struggle.[92] The political context in Ireland prior to and at the very beginning of the war is well known. There was the apparent march toward civil conflict in 1912 and 1913, marked by the creation of the unionist Ulster Volunteer Force and the nationalist Irish Volunteers. This was by the outbreak of war and the decision announced by John Redmond in his Woodenbridge speech to support allied war efforts. The split in the Irish Volunteers The split in the Irish Volunteers was immediate, with the Irish Volunteers opposing Redmond`s decision and were led by Eoin MacNeill, and the Nationalist Volunteers, led by John Redmond.[93]

Through the Gaelic League MacNeill met members of Sinn Féin, the Irish Republican Brotherhood (IRB) and other nationalists and republicans. One such colleague, The O'Rahilly, was editor of the League's newspaper, "An Claidheamh Soluis," and in October 1913 they asked MacNeill to write an editorial for them on a subject wider than Irish language issues. MacNeill submitted an article entitled "The North Began," encouraging the formation of a nationalist volunteer force for Irish Home Rule, much as unionists had done earlier that year with the Ulster Volunteers to defeat Home Rule. Bulmer Hobson, a member of the IRB, approached MacNeill with a view to bringing the idea to fruition and, through a series of meetings, MacNeill became chairman of the council that formed the Irish Volunteers and later became its chief of staff. Unlike the IRB, MacNeill was opposed to the idea of armed rebellion, except to resist any suppression of the Volunteers. He saw little hope of success in open battle against the British Army. The Irish Volunteers had been infiltrated by the Irish Republican Brotherhood, whose plan was to use the organization to stage an armed rebellion for the separation of Ireland from Britain and the establishment of an Irish Republic. They saw Britain's entry into the First World War as the perfect opportunity to do this. Working with James Connolly and the Irish Citizen Army, a secret council of IRB officials plotted to stage a general rising at Easter 1916. On the Wednesday before Easter, they presented MacNeill with a letter—allegedly stolen from senior British staff at Dublin Castle—stating that the British were going

---

92 See: F. X. Martin, E. MacNeill, *Eoin MacNeill on the 1916 Rising*, "Irish Historical Studies," Vol. 12, No. 47, March 1961, pp. 226–271.

93 See: P. Ranger, *The World in Paris and Ireland too: The French Diplomacy of Sinn Féin, 1919–1921*, "Etudes Irlandaises," number 36-2, February 2011, p. 3.

to arrest him and all the other nationalist leaders. Unknown to MacNeill, the letter—known as the Castle Document—was forged, as follows. When MacNeill learned of the IRB's plans, and that Roger Casement was about to land in County Kerry with a shipment of German arms, he was reluctantly persuaded to go along with them. He believed that British action was now imminent and that the mobilization of the Irish Volunteers would be justified as a defensive act. However, MacNeill countermanded the order for the Rising by sending written messages to leaders around the country and placing a notice in the "Sunday Independent" canceling the planned "maneuvers" after learning that the German arms shipment had been intercepted and Casement arrested, and after confronting Patrick Pearse who refused to back down. This greatly reduced the number of volunteers who reported for duty on the day of the Easter Rising. Pearse, Connolly and the others agreed that the Rising would go ahead anyway, but that it would start a day later than originally planned to ensure that the authorities got caught.

The Rising began on Easter Monday, April 24, 1916 and lasted less than a week. After the rebels surrendered, MacNeill was arrested, although he had not taken part in the rebellion.[94]

It was the most significant event for the resurgent Irish republican movement in the twentieth century. It broke out on April 24, 1916 with the Easter Rising and finished with the Proclamation of the Irish Republic. The Rising remains a point of reference for modern Irish republicans in terms of the cause they are fighting for, although it was militarily unsuccessful. The Irish Republic, which covers the whole of the island and was proclaimed by the rebels themselves at Easter 1916, is a republic whose jurisdiction they continue to legitimize. The Rising lasted only six days and was the shortest in the history of the Irish struggle for national liberation, while at the same time it was the most significant to date.[95]

Several very important developments took place during the Troubles. Firstly, the Irish Republic was established and its army became the Irish

---

[94] See: Ch. Townshend (review), *Patrick Pearse. The Triumph of Failure* by Ruth Dudley Edwards, "The English Historical Review," Vol. 95, No. 374, January 1980, pp. 168–170.

[95] Detailed events of Easter Rising in: G. Allwood, *Ireland On Stage – The 1916 Easter Rising*, published online: https://www.forces.net/heritage/wwi/ireland-stage-1916-easter-rising [accessed 9.05.2023].

Republican Army (IRA, Gaelic: *Óglaigh na hÉi-reann*).[96] This organization, which still exists and is widely regarded as terrorist, legitimized its use of violence through the events of Easter 1916.

Secondly, the proclamation of the Irish Republic—whatever its legitimacy—was in fact the fulfillment of the republican dream of a free, sovereign and indivisible homeland. The Proclamation of Independence gave republicans a vision of Ireland to strive and fight for decades to come.

Thirdly, the Easter Rising brought the cause of Irish independence and the sacrifices of the fighting rebels to the international stage. The British had to reassess their views of Irish independence aspirations (within the limits of their national interest, of course) and moderate their initially violent reactions to the Rising, influenced by international opinion, particularly the large Irish minority in the United States.

Fourthly, despite the military defeat of the insurgents, and what initially appeared to be a moral defeat as well, the heroic sacrifice of the fighters changed the attitudes of the majority of Irish society toward the insurgency and the republican movement as a whole, from initially very hostile to downright affirmative. Such an evolution was due to the brutal British retaliation against the insurgents, which was counterproductive. The British terror against the republicans paradoxically gained them supporters as it sanctified the Irish insurgent victims, making them heroes and martyrs. Pearse and Connolly's messianic views of "redeeming Ireland through bloodshed" awakened the Irish people's independence-minded attitudes, and their belief in the sense of continuing the armed struggle. On the other hand there is the opinion of Prof. MacGarry, with reference to O'Hegarty, that few periods in Irish history have generated as much historiographical controversy as the revolutionary period. The key issues were identified as early as 1924 by P. S. O'Hegarty, who in a pessimistic pro-Treaty polemic, Victory of Sinn Féin, claimed that the unnecessary use of political violence after the Easter Rising had destroyed the spirit of the national movement and demoralized the Irish people.[97]

---

[96] See more on IRA origins: R. English, *Armed Struggle, The history of the IRA*, London 2003, p. 1 and p. 2.

[97] See: F. Mc Garry, *Revolution, 1916– 1923*, in: T. Bartlett, (ed.), *Cambridge History of Ireland, Volume 1V:* from the 1880s to the present, Cambridge 2018, p. 258, and P. S.

Between the Easter Rising in 1916 and the December 1918 House of Commons elections, the British government's stance toward Sinn Féin evolved from one of harsh repression to a more conciliatory approach. In the immediate aftermath of the Easter Rising, the British authorities took a hard line against Sinn Féin and its supporters, arresting and interning thousands of Irish nationalists. The government also imposed martial law in Dublin and other parts of Ireland, and the military courts handed down harsh sentences, including death penalties, to those accused of involvement in the rebellion. The rebellion was widely condemned by the British public. It was seen as a betrayal by Irish nationalists who had sworn allegiance to the British Empire. The leaders of the rebellion were quickly arrested and court-martialed. The executions of the leaders of the Easter Rising[98] sparked outrage in Ireland and sympathy for the nationalist cause grew. In Britain, however, the executions were initially supported by many, including the mainstream press, who saw the rebellion as a threat to the stability of the British Empire. In time, however, the British government came to realize that the harsh repression of Irish nationalism was not working. A more conciliatory approach was needed.

As F. MacGarry writes the first evidence of growing sympathy for the rebels was the sight of crowds flocking to requiem Masses for the executed leaders who were almost instantly memorialized in ballads, mass cards, badges, flags, picture postcards and other relics.[99] At the end of 1916 the new Prime Minister of the British government, David Lloyd George, decided to make a gesture toward the republicans by releasing from prison, among others, the President of Sinn Féin, Griffith, and two young activists, Cathal Brugha and Michael Collins. Both soon became leaders who took control of

---

O'Hegarty, *The Victory of Sinn Féin* (new edn., University College Dublin Press) Dublin 2015.

98 Sixteen of the Rising's leaders were executed starting in May 1916, most notably: Roger Casement, Éamonn Ceannt, Thomas James Clarke, James Connolly, Seán MacDiarmada, Thomas MacDonagh, Patrick Pearse, Joseph Mary Plunkett. See: https://www.gov.ie/en/publication/583995-the-executed-leaders-of-the-1916-rising.

99 See F. MacGarry, *Easter Rising (Great Britain and Ireland)*, published online: https://encyclopedia.1914-1918-online.net/article/easter_rising_great_britain_and_ireland, https://www.theirishstory.com/2011/04/22/the-easter-rising-%e2%80%93-a-brief-overview/#.ZFycsHZByUk [both accessed 9.05.2023].

the entire armed republican movement. The third person who was responsible for the political direction and consolidation of the movement as a whole was another participant in the uprising, an Irishman with American citizenship—Éamon de Valera. By 1917 Sinn Féin was attracting more and more supporters. Its widespread association with the Easter Rising gave its members strength and verve in the creation of new party circles and local outposts, as well as in the promotion of the party's programme. The role of previously imprisoned activists was also important.[100]

At the convention (Gaelic: *ard-fhéis*) of Sinn Féin on Oct. 25, 1917, Éamon de Valera succeeded Arthur Griffith as party chairman. Griffith became its vice chairman. The change in the party's leadership was evidence of the party's evolution toward republicanism. Michael Collins, Rory O'Connor, William T. Cosgrave and Countess Constance Markievicz were appointed to Sinn Féin's coordinating committee.[101] They were republican-minded. From then on, Sinn Féin sought to secure international recognition of Ireland as an independent Irish Republic. The party's convention stressed the importance of applying the principle of abstentionism. Two days later—on October 27th, 1917, at the convention of the Irish Volunteers—de Valera became chairman, Brugha became the organization's chief of staff, and Collins—as organizational director and IRB member—focused on rebuilding IRB control over the Volunteers. These personnel and organizational decisions again emphatically confirmed the traditional link between political and military structures that had long existed within the Irish Republican movement.

Over a year-long period—preceding the British parliamentary elections—most Sinn Féin activists spent in detention and prison, suspected by the British authorities of successive attempts to conspire with the Germans and a desire to provoke another uprising. It is noteworthy that British repression only lent Sinn Féin supporters, Sinn Féin won six of nine by-elections to the House of Commons between February 1917 and June 1918, and boycotted the Irish Convention on the Future of Ireland (*Irish Convention*). Sinn Féin, despite large-scale British repression, was a well-organized party, as it had some 1,250 clubs in Ireland at the end of 1917. By the spring of 1918, these clubs were already approx. 1,700 in the country. According to the RIC (*Royal*

[100] See more: B. Feeney, op. cit., pp. 67–69.
[101] J. O'Beirne Ranelagh, op. cit., p. 184.

Irish Constabulary), Sinn Féin membership increased by 29 % between March and May 1918. At the time, Sinn Féin may have had as many as approx. 120–130,000 members. Given Ireland's population of less than four and a half million people at the time (1918), the number of about 130,000 Sinn Féin members was significant.[102]

The elections to the British House of Commons, held after the end of World War I on December 14, 1918, were a huge success for Sinn Féin, as the party won a whopping 73 of the 105 seats allocated to Ireland at Westminster.[103] However, the harsh repression by British government only served to increase support for Sinn Féin and other nationalist groups. In the 1918 general election, Sinn Féin won a landslide victory, and establishing the first *Dáil Éireann* (Irish Parliament). Mandates were obtained by, among others: Éamon de Valera, Arthur Griffith, Constance Markievicz.[104] Following the election, the British government began to reassess its policy toward Sinn Féin. The government's new approach was partly driven by the desire to avoid further bloodshed and partly by the recognition that Sinn Féin had won a democratic mandate from the Irish people.

On the initiative of Sinn Féin, the *Dáil Éireann*, or self-appointed Irish Parliament, was constituted in Dublin on 21st of January 1919 as an alternative form of activity to the Irish MPs at Westminster. However, the Irish faction and the Unionists did not respond to the invitation of their elected representatives to participate in the new body. The British also ignored the Dáil, recognizing by law that democratically elected MPs could not be prevented by anyone from meeting in any group outside parliament. The first meeting of the Dáil was attended by 27 Sinn Féin MPs, as the rest of those elected were either in prison or had special assignments to carry out. Those who were not in prison on 21 I 1919 met at Mansion House to take the oath to the Republic, adopt the "Democratic Programme" and re-declare

---

102 B. Feeney, op. cit., pp. 91–92.

103 See. A. Pawłowska, *Mit niezawodności – brytyjski wywiad na terenie Irlandii w przededniu wojny o niepodległość* [The myth of reliability – British intelligence in Ireland in the eve of War of Independence], "Acta Universitatis Lodziensis. Folia Historica," Issue 111, 2022, pp. 143–160.

104 B. O'Brien, *A Short History of the IRA: From 1916 Onwards*, Dublin 2019, p. 19.

Irish independence (this was first done on 24 IV 1916 during the Easter Rising).[105] The Democratic Programme was intended to bring the Irish cause to the attention of the Socialist International, then meeting in Bern, and the Declaration of Independence was intended to put pressure on the American government. The Dáil meeting was being prepared in great haste in order to still have time to present the Irish case to the Paris Peace Conference, which was inaugurated on eighteenth of January 1919.[106] However, the Irish case had no place at the Paris Conference.[107] Late in 1919, the British government invited Sinn Féin representatives to a peace conference in London, but the talks broke down over the issue of Irish independence. The government then declared martial law in Ireland, and the Irish War of Independence began in earnest.[108]

Cathal Brugha was appointed President of Dáil Éireann and Prime Minister of the Provisional Government, but he was to step down for de Valera when he was released from prison. The next meeting of Dáil Éireann was held in April 1919. It elected a new Prime Minister, who became Éamon de Valera, who had been released from prison by Collins. De Valera appointed a new government with, among others: Collins, Brugha, Griffith, MacNeill and Markiewicz. The reaction of the British authorities to such unceremonious actions by the Sinn Féin separatists did not come until

---

105 Text of declaration of independence 1919 in: https://www.difp.ie/volume-1/1919/declaration-of-independence/1/#section-documentpage [accessed 10.05.2023].

106 See also: G. Keown, *First of the Small Nations: The Beginnings of Irish Foreign Policy in the Inter-War Years*, 1919–1932, Oxford 2016, passim; G. Keown, *Knocking on the Door: The Irish Presence at the Paris Peace Conference of 1919*, "Irish Studies in International Affairs," Vol. 30, 2019, pp. 41–57.

107 A. Maillot, *The New Sinn Fein: Irish Republicanism in the Twenty-First Century*, New York 2004, p. 130. The problem, according to the author, was that republican ideas of Irish foreign policy were always dictated by the current international conjuncture, and at the time the only state that could support Ireland was an undesirable ally in the form of Soviet Russia. See also: S. Bachrynowski, *Sojusznicy i wrogowie Irlandii na arenie międzynarodowej w myśli politycznej irlandzkiego ruchu republikańskiego* [*Allies and Enemies of Ireland on International Scene in the Political Thought of Irish Republican Movement*], "Facta Simonidis," 2008, nr 1 (1), pp. 121–139.

108 See also: J. Dorney, *Peace after the Final Battle: The Story of the Irish Revolution, 1912–1924*, New Island 2014; J. Dorney, *The Civil War in Dublin: The Fight for the Irish Capital, 1922–1924*, Dublin 2017, passim.

September 10, 1919, when it was recognized that Dáil Éireann was an insecure organization and a threat to the interests of the United Kingdom. In these circumstances, most republicans realized that armed solutions might soon follow, not even ruling out British intervention on the island. Michael Collins, the head of the IRB and the IRA, wanted to obstruct British rule over Ireland and thought that the time had come to use the armed argument.

The Irish War of Independence was basically a guerrilla conflict between the British state and its forces in Ireland and Irish republican guerrillas in the Irish Volunteers or Irish Republican Army. The war is usually said to have run between 1919 and 1921, but violence both preceded these dates and continued afterwards. Parallel with the military campaign was the political confrontation between the separatist Sinn Féin party, who after winning the General Election of 1918, declared an Irish Republic, and the British administration based in Dublin Castle. Another strand of the conflict lay in the northern province of Ulster, which was majority unionist or pro-British and which opposed Sinn Féin. This led to violence between the majority Protestant unionists and the mainly Catholic Irish nationalist minority in the north. On the same day that the Dáil met for the first time, two RIC constables were shot dead by Irish Volunteers under Dan Breen at Soloheadbeg in Tipperary.[109] The explosives they were carrying were confiscated. This is commonly portrayed as the opening shots of the war, but there had been deaths in 1918 and only 17 more deaths in 1919.

The reaction of Dáil Éireann and Sinn Féin politicians to the IRA's use of force was highly critical. The official commander of the Irish Volunteers and Defense Minister in the De Valera government, Cathal Brugha, dissented from the attack. There was a very serious difference of opinion between the civilian and military factions of the Nationalist movement about the future of Ireland, so that by March 11, 1921 Dáil Éireann did not approve of the

---

[109] Daniel Breen joined the Irish Republican Brotherhood in 1912 and the Irish Volunteers in 1914. On January 21, 1919, the day the First Dáil met in Dublin, Breen took part in an ambush at Soloheadbeg. The ambush party, led by Seán Treacy, attacked a group of Royal Irish Constabulary men who were escorting explosives to a quarry and two policemen were shot dead during the engagement. The ambush is considered to be the first action taken in the Irish War of Independence. See more (statement by Dan Breen): https://www.militaryarchives.ie/collections/online-collections/bureau-of-military-history-1913-1921/reels/bmh/BMH.WS1739.pdf [accessed 11.05.2023].

IRA's methods of warfare, namely ambushes and stealth killings of police officers and soldiers. However, between 1920 and 1921, British reaction in the form of sending additional police and army troops to Ireland forced the Dáil to change its attitude and accept the IRA's actions. Collins, organizing so-called IRA flying columns, was quite successful in attacking.

The reaction of the British authorities to this turn of events was unequivocal: no concessions to the IRA. Retaliations by the police and army often affected the innocent civilian population of the island. The British authorities responded to this situation in an extraordinary way, recruiting first ex-soldiers and then ex-officers in England to join the RIC and bring their recent experience of weapons and warfare to what had previously been a distinctly Irish police force. Known respectively as the "Black and Tans" and the "Auxiliaries," these two elements of the RIC became notorious for using their war experience to terrorize the civilian population of Ireland, particularly the Catholic Irish majority, in the name of the Crown and supposedly in the cause of law, order and British justice.[110]

It is worth noting that over ten thousand Britons fought as police in the First Irish War (1920–21). Most of these British policemen were ex-soldiers, veterans of the First World War and members of the Royal Irish Constabulary (RfC), known as the "Black and Tans" for their mixed uniforms of dark police green and military khaki. Heavily armed and organized into military-style companies, the ex-officers joined a separate force, the Auxiliary Division (ADRIC), a special emergency gendarmerie. In combat with Irish Republican Army (IRA) guerrillas, the Black and Tans and Auxiliaries carried out many "reprisals," assassinations of Irish republicans and the burning of their homes and businesses. As a result, their name became synonymous with crime and violence, and the ghost of the Black and Tans has haunted Ireland ever since. It is crucial to recognize how difficult the position of the British government was in the early 1920s. The British had more potentially explosive problems to deal with at the end of the First World War and then the continuing administration and pacification of the mandates. There was inflation, industrial unrest, political unrest and fighting in Russia, Persia,

110 See: J. Ainsworth, *The Black & Tans and Auxiliaries in Ireland, 1920–1921: Their Origins, Roles and Legacy*, A paper presented to the Annual Conference of the Queensland History, pp. 1–8.

Afghanistan and Africa, having lost many of its overseas markets to America, and then there was Ireland. The problems at home meant that they had to control the territory and control the population—or at least prevent them from actively supporting the rebel cause. Moreover, you would expect the Cabinet to have directed the means of carrying out their policy of granting Home Rule in accordance with the Home Rule Act of 1914.[111]

Home Rule Act of 1914, it provided almost no guidance on how to stabilize Ireland long enough to do so. But the British forces had to operate without this guidance and with inadequate manpower, with restrictions on their authority and powers. with restrictions on their authority and powers, and with no political or military theory of how to deal with the rebellion. The lack of guidance is inexplicable, especially given the opinion of the Chief of the Imperial General Staff, Sir Henry Wilson, who said that to lose Ireland was to lose the realm. However, at the other end of the scale, according to W. H. Kautt—one might say that Sinn Féin and the IRA had a much easier yardstick, though they had different commitments. They achieved a measure of success simply by not losing. Their very existence demonstrated the "impotence" of British rule in Ireland, and each act seemed to reinforce this view. While their ultimate goal of a republican Ireland was concrete and in theory non-negotiable, their steady progress toward that goal was easier to see than the Castle's successes in its prevention.[112]

Between 1919 and 1920 there was a further escalation of violence from both sides. IRA Volunteer or Intelligence Director Michael Collins formed a "squad" In Dublin to assassinate detectives coordinating arrests of republican activists. Late in the year his men tried but failed to kill John French, the Lord Lieutenant of Ireland. Alongside the limited armed campaign, there was significant passive resistance, including hunger strikes by those imprisoned (many of whom were released in March 1920) and a boycott by railway workers of carrying British troops. Rural unrest, with small farmers attempting to seize parts of large "ranches," was also significant.

---

[111] https://www.parliament.uk/about/living-heritage/evolutionofparliament/legislative-scrutiny/parliamentandireland/collections/home-rule-1914/gov-of-ireland-act-1914/ [accessed 11.05.2023].

[112] See: W. H. Kautt, *Militarising Policemen. The various members of the RIC and their response to IRA violence in Ireland, 1919–21*, Conference Paper, May 2003, p. 2.

Violence intensified in early 1920. Much of Sinn Féin's political leadership was arrested. Éamon de Valera, the President of the Republic, had gone to America to raise funds. The two leaders of the IRA, Collins and Richard Mulcahy, ordered volunteer units across the country to raid RIC barracks for arms. The Dáil finally endorsed the IRA's campaign in 1921. However, some Sinn Féin figures, such as Arthur Griffith, were opposed to the use of violence. A series of attacks on rural police barracks followed in early 1920. On the night of Easter Sunday 1920, the RIC withdrew from its smaller stations to fortified barracks in towns and the abandoned posts were systematically burned down by the IRA across the country. By the summer of 1920, many RIC men had resigned their commissions and in many places the IRA was in the ascendancy. Elsewhere the RIC responded to attacks on them by assassinating republicans such as Tomas MacCurtain, Lord Mayor of Cork. The murder was the subject of widespread public outrage.[113]

At the same time, in the summer of 1920, Sinn Féin won local elections in most of Ireland and took over state functions such as collecting taxes and enforcing the law. In some places the RIC was replaced by the Irish Republican Police and the court system by Sinn Féin or Dáil courts. To put down this insurgency, the British government under Lloyd George proposed autonomous governments in Northern Ireland and Southern Ireland, and also used new corps of paramilitary police from Britain, the Black and Tans and the Auxiliary Division, made up largely of veterans of the First World War. Lloyd George also passed the Restoration of Order in Ireland Act, which gave special powers to the police and military. This led to a serious escalation of the conflict as the new forces carried out reprisals against the civilian population for IRA attacks—for example, in the summer of 1920, large parts of the towns of Balbriggan and Tuam were burned to the ground. The IRA responded by forming full-time Flying Columns[114] (also known as *Active Service Units*), which became

---

[113] See: D. J. O'Sullivan, *The Irish Constabularies, 1822–1922: A Century of Policing in Ireland*, Brandon 1999, p. 303.

[114] https://www.waterfordmuseum.ie/exhibit/web/Display/article/318/3/The_Irish_War_of_Independence_1919__21_The_Decies_Brigade__The_Flying_Column.html [accessed 12.05.2023].

much more ruthless and efficient at guerrilla warfare in some parts of the country. The British military-police force outnumbered the Irish guerrillas many times over in terms of numbers and weaponry. For Collins (the instigator of the IRA's military actions), it was the lack of guns and ammo that posed the most serious problem. Even the most spectacular guerrilla actions could not erase the impression that the guerrillas were already at the end of their tether.

The people of the south of Ireland were tired of the war and the scale of the terror of the British forces of law and order. In the north of the island, on the other hand, there was violence against the Catholic population. Given these facts, Collins was aware that such an unequal struggle would not last long. British public opinion was also weary of the conflict and demanded that the state authorities take appropriate steps to stabilize the situation in Ireland. In the north, after the IRA killed two northern Protestant policemen in separate incidents, loyalists attacked Catholic areas in Belfast, Derry and Lisburn, causing serious rioting. Up to 100 people were killed and hundreds of Catholic homes were burned. Another 7,000 Catholics were forced out of their jobs in the Belfast shipyards. The Northern Ireland authorities also set up the Ulster Special Constabulary to provide an armed police force for the mostly unionist population.

Under the 1920 Act, Sinn Féin contested the parliamentary elections for the 26 southern counties, creating two separate parliaments: the South and the six counties of the unionist North. Sinn Féin made significant gains in the South. It won 124 out of 128 seats. Traditionally, it did not contest any seats, as it did not wish to sanction the partition of the island. The autumn and winter of 1920 saw a new ruthlessness on both sides. On November 21, IRA units in Dublin launched a mass assassination of British intelligence officers, killing 14 men, at least 8 of them. In revenge, a force of RIC Black and Tans and Auxiliaries shot dead 15 civilians at a football match in Dublin's Croke Park on a day known as Bloody Sunday. A week later, a patrol of 17 Auxiliaries was ambushed and killed by the IRA in Kilmichael, County Cork, and shortly after that much of Cork city center was destroyed in a fire set by Crown forces.

A blatant example of a situation where the British forces over-reacted in their use of terror and thus lost so much control over what was happening in

Ireland in 1920–1921 was the Kevin Barry case.[115] Kevin Barry was 18 years old when he was hanged in Mountjoy Jail on November 1, 1920. His death at such a young age is perhaps the most poignant in recent Irish history. Born in Dublin in 1902, he grew up both in the capital and in County Carlow. He entered Belvedere College in 1916 and joined the Irish Volunteers, a nationalist organization. In 1919 he enrolled at Dublin University to study medicine. The War of Independence under the leadership of Michael Collins was in full swing and Barry, as a section commander, did his part in various raids around Dublin city. On September 20, 1920 he took part in one such raid which went badly wrong. A street firefight ensued and three British soldiers were killed. This was significant as it was the first British soldier deaths in Ireland since the 1916 Easter Rising led by Pearse and Connolly. Barry hid under a lorry during the British search for him but was discovered when a passer-by, concerned for his safety under the huge vehicle, inadvertently alerted the soldiers to his whereabouts. Reports of his torture in Mountjoy prison soon circulated, but Barry refused to name his comrades. He was sentenced to death, but there was widespread belief that the sentence would be commuted and that the British authorities would not have the courage to execute an eighteen-year-old. As the deadline approached it became clear that Kevin Barry would be executed. A planned rescue by Michael Collins failed when reinforcements from Dublin Castle were called to the prison because of the large crowds gathered outside. It was reported that Barry had asked to be shot by a firing squad rather than be hanged, which he considered to be a death unworthy of a soldier. The hangman, Ellis, had to be brought into the country from England as no one in Ireland could be found for the job. The calm and courage shown by young Barry in the hours leading up to his execution is legendary. Despite the protestations of clergy and politicians alike, he was hanged in Mountjoy Jail on November 1, 1920. Just as they had in the aftermath of the Easter Rising of 1916, the British military in Ireland had made a serious error of judgment. Had it simply been a case of imprisonment of the leaders of 1916, it is likely that there would not have been such a huge upsurge in support for Irish nationalism. By executing someone as young as Kevin Barry in 1920, they handed the Irish Republican Army a

115 See: M. A. Doherty, *Kevin Barry and the Anglo-Irish Propaganda War*, "Irish Historical Studies," Vol. 32, No. 1November 26, 2000, pp. 217–223.

huge propaganda victory. Young recruits flocked to join the IRA in the War of Independence. This in turn led to the Treaty, the partition of Ireland, the civil war, independence and everything that has happened since.[116]

By the end of 1920 terror continued, around 500 people had been killed. Attempts at a ceasefire in December were blocked by the British government, particularly Hamar Greenwood, the Chief Secretary for Ireland, who insisted that the IRA first disarm.[117] In the first 6 months of 1921, around 1,000 people were killed in the fighting. The violence was most intense in Dublin city, south Munster and Belfast, although there was some guerrilla activity in most areas. Almost 500 people were killed in County Cork (in actions such as the Upton ambush) and 300 in Dublin, while at the other end of the spectrum there were only nine deaths in County Cavan and Wicklow. In addition, some 6,000 republicans were imprisoned. Martial law was declared in the province of Munster. The regular British Army was deployed in greater numbers, mounting "sweeps" across the countryside, and the British authorities began "official reprisals," including house burnings and executions, in response to IRA attacks. The IRA retaliated with an increase in shootings of informers (real and alleged), eventually extending attacks to off-duty British personnel and the burning of loyalist property. When the British began executing prisoners, the IRA also began shooting captured British soldiers and police.

By summer 1921 the IRA was short of ammunition and weapons and many fighters had been arrested, notably in the Dublin Customs House raid. British forces claimed they were on the verge of defeat, but the guerrillas had also improved their bomb-making skills, were still inflicting casualties and there was no immediate end in sight. However, the fighting came to an end on July 11, 1921 when a ceasefire was negotiated between British and Irish republican forces so that talks on a political settlement could begin. In the North, however, the second half of 1921 was more violent than the first. There was extensive fighting between republicans and loyalists, Catholics and Protestants, particularly in Belfast.[118]

---

116 See: https://www.ireland-information.com/articles/kevinbarry.htm [accessed 12.05.2023].

117 *Kenny Barry and his times*, https://www.ucd.ie/t4cms/KBpanel2.pdf [accessed 12.05.2023].

118 See: Public Record Office of Northern Ireland, *Ireland 1900–1925: Crisis, War and Revolution A Resource for 'A' Level Students*, Belfast 2021, p. 90–100.

A ceasefire between the two sides in the conflict was signed on July 11, 1921, while peace talks began on October 11, 1921. The main issues were both the question of Irish unity and the future political status of the island. The British proposed to establish a British dominion in the southern 26 counties of Ireland, but with its own constitution, while the six most Protestant counties of Ulster—as Northern Ireland—would remain in union with Great Britain. The two proposals were hotly debated in the Republican camp. The ceasefire allowed the IRA to regroup, recruit and train openly. Many of its activists initially believed that this was only a temporary end to hostilities. But in December 1921, an Irish delegation led by Michael Collins and Arthur Griffith signed the Anglo-Irish Treaty, which abolished the Irish Republic of 1919 but created the Irish Free State. 26 of Ireland's 32 counties were given much more independence than the Home Rule Act of 1912 would have allowed.[119] The treaty negotiations were the culmination of more than two years of bitter conflict which ended with the declaration of an armistice on July 11, 1921. A few days later Sinn Féin leader Éamon de Valera traveled to London for a meeting with Prime Minister Lloyd George at Downing Street, where an enthusiastic crowd had gathered to support the Irish leader with songs and prayers. The talks lasted a week but failed to produce a meeting of minds. Then, in September 1921, the British government made an offer to negotiate to ascertain how an association of Ireland with the community of nations known as the British Empire can best be reconciled with Irish national aspirations, which was accepted.

British Prime Minister David Lloyd George convinced Irish delegates to sign the treaty on December 5, 1921, threatening a British military invasion of the island within three days. Signed Anglo-Irish Treaty, sanctioned the partition of the island and established the Irish Free State. It also soon became the cause of the first split in the Irish republican movement. The division of Ireland consequently led to the outbreak of civil war in Ireland on June 28, 1922. The republican movement (Sinn Féin and the IRA) suffered a fateful

---

[119] See: S. Bachrynowski, *Od centralizmu do autonomii. Problem ustanowienia i funkcjonowania samorządu w brytyjskiej prowincji Irlandii Północnej w latach 1921–1999* [*From Centralism to Autonomy. The Problem of Establishing and Functioning of Self-Government in the British Province of Northern Ireland in 1921–1999*], "Annales UMCS, Sectio K, Politologia," Vol. XIII, 2006, pp. 47–49.

split into two wings: 1) free-staters (pro-Treaty); 2) irregulars (anti-treaty). However, much of the IRA was unhappy with the settlement and this eventually led to civil war between nationalists in 1922–1923 before the new Irish Free State government was established. According to David Mulhall, already quoted on another occasion, the outcome of the London negotiations thus went far beyond the Home Rule arrangements of 1914. However, Ireland had changed dramatically over the years and the treaty, and particularly the introduction of the oath of allegiance to the British Crown, proved deeply divisive. This led to a disastrous civil war and sparked political animosities that lasted for generations. However, the Treaty allowed Ireland to develop its international profile and therefore all the achievements of Irish foreign policy in the last century stem from that fateful set of negotiations in London in the last weeks of 1921. It is worth adding, following cited D. Mulhall, that none of those who participated in the Irish delegation went on to have long careers in Irish politics or diplomacy. Collins and Griffith died within a year of each other. Erskine Childers was executed in November 1922. This was during the Irish Civil War. George Gavan Duffy served as Ireland's first foreign minister but soon returned to his legal career. On the British side, Lloyd George was sacked as Prime Minister within a year and Churchill was to have a turbulent career until the crisis of 1940 gave him a chance to shine as a wartime leader. Meanwhile de Valera, absent from the Treaty negotiations, was leading from Dublin, maintaining Ireland's neutrality as the Second World War crisis unfolded.[120]

The violence did not come to a complete end with the ceasefire in the south of Ireland. British troops remained in garrisons until the spring of 1922 and the last 6,000 soldiers did not leave until December 1922. There were a significant number of killings of serving and former RIC personnel by the IRA, and some killings of civilians—notably 13 Protestant civilians around Dunmanway in Cork in April 1922,[121] thought to be suspected informers—but the last major outbreak of violence was in Northern Ireland, whose existence was confirmed by the Treaty. In early 1922, both pro- and anti-Treaty

---

[120] See: D. Mulhall, *Our History 1921 – London October-December 1921*, published online https://www.dfa.ie/about-us/ourhistory/100years/1919-1929/1921,

[121] See: "History Ireland" published online: https://www.historyireland.com/massacre-west-cork-dunmanway-ballygorman-killings [accessed 12.05.2023].

wings of the IRA waged a clandestine campaign against Northern Ireland, tacitly supported by elements of the Provisional Free State government led by Michael Collins. This culminated in an abortive IRA offensive in May 1922, in which the guerrillas fought a number of major battles with British troops in the villages of Pettigo and Beleek in Fermanagh, but overall failed to coordinate their actions and were arrested in large numbers by the Northern government. Loyalists, in a number of cases with the help of the RIC and the Ulster Special Constabulary, launched reprisal attacks on Catholic areas of Belfast. On one occasion, the male members of a Catholic family—the McMahons[122]— were wiped out to avenge the murder of a police officer. The IRA in Belfast also carried out killings of Protestants, including bombing the trams taking workers to the shipyards.

Initially, both de Valera and Collins wanted to prevent the outbreak of civil war. They signed a pact on May 20, 1922, known as the "Collins—de Valera Pact," in which they called for unity in the republican movement and proposed a joint coalition electoral list for Sinn Féin. This pact was completely rejected by both wings of the republican movement. On June 16, 1922, a general election was held in the 26 southern counties. Supporters of the Treaty received 58 seats, while its opponents received 35 seats. Two days after the results were announced, the Civil War began. The war was won by Treaty supporters. The main opponent of the Treaty at the time, Éamon de Valera, remained formally chairman of Sinn Féin until March 1926. By then, the party, which by then was comprised exclusively of Treaty opponents, was divided, divided, and had almost no financial resources left. De Valera, tired of the abstentionist stance of the anti-treaty fundamentalists (Michael O'Flanagan, Mary MacSwiney, J. J. Scelig O' Kelly or Austin Stack), decided in May 1926 to found the Fianna Fáil party, which has been active in the Irish political arena to this day, and for many years (along with Fine Gael) was one of the two main parties in the South.

However the civil war in the south that broke out in June 1922 and the Northern government's introduction of wholesale internment led to the complete defeat of the republicans there by mid-1922. If taken from 1917 up to mid-1922, the conflict produced in the region of 2,500 deaths. Its political

---

122 See: "Slugger O'Toole" portal, published online: https://sluggerotoole.com/2020/07/21/the-forgotten-troubles-1920-1922-the-mcmahon-murders/ [accessed 12.05.2023].

results were the creation of the substantially independent Irish Free State (since 1948, the Republic of Ireland and fully independent) and Northern Ireland, which remained part of the United Kingdom. The Irish Free State and later Republic was the first fully independent functional Irish state in recorded history. This is why the years from 1920 to 1923 are so crucial to the subsequent 100 years of the history of a divided but sovereign Ireland. In addition, the memory of the War of Independence was tarnished by the subsequent civil war but it was openly celebrated up to the 1970s as marking the foundation of the Irish state. After the outbreak of the Northern Ireland conflict in 1969, public memory began to be more critical with more focus on the killing of civilians and the lack of democratic endorsement of the IRA campaign. However since end of the Northern conflict after the late 1990s, more positive views of the 1919–1921 period are again in the ascendant in nationalist Ireland.

Professor Gavin Foster in a discussion with the author of a book on the "Irish Civil War," John Dorney, argues that in debates surrounding the Anglo-Irish Treaty, signed in December 1921 between the British Government and those representing the revolutionary Irish Republic proclaimed by Sinn Féin in 1919, two issues stand out prominently:

1) The first of these was the extent to which the new Irish Free State would be independent of Britain. The oath of allegiance that future Irish parliamentarians would have to swear to the British monarch was the most powerful symbol of this. The idea of a civil war being fought over something as abstract as an oath is often scoffed at, but as we shall see, the oath "represented" or represented the question of where sovereignty in independent Ireland would actually lie—with the people—as classic republican theory would have it—or in the person of the British monarch. Furthermore, if the Oath was irrelevant, as the pro-Treaty side and many later commentators would argue, we raise the question of why the British negotiators were so adamant about insisting on it during and after the Treaty negotiations.

2) The second major issue crucial in this history is that of partition and the separation of the six north-eastern counties as Northern Ireland. This played an important but highly complex and indirect role in the outbreak of the war, although it is popularly seen as the cause of the southern civil war. Both sides claimed to be anti-partitionist, and in fact it was the pro-Treaty side, led by Michael Collins, who were at the forefront of a clandestine military assault

on the Six Counties in early 1922. As a result, the Free State side won over much of the Northern IRA, some of whom paradoxically were instrumental in the defeat of the anti-Treaty side in the south in 1922–1923.[123]

The Anglo-Irish Treaty and the subsequent partition of Ireland were significant events which had a lasting impact on political relations between Ireland and the United Kingdom for at least four reasons:

1) The Treaty was controversial in Ireland. Some saw it as a betrayal of the republican cause, while others saw it as a pragmatic compromise that would lead to greater independence in the long term.
2) The partition of Ireland was a result of the Treaty, with Northern Ireland remaining part of the United Kingdom and the rest of Ireland becoming the Irish Free State. This led to the island becoming divided along religious and political lines, with Protestants in the North and Catholics in the South.
3) The partition and the resulting violence and political instability in Northern Ireland led to strained relations between the UK and Ireland for many decades. The IRA waged a campaign of violence against British forces and infrastructure and there were frequent clashes between British soldiers and protesters in Northern Ireland.
4) The events surrounding the Treaty and partition strained political relations between Ireland and the UK. The UK was seen by many Irish nationalists as an occupying power and relations between the two countries were marked by violence and terrorism for many years.

***

Irish and British history are strongly influenced by the Anglo-Irish Treaty and the partition of Ireland. They have had a lasting impact on their political relationship. While progress has been made in recent years, these events continue to shape the relationship between the two countries. This is especially after GFA (Good Friday Agreement 1998), or even Brexit in 2016. However, the

---

[123] https://www.theirishstory.com/2013/07/28/making-sense-of-the-irish-civil-war-a-conversation-with-gavin-foster/#.ZFytLXZByUk [accessed 12.05.2023].

resulting Anglo-Irish Treaty, signed in December 1921,[124] established the Irish Free State as a self-governing dominion within the British Commonwealth. The treaty was controversial, however, as it fell short of full independence demanded by Irish republicans. This led to a split in the pro-independence movement between those who accepted the treaty and those who rejected it. The Irish Free State initially remained within the British Commonwealth, with the British monarch as head of state, and was founded in December 1922. However, in 1937 an amended constitution established Ireland as a fully independent republic with its own president as head of state. It is important to examine this period in Irish history—the emergence of statehood and the relationship of the young state with its former colonizer, Britain, as well as the developing foreign policy of Éire.

---

[124] See: D. Lowry, *The captive dominion: imperial realities behind Irish diplomacy, 1922–49*, "Irish Historical Studies," Volume XXXVI, No. 142, November 2008, p. 202.

Ireland and UK Political Relations from Anglo-Irish Treaty to EEC Accession (1921–1972)

2.1. Ireland and UK political relations from Anglo-Irish Treaty to the proclamation of the Republic of Ireland (1921–1949)

2.1.1. Political relations since Anglo-Irish Treaty. Early 1920s and pro-treaty rule

The period from the Anglo-Irish Treaty in 1921 to the proclamation of the Republic of Ireland in 1949 was marked by significant political developments and tensions between Ireland and the United Kingdom. The Anglo-Irish Treaty, as already highlighted, was signed on December 6, 1921, between the British government and representatives of the Irish Republic during the Irish War of Independence (1919–1921). The treaty established the Irish Free State, an independent dominion within the British Commonwealth. While it granted self-governance to most of Ireland, it also allowed Northern Ireland to opt-out of the Free State and remain part of the United Kingdom, which it did. The signing of the Anglo-Irish Treaty led to a split among Irish nationalists. Some, including prominent figures like Michael Collins and Arthur Griffith, supported the treaty and the establishment of the Irish Free State. Others, led by Éamon de Valera, opposed it because it fell short of a fully independent republic. This disagreement resulted in a bitter civil war from 1922 to 1923, with the pro-treaty forces ultimately prevailing. Initially, both de Valera and Collins wanted to prevent the outbreak of civil war. They signed a pact on May 20, 1922, known as the Pact Collins—de Valera, in which they called for unity in the republican movement and proposed a joint coalition electoral list for Sinn Féin.

This pact was completely rejected by both wings of the republican movement. On June 16, 1922, a general election was held in the 26 southern counties. Supporters of the Treaty received 58 seats, while its opponents received 35 seats. Two days after the results were announced, the Civil War began. The war was won by Treaty supporters. The main opponent of the Treaty at the time, Éamon de Valera, remained formally chairman of Sinn Féin until March 1926. By then, the party, which by then was comprised solely of Treaty opponents, was divided, divided, and had almost no financial resources left. De Valera, tired of the abstentionist stance of the anti-treaty fundamentalists (Michael O'Flanagan, Mary MacSwiney, J. J. Scelig O' Kelly or Austin Stack), decided in May 1926 to found the Fianna Fáil party.[125]

Irish Free State was a historical entity that existed from December 1922 until December 1937. It was a self-governing dominion within the British Commonwealth (with its own written constitution),[126] and it was established as a result of the Anglo-Irish Treaty signed on December 6, 1921. The Anglo-Irish Treaty was an agreement between the British government and representatives of the Irish Republic, including Michael Collins and Arthur Griffith. The treaty resulted in the partition of Ireland into two separate jurisdictions: Northern Ireland (comprising six counties in the northeast) and the Irish Free State (encompassing the rest of the island). Under the terms of the treaty, the Irish Free State retained nominal allegiance to the British Crown, recognizing the British monarch as its head of state. However, the Free State was granted significant autonomy and self-governance in most internal matters, similar to other dominions within the British Commonwealth, such as Canada and Australia. The British Crown's involvement in the Irish Free State's affairs

---

[125] See: R. Dunphy, *The Making of Fianna Fáil Power in Ireland 1923–1948*, Oxford 1995, pp. 30–73.

[126] The Irish Free State Constitution Act 1922 (Session 2) was an Act of the Parliament of the United Kingdom, passed in 1922 to enact in UK law the Constitution of the Irish Free State, and to ratify the 1921 Anglo-Irish Treaty formally. An Act to provide for the Constitution of the Irish Free State. See: https://www.irishstatutebook.ie/eli/1922/act/1/enacted/en/print [accessed 18.08.2023]. Further read: T. Mohr, *British Imperial Statutes and Irish Sovereignty: Statutes Passed After the Creation of the Irish Free State*, "Journal of Legal History," nr 32 (1), 2011, pp. 61–85; O. Doyle, D. Kenny, C. McCrudden, *The Constitutional Politics of a United Ireland*, in: O. Doyle, A. McHarg and J. Murkens (eds.), *The Brexit Challenge for Ireland and the United Kingdom: Constitutions under Pressure*, Cambridge 2021, passim.

was largely symbolic, and the Irish Free State functioned as a sovereign state in most respects. The Governor-General, representing the British Crown, was the official head of state in the Irish Free State, but the actual executive power was vested in the Irish government. In 1937, the Irish Free State was replaced by a new constitution that proclaimed Ireland as a fully sovereign state, named "Ireland" or "Éire" in the Irish language, and removed any remaining constitutional links with the British Crown. This marked the beginning of the modern-day Republic of Ireland, as we know it today.[127]

It is worth emphasizing that the period from the Anglo-Irish Treaty in 1921 to the proclamation of the Republic of Ireland in 1949 was marked by significant political developments and tensions between Ireland and the United Kingdom. The Treaty also led to the partition of Ireland. Northern Ireland remained part of the United Kingdom, while the rest of Ireland became the Irish Free State. This partition created ongoing tensions and conflicts, as nationalists in Northern Ireland sought reunification with the Free State. While the Irish Free State was technically independent, it maintained close ties to Great Britain due to its membership in the British Commonwealth. The British monarch remained the head of state, represented in Ireland by a governor-general. While the Treaty granted Ireland considerable autonomy, it still recognized the British monarch as the head of state and included a controversial oath of allegiance. The treaty required members of the Irish Free State's parliament (Oireachtas) and other public officials to take an oath of allegiance to the British monarch.[128] This oath was a source of controversy and led to divisions within the Irish political landscape.

It worth noting that Cumann na nGaedheal party played a crucial role in the political landscape of an Irish Free State since 1923. Cumann na nGaedheal (meaning "Society of the Gaels" in Irish) was a political party in Ireland that existed from 1923 to 1933. It was named after the original Cumann na nGaedheal organization which merged with the Dungannon Clubs and the

---

127 See: E. Féron, *Prisoners of History? British-Irish Relations and the Conflict in Northern Ireland*, "European Review of International Studies," Volume 1, Issue 3, 2014, pp. 3–15.

128 See: D. K. Coffey, *The Commonwealth and the Oath of Allegiance Crisis: A Study in Inter-War Commonwealth Relations*, "The Journal of Imperial and Commonwealth History," 2016, vol. 44, no. 3, pp. 492–512.

National Council to form Sinn Féin in 1905. In 1933 it merged with a number of smaller groups to form the Fine Gael party.[129]

It played a significant role in Irish politics during the early years of the Irish Free State, which was established in 1922 following the Anglo-Irish Treaty. After the Anglo-Irish Treaty was signed in December 1921, Ireland was partitioned, and the majority of the island became the Irish Free State, a self-governing dominion within the British Commonwealth. The treaty led to a bitter division among Irish nationalists, with some supporting the treaty and the establishment of the Free State and others opposing it as they believed it fell short of full independence and failed to address the issue of partition. The Anglo-Irish Treaty promised a Boundary Commission to review the border between Northern Ireland and the Free State. However, the Commission's findings were never implemented, leading to disappointment among some nationalists who felt that the Free State should have a more extensive territory.

Those who supported the treaty and the Free State formed Cumann na nGaedheal in April 1923, with W. T. Cosgrave as its leader. The party aimed to establish a stable, constitutional government and to work within the framework of the new Free State. It drew support from pro-Treaty supporters and conservative elements of Irish society, including farmers, businesspeople, and the Catholic Church. Cumann na nGaedheal played a crucial role in shaping the early years of the Irish Free State. Its governance, policies, and response to challenges laid the groundwork for the political landscape that followed in Ireland. Cumann na nGaedheal was the dominant party in the Irish Free State during this period. It won the 1923 general election and formed the government. W. T. Cosgrave became the first President of the Executive Council (prime minister) of the Free State. Party's formation was closely tied to the Anglo-Irish Treaty of 1921, which ended the Irish War of Independence and led to the establishment of the Irish Free State. The party's members were generally supportive of the Treaty and believed in the necessity of compromise to achieve a degree of self-governance for Ireland within the British Commonwealth. The party's initial leader was W. T. Cosgrave, who later became the first President of the Executive Council (the head of

---

[129] M. Laffan, op. cit., pp. 25–26.

government) of the Irish Free State. Cosgrave and other party leaders were key figures in negotiating the Treaty and were committed to stabilizing the country after years of conflict. Cumann na nGaedheal faced numerous challenges during its time in power. The party had to contend with ongoing tensions between pro-Treaty and anti-Treaty factions, which ultimately led to the Irish Civil War (1922–1923). Additionally, the party inherited a country grappling with economic instability, a legacy of the War of Independence, and the difficulties of nation-building. The party's policies during its time in power focused on nation-building, economic development, and maintaining law and order. Cumann na nGaedheal sought to establish a stable and secure Irish Free State by strengthening government institutions, establishing a national police force (the Garda Síochána), and pursuing economic policies aimed at fostering industrial growth. The party pursued a conservative economic approach that favored free trade and private enterprise. They sought to attract foreign investment and encourage domestic industries. However, the global economic downturn in the late 1920s, followed by the Great Depression, posed significant challenges to their economic plans.

2.1.2. Cumann na nGaedheal decline, and Fianna Fáil rise to power: relations with the UK

Cumann na nGaedheal won the general elections of 1923 and 1927. However, by 1932, it was facing increased criticism for its handling of economic issues and social inequality. As a result, the party faced electoral defeat in 1932. While Cumann na nGaedheal's time in power was relatively short-lived, it laid the foundation for the Irish political system and institutions. The party's successors, Fianna Fáil, led by Éamon de Valera, took power in 1932 and pursued a different policy direction. Despite its electoral defeat, Cumann na nGaedheal's legacy endured in the form of the Fine Gael party, which evolved from a merger of Cumann na nGaedheal with other political groups in 1933. Cumann na nGaedheal played a crucial role in shaping the early years of the Irish Free State. Its efforts to stabilize the country, establish institutions, and promote economic growth laid the groundwork for subsequent developments in Irish politics. The party pursued conservative economic policies, focusing on fiscal responsibility, promoting agriculture, and encouraging foreign investment. They aimed to stabilize the economy after the tumultuous events of the Irish War of Independence and the subsequent Civil War. One of Cumann na nGaedheal's main objectives was to establish law and order after years of violence and unrest. They sought to dismantle the paramilitary groups involved in the Irish Civil War and create a professional police force, the Garda Síochána.[130]

Cumann na nGaedheal faced opposition from Fianna Fáil, a party founded by Éamon de Valera in 1926, which rejected the treaty and sought to achieve a united Ireland. In 1932, Fianna Fáil won the general election, and Cumann na nGaedheal, along with two other parties, merged to form Fine Gael, a center-right political party that continues to exist in Irish politics today. Cumann na nGaedheal was a political party in Ireland that played a significant role in Irish politics from 1922 to 1932. It was the first government of the newly established Irish Free State and was instrumental in shaping the country's early political landscape. The party's support base gradually shifted to Éamon de Valera's new party, Fianna Fáil, after it was formed in 1926. While Cosgrave's Cumann na nGaedheal appeared to be preoccupied with public safety, it became identified solely with the protection of the Treaty and the defense of the new state. Economically, the party was in favor of balanced budgets and free trade at a time when its opponents were in favor of protectionism. The Free State's fragile economy suffered during the Great Depression.

Nevertheless, it came as a surprise when Cumann na nGaedheal was defeated by Fianna Fáil in the February 1932 general election. Cumann na nGaedheal won only 57 seats to Fianna Fáil's 72. Cumann na nGaedheal was ill-prepared for a role in opposition, having spent its entire existence before 1932 in government. Its support base shrank further in the January 1933 general election, when it won 48 seats to Fianna Fáil's 77. The party found itself increasingly unable to counter de Valera's populism and was increasingly labeled the party of the middle classes. Fianna Fáil then began discussing the possibility of merging with the National Centre Party and the ultranationalist Blueshirts. This came about in September 1933 with the formation of Fine Gael from the three parties. Fine Gael was formed in September 1933 from the merger of Cumann na nGaedheal ("Party of the Irish")—the party of William Thomas Cosgrave, the first President of the Irish Free State— and

[130] See more: J. Knirck, *Afterimage of the Revolution. Cumann na nGaedheal and Irish Politics, 1922–1932*, Madison 2014, pp. 304, passim.

two smaller parties, the Centre Party (formerly the Farmers' Party) and the National Guard (formerly the Army Comrades Association), also known as the Blueshirts. Cumann na nGaedheal represented the supporters of the Anglo-Irish Treaty of 1921 which established the Irish Free State. Identifying itself as the party of peace and stability, Cumann na nGaedheal won 41 % of the seats in the first Free State election in 1923 and formed a minority government under Cosgrave. It remained in power until it was defeated by its main opposition, Fianna Fáil, in 1932. In response, Cosgrave created a larger and more heterogeneous party in 1933, which he called Fine Gael. However, it was not until 1948 that the new party won national office. John Costello formed a five-party coalition government (1948–1951).[131]

Over time, the role of the party that dominates in Ireland was taken by the anti-Treaty party Fianna Fáil. Their rise in popularity was spectacular. They completely took over the patriotic and nationalistic electors and caused the downfall of Cumann na nGaedheal. The Fianna Fáil party's rise in the Irish Free State (now the Republic of Ireland) from 1928 to 1937 was a significant period in Irish history. Founded by Éamon de Valera in 1926, the party emerged as a formidable political force, representing a departure from the traditional pro-Treaty and more conservative politics of the Cumann na nGaedheal (later Fine Gael) party. De Valera was a prominent figure in the struggle for Irish independence and had previously been a leader of Sinn Féin.[132]

During this time, Fianna Fáil capitalized on various factors that contributed to their popularity and eventual electoral success:

1) Anti-Treaty Sentiment: Fianna Fáil appealed to those who were dissatisfied with the Anglo-Irish Treaty of 1921 and the subsequent Civil War (1922–1923) that followed between pro-Treaty forces and anti-Treaty republicans. The party sought to reunite the country and bring an end to the partition of Ireland, which was a contentious issue at the time.
2) Economic Policies: Fianna Fáil adopted populist economic policies, advocating for increased government intervention and social welfare

---

[131] See more: C. Bouyoux Barthélémy, The Role of Minor Political Parties in the Republic of Ireland, "Nordic Irish Studies," Vol. 17, No. 2 (2018), pp. 167–184.

[132] On de Valera see: P. Toboła-Pertkiewicz, *De Valera. Gigant polityki irlandzkiej i jego epoka* [*De Valera. The giant of Irish politics and his era*], Warszawa 2014, pp. 246, passim.

measures. They promised land reform, protection of agricultural interests, and economic policies that aimed to improve the living conditions of the rural population.

3) Republicanism: The party's core ideology was grounded in Irish republicanism and a commitment to achieving full Irish independence from Great Britain. While the Irish Free State had been established in 1922 with dominion status within the British Commonwealth, Fianna Fáil sought complete sovereignty and the establishment of a republic.
4) Electoral Strategy: Fianna Fáil worked diligently to build a nationwide grassroots organization and fostered a strong sense of party loyalty among its members. They made effective use of propaganda and rhetoric, presenting themselves as the true defenders of Irish interests against perceived British interference.
5) Opposition to the Oath of Allegiance: One of the critical issues that helped Fianna Fáil gain support was its opposition to the requirement that elected officials in the Irish Free State had to take an Oath of Allegiance to the British Crown. Fianna Fáil argued that the oath was a symbol of continued British influence over Irish affairs.

Regarding their attitude toward Great Britain, Fianna Fáil's stance was characterized by a desire for increased independence and a distancing from British influence. While they sought to establish friendly relations with Britain, they were determined to assert Ireland's sovereignty and pursue an independent foreign policy. Despite occasional tensions in Anglo-Irish relations, particularly over issues such as partition and neutrality during World War II, Fianna Fáil's attitude toward Britain was generally focused on establishing Ireland as a separate and self-governing nation. They pursued a policy of "external association" with the British Commonwealth, intending to cooperate with Britain on common interests while avoiding undue interference in Irish affairs.

During this period, the Irish Free State was still closely connected to Great Britain through the Anglo-Irish Treaty of 1921, which established the dominion status of Ireland within the British Commonwealth. The treaty had led to the Irish Civil War, with some factions accepting the dominion status, while others wanted a complete break from the British Empire. Fianna Fáil, as a political party, sought to reconcile the opposing views on the treaty and consolidate the Irish nation by working toward a united Ireland, which included Northern Ireland. They advocated for a new constitution, economic protectionism, and social reforms. They also pledged to abolish the Oath of Allegiance to the British Crown, which was required of members of the Oireachtas (the Irish parliament) and civil servants.

In the 1927 general election, Fianna Fáil emerged as the largest party in the Dáil Éireann (Irish parliament) but did not have enough seats to form a government. Nonetheless, they remained a powerful opposition force. In the 1928 general election, Fianna Fáil secured more seats than any other party, and Éamon de Valera became the head of a minority government. One of the defining moments of Fianna Fáil's rise to power was their decision to drop their abstentionist policy in 1927, which had previously prevented them from taking their seats in the British Parliament. De Valera and Fianna Fáil decided to participate in the Dáil Éireann to work within the system and pursue their goals of furthering Irish sovereignty.

In 1932, Fianna Fáil won a landslide victory in the general election, securing a majority government. As the ruling party, they began implementing significant policy changes, including economic protectionism, land reforms, and social welfare initiatives. In 1937, Fianna Fáil introduced a new constitution that declared Ireland a sovereign, independent state and officially renamed the country "Éire" (Ireland). In 1932, Fianna Fáil won the general election and formed the government under Éamon de Valera's leadership. During their time in power (1932–1948, and again from 1951 to 1954), Fianna Fáil worked to strengthen Irish national identity, implement social and economic reforms, and assert Irish sovereignty in various ways. They abolished the Oath of Allegiance in 1933 and passed the External Relations Act of 1936, which effectively removed the British monarch as the head of state in Irish external affairs.[133]

Throughout their rule, Fianna Fáil remained committed to maintaining Ireland's neutrality during World War II, despite being under significant pressure from Britain to join the war effort. This stance reinforced their independent and assertive attitude toward Great Britain and other external influences. In summary, the rise of Fianna Fáil in the Irish Free State from

---

[133] See more: R. Dunphy, op. cit., 74–144.

1928 to 1937 was marked by their efforts to consolidate Irish sovereignty, challenge provisions of the Anglo-Irish Treaty, and promote the idea of a united Ireland. Their attitude toward Great Britain was one of cautious cooperation and assertive independence, aimed at safeguarding Ireland's national interests and identity.

2.1.3. Fianna Fáil inter-war government and the UK

Throughout its history, the Irish Free State (later the Republic of Ireland) evolved politically, economically, and socially. It transitioned from a dominion within the British Commonwealth to a fully independent republic, weathered conflicts, embraced European integration, and experienced periods of economic growth and transformation. Today, Ireland is a modern, democratic nation with a strong global presence. Since the foundation of the Irish state in 1922, politics has been the preserve of two political giants. The modern Fine Gael party and its historic rival, Fianna Fáil, both trace their origins to the 1917–1921 independence movement. When Sinn Féin agreed to enter into talks with David Lloyd George's government in the autumn, Éamon de Valera, Arthur Griffith, Michael Collins, Cathal Brugha, Austin Stack, W. T. Cosgrave and Robert Barton formed the seven-member cabinet of the Second Dáil. Every government since the first change of government in 1932 had been led by one party or the other, while Cumann na nGaedheal, Fine Gael's parent party, had governed the state for the first ten years of independence. According to Mel Farrell during the twentieth century, Fianna Fáil and Fine Gael remained bitter rivals, both nationally and locally. Each party developed and maintained an organizational presence in every constituency in the state, a factor which certainly shaped the nature of the intense rivalry between them.[134] This political dichotomy and dominance of the two parties is enduring and has been a feature of the Irish party system since at least the 1930s (despite the fact that contemporaries of these two parties and the Greens have formed a German-style grand coalition since June 2020 to

[134] M. Farrell, *Fine Gael and Fianna Fáil: 'Civil War' Parties?* Published online: https://www.theirishstory.com/2020/05/26/fine-gael-and-fianna-fail-civil-war-parties [accessed 10.08.2023].

prevent a Sinn Féin government and form two consecutive governments, a M. Martin cabinet and a second L. Varadkar cabinet).[135]

In 1931, the British Parliament passed the Statute of Westminster, which granted full legislative independence to the dominions, including the Irish Free State. This statute allowed the Irish Free State to make its own laws without requiring British approval, further strengthening its autonomy. It is worth noting that the Statute of Westminster granted legislative independence to the Dominions of the British Commonwealth, including the Irish Free State. The recognition of the autonomy of the Dominions was a further factor in the transformation of the relationship.[136]

In 1932, Éamon de Valera's Fianna Fáil party came to power in Ireland, ending Cumann na nGaedheal's long dominance. De Valera's government sought to assert Irish sovereignty and reduce British influence in Irish affairs. In 1933 De Valera abolished the oath of allegiance (to the Constitution of the Free State and to George V as "King in Ireland") required by the 1922 Constitution. The 1921 Anglo-Irish Treaty established the Irish Free State as a self-governing dominion within the Commonwealth. However, tensions remained over issues such as allegiance to the British monarch. De Valera's government abolished the oath in 1932, symbolizing a break with the Treaty era. In late 1936, he passed the Executive Powers (External Relations) Act 1936 and the Executive Powers (Consequential Provisions) Act 1937, taking advantage of the crisis over Edward VIII's abdication. This had the effect of ending the role of the Governor-General of the Irish Free State in Irish internal affairs and replacing him with the government of the day. The Irish government passed the External Relations Act 1936 to assert its right to conduct foreign policy independently of the British government. This act allowed Ireland to accredit its own envoys abroad. In the years 1934–1936, the government, concerned about the legislative delays caused by the Senate (*Seanad Éireann* in Irish), passed the Constitution (Amendment No. 24) Act

---

[135] See: "The Irish Times" 26th of June 2020: https://www.irishtimes.com/news/politics/coalition-or-political-crisis-verdict-of-ff-fg-and-green-members-to-be-revealed-this-evening-1.4288833 [accessed 10.08.2023].

[136] See: T. Mohr, *The Statute of Westminster, 1931: An Irish Perspective*, "Law and History Review," 31 (4), 2013, pp. 749–791.

1936. The modern Seanad Éireann was created by the 1937 Constitution and met for the first time in January 1939.[137]

It is remarkable that, despite the general economic difficulties, the vote for the government held up in 1932–1938. Firstly, de Valera had called the 1933 election within a year of taking office, before the worst effects had been felt. By the July 1937 election, support for him and his main rival, Fine Gael, had collapsed and he remained in office with the silent support of Labour. The number of Dáil seats contested in 1937 had been reduced from 153 to 138. This meant that smaller parties had less chance of winning seats. On the same day as the 1937 election, the Irish Constitution was adopted by plebiscite, moving the state further away from the constitutional position envisaged in the 1921 Anglo-Irish Treaty. The new Constitution was approved by 56.5 % of the electorate, which, because of the large number of abstentions and spoiled ballots, represented only 38.6 % of the total electorate. Overall, the period from 1932 to 1937 saw a gradual easing of tensions between the United Kingdom and Ireland. Both countries took steps to assert their sovereignty and establish more amicable relations. The foundations for the development of relations in the following decades were laid by the Anglo-Irish Trade Agreement and other diplomatic efforts during this period.[138]

A major conflict in the period 1932–1938 was the trade dispute between Ireland and Britain. This had the greatest impact on the young Irish state's relationship with the former metropolis in imperial terms, along with the border conflict between south and north and constitutional changes in Ireland. In 1932, the Irish Free State underwent a significant change when Fianna Fáil came to power under Éamon de Valera. The Anglo-Irish Treaty's provisions were gradually dismantled, and in 1937, a new constitution was adopted, formally renaming the country as "Éire" (in English, "Ireland") and asserting its status as a sovereign republic outside of the British Commonwealth. The

---

[137] See: Documents of Irish Foreign Policy (years 1932–1936), https://www.difp.ie/volume-4/1932/british-irish-relations/1505 [accessed 10.08.2023] and A. Dolan, *Politics, Economy and Society in the Irish Free State, 1922–1939*, in: T. Bartlett, (ed.), *Cambridge History of Ireland, Volume 1V:* from the 1880s to the present, Cambridge 2018, pp. 323–348.

[138] See more: R. Fanning, *Anglo-Irish Relations: Partition and the British Dimension in Historical Perspective*, "Irish Studies in International Affairs," Vol. 2, No. 1 (1985), pp. 1–20; B. Chubb, *The Politics of the Irish constitution*, Dublin 1991, p. 153.

period between 1922 and 1932 was characterized by the Irish Free State's efforts to establish itself as a self-governing entity within the framework of the British Commonwealth, while also navigating the complexities of its relationship with the British Empire. The tensions and conflicts during this time ultimately set the stage for the Free State's evolution into a fully sovereign republic.

Another important factor was The Anglo-Irish Trade War, also known as the Economic War, occurred between 1932 and 1938 and involved a series of trade restrictions and economic sanctions imposed by the Irish Free State against the United Kingdom. The conflict was a result of political and economic tensions between the two nations following Ireland's declaration of independence in 1922. After gaining partial independence from Britain in 1922 and becoming the Irish Free State, Ireland maintained a close economic relationship with the UK. However, disagreements arose over issues such as the status of Northern Ireland and the payment of land annuities to the UK for land purchased under the Irish Land Acts.[139]

In 1932, Éamon de Valera's Fianna Fáil party came to power in Ireland and adopted a more nationalist and protectionist stance. One of the first acts of the new government was to halt payments on land annuities to the UK, which were seen as a symbol of Ireland's colonial past. In response to Ireland's refusal to pay the land annuities, the UK imposed tariffs on Irish exports, particularly agricultural products such as cattle and butter. In retaliation, Ireland introduced its own tariffs on British goods, leading to a reduction in bilateral trade. The trade restrictions had a negative impact on both economies. Ireland, heavily dependent on agricultural exports, suffered from reduced access to the UK market. In the UK, industries relying on Irish imports were also affected. The trade war continued to escalate over the years, with both sides introducing additional tariffs and sanctions on various goods. This strained diplomatic relations between the two nations.

Britain and Ireland signed in 1935 the Coal-Cattle Pact which meant that buying these commodities would be cheaper and easier to get. The Coal-Cattle Pact indicated a willingness to end the Economic War. The resolution of the

[139] See: D. Lowry, *New Ireland, Old Empire and the Outside World, 1922–49: The Strange Evolution of a Dictionary Republic*, in: Cronin, M., Regan, J. M. (eds.), Ireland. The Politics of Independence, London 2000, p. 175.

crisis came after a series of talks in London between the British Prime Minister Neville Chamberlain and de Valera, who was accompanied by Lemass and James Ryan. An agreement to reach an acceptable settlement was drawn up in 1938, enacted in Britain as the Éire (*Confirmation of Agreements*) Act. Under the terms of the three-year Anglo-Irish Trade Agreement, all duties imposed during the previous five years were lifted.

In 1938, the Anglo-Irish Trade War was effectively ended through negotiations. The trade restrictions were gradually lifted, and an agreement was reached regarding the land annuities. The signing of the Anglo-Irish Trade Agreement marked the resolution of the conflict. The trade war highlighted the economic vulnerabilities of both nations and underscored the complex nature of their relationship. It also demonstrated Ireland's determination to assert its independence and sovereignty in economic matters.

Anglo-Irish Trade War was a significant episode in the history of Ireland's relationship with the United Kingdom. It reflected the broader challenges of post-colonial relations and the complexities of balancing economic interests with national sovereignty. Although the period of the Economic War caused great social suffering and financial loss to Ireland, its outcome was publicized as favorable. Ireland retained the right to impose tariffs on British imports to protect new Irish industries. The treaty also settled the potential liability of £3 million a year in land rents by a one-off payment of £10 million to Britain and a waiver by both sides of all similar claims and counterclaims. Since it was known in the 1930s that the land annuity payments in Northern Ireland of some £650,000 a year were retained by the government and not passed on to London, it remains unclear why the Irish government did not mention this in the course of the negotiations. It also included the return to Ireland of the Treaty ports, which had been retained by Britain under a provision of the 1921 Treaty. Returning these enabled Ireland to remain neutral when the Second World War broke out in 1939.[140] Ireland's neutrality during

[140] See further: P. M. Canning, Paul, *The impact of Éamon de Valera: domestic causes of the Anglo-Irish economic war*, "Albion," 15.3 (1983), pp. 179–205; K. O'Rourke, *Burn everything British but their coal: the Anglo-Irish economic war of the 1930s*, "Journal of Economic History," 51.2 (1991), pp. 357–366; M. E. Daly, *The Irish Free State and the Great Depression of the 1930s: the interaction of the global and the local*, "Irish Economic and Social History," Vol. 38 (2011), pp. 19–36.

World War II shaped its relationship with Great Britain by maintaining a stance of non-involvement in the conflict, which both reflected its desire for independence and impacted its diplomatic standing in the post-war world.

2.1.4. War, Ireland, and the UK. Question of neutrality

The issue of Irish neutrality (an inherent and constitutive aspect of Irish republicanism) was also contentious and problematic in Ireland's relationship with Great Britain during WWII, played a significant role in shaping its relationship with Great Britain and the broader global conflict.[141] Ireland officially declared its neutrality at the outbreak of World War II on September 2, 1939.[142] The decision to remain neutral was largely influenced by Ireland's desire to avoid becoming embroiled in another global conflict after the devastation of World War I and its struggle for independence from British rule. The government, led by Prime Minister Éamon de Valera, believed that neutrality was in the best interest of Ireland's security and independence.

Ireland's decision to remain neutral during the Second World War affected how it would relate to Britain. Historically, Ireland had a complex and contentious relationship with Britain due to its history of British colonial rule and the struggle for Irish independence. Tensions between the two countries remained despite Ireland's independence from Britain in 1922 (with the exception of Northern Ireland). Relations between Ireland and Britain as we said were historically strained by the Irish War of Independence and the subsequent establishment of the Irish Free State in 1922. The Anglo-Irish Treaty of 1921 had led to the partition of Ireland and the creation of Northern Ireland within the United Kingdom. Ireland's decision to remain neutral during the Second World War and President De Valera policy was strongly influenced by these historical factors.[143]

Britain, as part of the Allied powers in the war, hoped to secure Irish cooperation and assistance in various forms, such as the use of Irish ports

---

141 P. Ollerenshaw, *Neutrality and Belligerence: Ireland, 1939–1945*, in: T. Bartlett, (ed.), *Cambridge History of Ireland, Volume 1V: from the 1880s to the present*, Cambridge 2018, pp. 349–378.

142 See: D. Lowry, *The Neutral Dominion: Ireland and the British Empire in the Second World War*, "Global War Studies," Volume 7, Number 1, 2010, pp. 37–46.

143 T. Ryle Dwyer, *De Valera: The Man & the Myths*, Dublin 1992, p. 372.

and airspace. However, Ireland refused British requests to use its facilities for military purposes and maintained a strict policy of non-participation in the war. Maintaining neutrality during the Second World War was not without its challenges for Ireland. Despite its declared neutrality, Ireland was not immune to the effects of the war. It experienced economic hardship, shortages of essential goods and the impact of German submarine activity in the Atlantic disrupting trade routes. In addition, Ireland's neutrality was tested by the presence of German spies and the potential for the country to be used as a base for espionage or sabotage activities. The Irish government took steps to monitor and counter these threats while avoiding direct involvement in the war. Ireland avoided the destruction and casualties suffered by many European nations during the Second World War through its policy of neutrality.

Despite their neutrality, Ireland and Britain worked together on some issues during the war. The Irish government entered into bilateral agreements with the British government to deal with certain issues. For example, in 1941 they negotiated the Economic War Settlement, which resolved trade and economic disputes between the two countries. Ireland continued to trade with both the Allies and the Axis powers, although trade with the Allies was on a larger scale. The British naval blockade made trade with Germany difficult. Ireland faced shortages of certain goods and rationing was introduced. The British government was initially concerned that Ireland's neutrality could be exploited by Nazi Germany for strategic purposes, such as submarine bases or airfields. However, as the war progressed and it became clear that Ireland would maintain its policy of non-involvement, these concerns diminished. While Ireland did intern a number of Axis personnel stranded on Irish soil, including German and Italian sailors and airmen, it treated them as prisoners of war rather than enemy combatants. It is worth noting that Northern Ireland participated actively in the war effort as part of the United Kingdom. Its strategic location and industrial capacity made it a major contributor to the British war machine. The government of Northern Ireland worked closely with Britain and its citizens volunteered for military service.[144]

[144] See: S. Paseta, *Northern Ireland and Second World War, an essay*, St. Hugh College, Oxford, published online: https://www.gale.com/binaries/content/assets/au-resources-in-product/northernireland_essay_ww2.pdf [accessed 18.08.2023].

Ireland's policy of neutrality during the Second World War meant that it maintained a cautious distance from both the Allied and Axis powers. There was some diplomatic cooperation between Ireland and Britain during the war, despite a history of tension. Ireland's decision to remain neutral was influenced by a desire to avoid the conflicts of the past and to protect its own interests in a turbulent global environment. However, its decision led to a degree of diplomatic isolation during the war and in the immediate post-war years. Nevertheless, Ireland's policy of neutrality laid the foundations for its continued pursuit of a distinct foreign policy and its emphasis on neutrality and non-alignment during the Cold War era.

2.2. Sovereign Ireland and the UK. Since WWII to the common accession to the EEC (1949–1972)

2.2.1. 1948–1949: Declaration of the Republic of Ireland and Ireland-UK relations after WWII

The period between 1945 and 1950 marked a significant time in the relations between Ireland and the UK, directly following the end of World War II. Ireland maintained a policy of neutrality during World War II. Despite being a neighbor and former part of the British Empire, Ireland chose not to join the Allied forces in the conflict against Nazi Germany and its allies. This decision had implications for relations between Ireland and the UK during the war years.[145] After the war, both the UK and Ireland, like many other countries in Europe, faced the challenges of post-war recovery and reconstruction. The UK was dealing with the economic and social aftermath of the conflict, including rationing and rebuilding efforts. Ireland, while not directly involved in the war, also had economic challenges and sought to develop its industries and infrastructure.

During this period, efforts were made to address these issues and improve relations between Ireland and the UK, but the historical context and ongoing complexities, especially concerning Northern Ireland, continued to influence the relationship. Throughout its history, the Irish Free State (later the Republic of Ireland) evolved politically, economically, and socially. It transitioned from

---

[145] See: M. Kennedy, *Irish Foreign Policy: 1919 to 1973*, in: T. Bartlett, (ed.), *Cambridge History of Ireland, Volume IV: from the 1880s to the present*, Cambridge 2018, pp. 611–621.

a dominion within the British Commonwealth to a fully independent republic, weathered conflicts, embraced European integration, and experienced periods of economic growth and transformation. Today, Ireland is a modern, democratic nation with a strong global presence. During the war itself, Ireland maintained a policy of neutrality, a decision that affected its relations with Britain and other Allied powers. This neutrality had repercussions in terms of strained relations, as the UK was part of the Allied effort against the Axis powers. In the post-war period, relations between Ireland and the United Kingdom remained complex. The Irish Free State (later the Republic of Ireland) had gained greater independence. But historical tensions remained, particularly over Northern Ireland. The issue of Northern Ireland, with its predominantly unionist (wanting to remain part of the United Kingdom) and nationalist (wanting to unite with the Republic of Ireland) communities, remained a major point of contention. The aftermath of the war did not immediately resolve historical tensions between the UK and Ireland. The legacy of Ireland's struggle for independence, the partition of the island, and differing political aspirations regarding Northern Ireland continued to shape their interactions. The partition of Ireland in 1921 had left Northern Ireland within the UK while the rest of the island became the Irish Free State (later the Republic of Ireland). Disputes over Northern Ireland's status and the treatment of the nationalist community there remained contentious issues.

Let us therefore recall, in 1937, a new constitution was adopted, which renamed the state "Éire" and asserted Ireland's claim over the whole island. However, it maintained the British monarch as head of state. In 1948, Fianna Fáil lost power, and a coalition government led by Fine Gael came into office. John A. Costello became Taoiseach. In 1949, Ireland formally declared itself a republic and left the British Commonwealth. This move emphasized Ireland's desire for full independence from the UK and symbolically solidified its status as a separate nation. On April 18, 1949, the Republic of Ireland Act was enacted, formally declaring Ireland a republic and severing its remaining ties to the British Crown. The country left the Commonwealth.[146] The decision of Ireland to declare itself a republic in

---

[146] See: J. Gibney, *Ireland leaves the Commonwealth, 1949*, in: "RIA Documents on Irish Foreign Policy," 18th April 2019, published online: https://www.ria.ie/news/documents-irish-foreign-policy/ireland-leaves-commonwealth-1949 [accessed 14.12.2023].

1949 further emphasized its distinct national identity separate from the UK. The years following World War II were marked by efforts to navigate the complexities of their historical relationship, and while some initiatives aimed at cooperation were undertaken, unresolved issues continued to affect their relations in the immediate post-war period.

Examining Irish politics and the dynamics between Éire and Great Britain in 1940s and 1950s reveals several pivotal aspects worth delving into. Firstly, the proclamation of the Republic of Ireland stands as a significant historical event, particularly considering its exclusion of the northern part of the island. This declaration not only asserted Ireland's sovereignty but also laid the groundwork for the complex relationship between the Republic and Northern Ireland, which has been marked by political tensions and intermittent conflict. Secondly, the pursuit of economic modernization in the southern region of Éire has been a central focus in shaping its trajectory as a nation. From agrarian reforms to fostering technological advancements and attracting foreign investment, Éire's efforts toward economic development have been instrumental in its evolution into a modern, thriving economy. However, these initiatives have also faced challenges such as balancing economic growth with environmental sustainability and addressing disparities in wealth distribution. Lastly, the decision of the Republic of Ireland to exit the British Commonwealth underscores its pursuit of an independent foreign policy and its desire to assert its distinct national identity. This move reflects a broader trend of decolonization and the reconfiguration of global power dynamics in the post-colonial era. Additionally, it has implications for diplomatic relations with other Commonwealth member states and signifies Ireland's aspirations for greater autonomy on the world stage. Analyzing Irish politics and relations between Éire and Great Britain straight , three key points can be noted. These are:

1) Question of Republic: During this period, the question of the republic remained a central issue in Irish politics. The 1937 Constitution of Ireland, adopted during this time, declared Ireland as a sovereign, independent, and democratic state, but it did not explicitly sever ties with the British monarchy. However, discussions and debates regarding Ireland's status as a republic persisted. In 1948, the Republic of Ireland Act was passed, formally declaring Ireland as a republic within the

Commonwealth. Finally, in 1949, Ireland officially declared itself a republic, fully asserting its independence from British rule.

2) Modernization: The 1940s and 1950s also witnessed efforts toward modernization in various aspects of Irish society and economy. These decades saw the beginnings of industrialization and economic development, as well as the implementation of social reforms. The government initiated policies aimed at stimulating economic growth, such as the establishment of the Industrial Development Authority (IDA) to attract foreign investment and promote industrialization. Social reforms, including the expansion of social welfare programs and improvements in healthcare and education, also contributed to the modernization of Ireland during this time.
3) Relation toward the Commonwealth: Ireland's relationship with the Commonwealth underwent changes during the 1940s and 1950s, particularly following its declaration as a republic in 1949. While Ireland had initially chosen to remain a member of the Commonwealth after gaining independence, the declaration of the republic marked a significant shift in its relationship with the organization. Ireland opted to stay outside the Commonwealth, asserting its status as a fully independent republic. Despite this, Ireland maintained diplomatic relations with Commonwealth member states and continued to engage in cultural, economic, and political cooperation with them on various levels.

In summary, the 1940s and 1950s were pivotal decades in Irish politics, marked by the declaration of Ireland as a republic, efforts toward modernization and economic development, and the evolution of its relationship with the Commonwealth. These developments shaped Ireland's trajectory as an independent nation in the mid-twentieth century and beyond. In essence, these three issues encapsulate the multifaceted nature of Irish politics and its intricate relationship with Great Britain, highlighting the complexities and nuances that continue to shape the dynamics between these neighboring nations.[147]

---

[147] See more: B. Girvin, *Stability, Crisis and Change in Post-war Ireland 1945–1973*, in: T. Bartlett, (ed.), *Cambridge History of Ireland, Volume 1V: from the 1880s to the present*, Cambridge 2018, pp. 381–406.

2.2.2. 1950s–1960s: economic development and social change, and Ireland-UK trade relations

From 1945 to 1973, Ireland stood at the crossroads of continuity and transformation. Despite maintaining a steadfast commitment to agrarian values and social conservatism, this era witnessed significant shifts in policies and outlooks. While Ireland remained distanced from the rapid industrialization seen in counterparts like Denmark, the period was marked by the dawn of more inclusive industrial policies, the dismantling of protectionist barriers, and a growing liberal minority. Moreover, Ireland embarked on a new chapter by embracing membership in the European Economic Community, opening doors to foreign engagement and economic integration. The landscape of Irish politics and society had undergone profound changes by 1945, following nearly four decades of tumult. The Ireland of this era was fiercely independent, steeped in nationalist fervor, and deeply rooted in Catholic tradition. Its democratic foundations were bolstered by a stable constitutional framework, a testament to the efforts of Éamon de Valera and the Fianna Fáil party since 1932. Their achievements, though not universally embraced, undeniably shaped the trajectory of Irish politics and social norms for the ensuing three decades. De Valera's formidable influence remained paramount during this time, with Fianna Fáil solidifying its dominance by securing a decisive majority in the 1944 elections, reaffirming its position as the nation's preeminent political force.

As Ireland navigated the complexities of post-war reconstruction, the government under de Valera's leadership contemplated ambitious plans for the nation's future. Despite challenges and diverging perspectives, the imprint of Fianna Fáil's governance and de Valera's vision left an indelible mark on the collective understanding and interpretation of this pivotal period in Irish history.[148]

The 1950s and 1960s saw a focus on economic development and modernization. Ireland's policy of neutrality and non-participation in NATO continued during the Cold War. Economic initiatives like the First Programme

---

[148] See: ibid. s. 381; F. Barry, *Ireland – Politics, Institutions and Post-war Economic Growth*, "CESifo Forum" 1/2008, pp. 1–12. More on Ireland's industrial policy in: F. Barry, *Industry and Policy in Independent Ireland, 1922–1972*, Oxford, 2023, p. 232.

for Economic Expansion (1958–1963) aimed to boost industrialization and create jobs, leading to some improvements in living standards. The period following World War II marked a significant transformation in Ireland's economic policy and approach to international trade. We excerpt highlights key aspects of this transformation, emphasizing the shift from a protectionist framework to one embracing interdependence with other economies. It is worth emphasizing several issues that constituted the situation of the Irish economy in the 1950s and 1960s:

1) Transition from Protectionism to Interdependence: Post-World War II, Ireland's economic policy shifted from protectionism, which favored shielding domestic industries from foreign competition, to one embracing interdependence with other economies. This shift was driven by several factors, including the recognition of the limitations of a protectionist approach in stimulating economic growth and the desire to capitalize on emerging opportunities in international trade.
2) Influence of Multilateral Trading Arrangements: there was initial resistance among some policymakers to accept multilateral trading arrangements that would challenge protected industries and Ireland's preferential access to British markets. However, the economic crises of the 1950s, coupled with changing global dynamics, compelled a reconsideration of this stance. Ireland recognized the potential benefits of participating in multilateral trade agreements for economic growth and stability.
3) Role of Economic Crisis in Shaping Policy: the severe economic crisis that plagued Ireland throughout the 1950s played a pivotal role in shaping the country's economic policy. The prolonged downturn forced policymakers to reevaluate existing strategies and adopt new approaches to address the challenges faced by the economy. This period of crisis served as a catalyst for embracing fresh economic thinking, both within the government and among non-governmental actors.
4) Inception of Corporatist Style Approach: the interactions between the government and various stakeholders, such as trade unions, employers' groups, and farmers' organizations, during this period marked the beginning of a corporatist style approach to national policymaking. This approach emphasized collaboration and dialogue between the

> government and different interest groups in formulating economic policies, aiming for consensus-building and mutual agreement.[149]

Additionally, in the years spanning from 1945 to 1973, Ireland's journey epitomized a delicate balance between tradition and change, with significant milestones shaping its economic, social, and political landscape.

As the world emerged from the devastation of World War II, Ireland found itself at a pivotal juncture, grappling with the dual imperatives of preserving its cultural heritage and embracing the winds of modernization sweeping across Europe. Despite its steadfast commitment to agrarian values and social conservatism, the country embarked on a trajectory marked by evolving policies and outlooks.

Throughout the 1950s and 1960s, Ireland's economic agenda took center stage as the government, under the leadership of Éamon de Valera and Fianna Fáil, pursued ambitious plans for development and modernization. The First Programme for Economic Expansion (1958–1963) emerged as a cornerstone initiative, aimed at propelling Ireland into the realm of industrialization and job creation. This marked a departure from the protectionist stance of previous decades, signaling a newfound willingness to engage with global markets and foster economic interdependence. Despite initial challenges and diverging perspectives, this era witnessed notable improvements in living standards, propelled by concerted efforts to diversify the economy and attract foreign investment. Ireland's policy of neutrality and non-participation in NATO during the Cold War remained steadfast, underscoring its commitment to sovereignty while navigating the geopolitical complexities of the era.[150]

The First Programme for Economic Advancement, 1958–1963, is generally regarded by historians as a major milestone and turning point in the economic and political history of the independent Irish state. It marked a departure

---

149 See: G. Murphy, *The Politics of Economic Realignment, Ireland 1948–1964*, Dissertation submitted for the degree of Ph.D. under the supervision of Professor Eunan O'Halpin, Dublin City University Business School Dublin City University, September 1996.

150 See: W. Crotty, *The "Celtic Tiger": Economic Modernization and its Social and Political Ramifications in Ireland*, in: Catherine Maignant (ed.) *Le Tigre celtique en question L'Irlande contemporaine : économie, État, société*, Caen 1999, pp. 119–136.

from the reliance on protective tariffs that had characterized Irish economic policy under the governments of Éamon de Valera and, to a lesser extent, his predecessor as Taoiseach, W. T. Cosgrave. T. K. Whitaker—on whose Economic Development report the programme was based—and Seán Lemass, who became Taoiseach in 1959 and gave his enthusiastic support to the new programme, were the two leaders most identified with it. T. K. Whitaker was Secretary to the Treasury when he wrote the Economic Development Report in 1958. He had been appointed to the post in 1956 by Gerard Sweetman, Minister for Finance in the 1954–1957 coalition government. Sweetman was also responsible for Ireland's application to join the IMF (*International Monetary Fund*) and the World Bank. He also set up the Capital Investment Advisory Committee. The change in policy that he initiated survived his government's loss of power in 1957 and became associated mainly with Seán Lemass, the Fianna Fáil Tánaiste and Minister for Industry and Commerce, who became Taoiseach in June 1959 on de Valera's retirement. Even before becoming Taoiseach, Lemass had chaired the cabinet committee that drew up the First Programme for Economic Expansion. He had presented the programme to the Fianna Fáil Ard-fheis in 1958. The first programme was essentially a five-year plan. The word "programme" was preferred because five-year plans were associated with communism and, in particular, with Stalin's Soviet Union. It identified grassland as Ireland's greatest natural resource (accounting for over 85 % of agricultural land) and sought to increase livestock numbers and the production of milk and milk products. But it was the move toward free trade and away from protectionism that was the biggest policy shift outlined in the document.

Other important issue was Anglo-Irish economic relations at that time. Anglo-Irish Free Trade Agreement was signed in 1965. It marked a significant shift in trade relations between Ireland and Britain by providing tariff-free access to each other's markets. This agreement was a pivotal moment in Irish economic policy during the 1960s, as it aimed to boost trade and economic growth between the two countries. After a long period when trade with Britain was regulated by quotas and tariffs, this agreement gave Irish industry tariff-free access to the British market. It also guaranteed a market for store cattle and sheep and an increased butter quota. Under the agreement, Ireland was to reduce its tariffs on imports from Britain—with 1975 set as the year when this process was to be concluded and full free trade between the two countries achieved. The agreement was an important element of Irish economic policy during the 1960s.

Additionally, in 1960 the government decided to join the GATT (General Agreement on Tariffs and Trade). Tariff barriers were gradually dismantled and in 1965 the Anglo-Irish Free Trade Area Agreement was signed with Britain. In 1961 Ireland and Britain applied to join the Common Market, but the Irish application was withdrawn when the French vetoed British entry in 1963.[151] Britain still dominated Ireland's export market. In industry, the programme aimed to achieve a large increase in investment in private industry through tax concessions and other measures such as export promotion. The cost of these measures was substantial, but the programme argued that risks had to be taken if future growth and prosperity were to be achieved. The programme was well timed to take advantage of the upturn in world economic activity that followed the economic depression of the post-war period. During the period of the first programme, national income grew by 4 %. The increase in prosperity was brought about by an increase in agricultural production (9 % in the 1960s) and in manufacturing, where the value of production rose by 82 % in the period 1959–1968. The value of exports in 1960 was the highest for 30 years. Unemployment fell as job prospects improved. Another sign of growing affluence was the increase in population. The 1966 census showed an increase of 62,411, the first increase since the Great Famine of the 1840s. Two more programmes followed, in 1963 and 1973, following which the 1973 Oil Crisis saw a period of economic depression begin.[152]

In the historical context of the 1950s and 1960s, Ireland found itself at a pivotal juncture, grappling with economic challenges while witnessing the rapid integration of European economies through organizations like the European Economic Community (EEC). The decision to apply for EEC membership in 1961 marked a significant shift in Ireland's economic and foreign policy. During this period, Ireland faced daunting economic hurdles characterized

---

151 See: G. Murphy, *A Measurement of the Extent of Our Sovereignty at the Moment': Sovereignty and the Question of Irish Entry to the EEC, New Evidence from the Archives Irish Studies in International Affairs*, "Irish Studies in International Affairs," Vol. 12 (2001), pp. 191–202.

152 See more: P. Perry, *Modernizing Ireland's Economy*, "Finance & Development," March 1965, p. 70.

by mass emigration and persistent unemployment. These challenges underscored the need for a departure from previous economic strategies centered on protectionism and self-sufficiency, toward a more open and interconnected approach to trade and economic development.

Prior to seeking EEC membership, Ireland's trade landscape was heavily reliant on the United Kingdom. The overwhelming majority of Irish exports, around 81 %, were destined for the British market, highlighting a vulnerability to changes in UK trade policies and economic conditions. In contrast, the six founding members of the EEC were experiencing a period of unprecedented post-war prosperity, driven by economic integration and cooperation within the European community. Recognizing the potential benefits of joining this burgeoning economic bloc, Irish policymakers embarked on a path toward greater international engagement and integration. The decision to apply for EEC membership reflected a broader shift in Ireland's foreign policy toward greater involvement in international organizations. By joining the United Nations in 1955 and subsequently becoming a member of the International Monetary Fund and World Bank in 1957, Ireland signaled its willingness to participate in global affairs and embrace multilateral cooperation.

The move toward EEC membership represented a strategic pivot for Ireland, not only in terms of economic policy but also in terms of its broader diplomatic and geopolitical orientation. Embracing European integration offered Ireland the opportunity to diversify its trade relationships, reduce dependency on the UK market, and access new avenues for economic growth and development. Overall, Ireland's decision to apply for EEC membership in 1961 reflected a pragmatic recognition of the changing realities of the global economy and a commitment to pursuing a more open and interconnected approach to trade and international relations.

When Seán Lemass became Irish Prime Minister in 1959, he decided to implement the ideas expressed in the government's White Paper. The new policy aims to increase Irish agricultural production and identify opportunities in higher-priced continental European food markets. Attempts have also been made to attract foreign investment into the manufacturing export sector to boost domestic employment. The European Economic Community's plan to develop a common agricultural policy is particularly attractive to Ireland because its price guarantees and export subsidies will benefit Ireland's agriculture-based economy. When Lemas learned that Britain might apply to join the European Economic Community, his government published a White Paper on the European Economic Community in July 1961, informing the six EEC member states that if Britain applied to join the European Economic Community, Ireland also applies. When the United Kingdom applied to become a full member of the European Economic Community in 1961, Ireland submitted a formal application letter on July 31, 1961.[153]

Although the September 1961 Ministerial Conference allowed Britain and Denmark to enter the negotiating stage, the six founding members of the EEC expressed doubts about Ireland's economic performance and how Ireland's military neutrality would affect its ability to become a full member of the EEC role. Lemas conducted intensive diplomatic efforts, including personal visits to six capitals, to provide reassurances about Ireland's neutrality and the economy's ability to meet the requirements of EEC membership. In October 1962, the Council of Ministers of the European Economic Community agreed to start accession negotiations with Dublin on the basis of full membership. However, when France vetoed Britain's accession to the European Community in January 1963, Ireland had no choice but to withdraw its application on economic grounds. With its main trading partner still outside the European Economic Community, Ireland cannot survive on its own.

2.2.3. 1970s troubles and EEC negotiation and accession

Ireland applied for full membership of the European Economic Community (EEC) on July 31, 1961. The possibility of associate membership was rejected because it implied that Ireland was economically underdeveloped. This application was submitted at the same time that British Prime Minister Harold Macmillan announced Britain's intention to apply for EEC membership.

The European Commission's response to Dublin did not specify a timeline for when Ireland's EEC entry negotiations might commence. Few in Brussels believed Ireland was economically developed enough for EEC membership. There was also a perception that Ireland's application was not serious, as many did not expect an Irish application independent of Britain's. Additionally,

[153] See: A. Neville, *Ireland and Denmark in the EU*, "BRIEFING," European Union History Series, EPRS – European Parliamentary Research Service, January 2022, https://www.europarl.europa.eu/RegData/etudes/BRIE/2022/698877/EPRS_BRI(2022)698877_EN.pdf.

Ireland's neutrality and non-membership in NATO posed problems, especially in light of European political integration efforts following the July 1961 Bonn Declaration. Consequently, the Community focused on the British and Danish applications, setting Ireland's aside.

In January 1962, Taoiseach Seán Lemass addressed the Community's concerns directly in a speech to the European Commission. He then visited the capitals of the Six in October 1962 to assert that Ireland was sufficiently economically developed for EEC membership and that its military neutrality and non-membership of NATO were not obstacles to entry. Lemass's personal diplomacy helped break the deadlock. In October 1962, the EEC Council of Ministers agreed to open entry negotiations with Dublin on the basis of full membership.

While five of the Six were in favor of opening negotiations, France remained hesitant, despite Lemass receiving positive indications from President Charles de Gaulle. Britain's entry negotiations took precedence, and Ireland's negotiations were not expected to begin before March 1963. However, on January 14, 1963, de Gaulle raised doubts about Britain's suitability for EEC membership and vetoed its application. Ireland's EEC application was effectively caught in the fallout of de Gaulle's "Non." Although de Gaulle did not veto Ireland's application, the exclusion of its main trading partner, Britain, rendered Ireland's solo entry impractical. Consequently, Ireland's EEC membership prospects were indefinitely postponed, and the country adopted a "wait and see" stance toward Europe.

Following de Gaulle's veto, Ireland's EEC application was shelved. Lemass continued to promote Irish economic modernization, and the economy grew at a rate of 3 % per annum, slightly below the anticipated 4.3 %. Additional trade barriers were removed, and the establishment of the Anglo-Irish Free Trade Area in 1966 created a conducive environment for Ireland's eventual EEC membership. Lemass aimed to demonstrate that Ireland was adapting to the economic transformations occurring in 1960s Western Europe. Attempts by Ireland to secure an interim trade deal with the EEC were unsuccessful. The European Commission expressed sympathy but offered little practical support. Domestically, there was some dissatisfaction regarding Ireland's seemingly directionless EEC policy. In reality, the EEC was not eager to welcome Ireland, and ongoing Anglo-French tensions continued to complicate the enlargement process.

Lemass resigned in November 1966 and was succeeded as Taoiseach by his Minister for Finance, Jack Lynch. When Lynch met British Prime Minister Harold Wilson in December 1966, he learned that Britain was considering a renewed EEC application. Wilson assured Lynch that if Britain reapplied, Ireland could also reactivate its application. On May 1, 1967, Wilson confirmed Britain's intention to reapply for EEC membership and assured Lynch of London's support for simultaneous British and Irish accession. Britain's application was submitted on May 11, and Ireland's application followed 15 minutes later. However, five days later, de Gaulle issued a "velvet veto," stating that conditions were not right for Britain's EEC membership. In the second half of 1967, Lynch visited the capitals of the Six, including a successful meeting with de Gaulle in early November. Despite these efforts, by the end of 1967, the prospect of EEC membership for Ireland remained distant. In December, the Council of Ministers decided against formally opening entry negotiations with any of the applicants. On December 19, Karl Schiller, President of the Council of Ministers, informed Dublin that the Six were not proceeding with Ireland's EEC application.

The UK reapplied in 1967, submitting its application on May 11, and Ireland submitted its application 15 minutes later. While Taoiseach Jack Lynch sought to protect Ireland's chances of joining the EEC through diplomacy, the Council of Ministers decided in December not to formally launch accession talks with any candidate country. The resignation of General de Gaulle in 1969 opened the possibility of joining the organization. In December 1969, the six agreed in The Hague that accession negotiations would begin in mid-1970. Ireland's accession negotiations finally began on June 30, 1970, and Ireland's first face-to-face negotiations with the European Commission began in September 1970.

Following General de Gaulle's resignation on April 28, 1969, the possibility of community enlargement within the European Communities (EC) resurfaced. Despite this political shift, Seán Morrissey, the Irish Ambassador to the European Communities, noted a lack of immediate enthusiasm in Brussels regarding enlargement, cautioning against expectations of swift progress. Ireland's accession to the EC would not be instantaneous.

In June 1969, Patrick Hillery succeeded Frank Aiken as Ireland's Minister for External Affairs following the Irish general election. Unlike Aiken, who had focused on the United Nations, Hillery's appointment underscored Dublin's renewed commitment to securing EC membership. Throughout the summer of 1969, Hillery and other officials embarked on ministerial visits to the European Commission and the capitals of the Six (the founding members of the EC), aiming to foster a favorable perception of Ireland within the European Communities. One significant challenge Hillery faced was overcoming a proposal to prioritize Britain's EC application over Ireland's, which could have jeopardized Ireland's economic ties with its primary export market. The December 1969 agreement of the Six at The Hague was a pivotal moment for Ireland. This agreement set the stage for entry negotiations to begin in mid-1970. The negotiations officially started on June 30, 1970, with the initial direct talks between Ireland and the European Commission occurring in September 1970.

The Hague Summit also marked a significant evolution in the European Communities. The decisions made there included completing the Common Market, initiating steps toward establishing a European Monetary System, and enhancing foreign policy coordination. Consequently, the EC that Ireland was negotiating to join in 1970 had become a more integrated and advanced entity compared to the original Common Market established in the 1950s. Hillery preceded Ireland's accession negotiations with further visits to the capitals of Community members to ensure they understood that Ireland would undertake the political and economic obligations of membership. To support this initiative, a White Paper titled Membership of the European Communities—Implications for Ireland was agreed upon by the Cabinet in April 1970 and subsequently published.

During the entry negotiations and the transitional period following entry, Ireland's primary concerns were to protect its interests in trade, agriculture, industry, and fisheries. The Committee of Secretaries, composed of the heads of senior government departments, emphasized that "the most important objective for us in these negotiations will be protection during the transitional period of our interests in the British market, particularly as regards agriculture."[154] Despite the fraught state of Anglo-Irish relations and the concurrent escalation of the Northern Ireland Troubles, Hillery collaborated closely with his British counterparts to ensure mutual understanding of matters of joint concern throughout the entry negotiations. The negotiating team,

[154] See: https://www.ireland.ie/en/eu50/history-of-ireland-in-the-eu/ [accessed 22.05.2024].

led by Hillery, was granted considerable freedom by Dublin. The Cabinet discussed European matters only when the most critical aspects of the negotiations required a decision. On September 15, 1970, the Cabinet agreed that the negotiators were "to signify the acceptance, without reservation, of the principle of equal pay for men and women." The negotiators had a broad outline of what needed to be concluded but had to fill in much detail and engage in hard bargaining during the course of the accession talks.

In 1971, Ireland faced significant concerns regarding the five-year transitional measures for industry and agriculture and the complex issue of the Common Fisheries Policy. The final negotiating session occurred on January 18, 1972. Jean Dondelinger, Luxembourg's Permanent Representative to the European Communities and the Chairman of the session, declared all outstanding problems solved, concluding the proceedings with appropriate toasts. The signing ceremony for Ireland's EC accession took place at the Palais d'Egmont in Brussels on January 22, 1972. Negotiations continued until January 1972, with a ceremony held at the Egmont Palace in Brussels on January 22, culminating in the signing of the first Accession Treaty in 1972 (effective January 1, 1973). Major changes in Irish policy therefore required constitutional ratification on May 10, 1972.[155]

In 1973, Ireland joined the European Economic Community (EEC), now the European Union (EU). EU membership brought significant economic benefits and helped transform Ireland into a more outward-looking and prosperous nation. Membership in the European Economic Community (EEC) in 1973 represented a watershed moment, opening doors to unprecedented foreign engagement and economic integration. This decision not only signaled Ireland's willingness to embrace a broader European identity but also facilitated access to vital markets and resources, further bolstering its economic standing on the global stage. Against the backdrop of these transformative shifts, the imprint of de Valera's vision and Fianna Fáil's governance remained palpable, shaping the collective understanding of this

---

[155] Some 83 % of Irish people voted "yes," and Article 29.4.3 of the Irish Constitution holds that: "The State may become a member of the European Atomic Energy Community (established by Treaty signed at Rome on the 25th day of March, 1957)." See: J. O'Mahony, *Ireland's EU Referendum Experience*, "Irish Political Studies," Vol. 24, No. 4, 429–446, December 2009, pp. 429–430.

pivotal period in Irish history. Their legacy, though not without controversy, undeniably left an indelible mark on the trajectory of Irish politics and society, laying the foundation for the nation's continued evolution in the decades to come.[156]

The 1970s witnessed a confluence of significant events in both Northern Ireland and the broader context of European integration. The Troubles began in the late 1960s, but the 1970s saw some of the most intense violence, with bombings, shootings, and riots becoming almost daily occurrences. The conflict primarily involved nationalist/republican groups, who were mainly Catholic and sought unification with the Republic of Ireland, and unionist/loyalist groups, who were predominantly Protestant and wanted Northern Ireland to remain part of the United Kingdom. The British government's presence in Northern Ireland, including the deployment of troops, further complicated the situation and often exacerbated tensions against the backdrop of the Troubles—a period of intense political and sectarian violence in Northern Ireland—the island of Ireland found itself at the intersection of domestic conflict and the evolving landscape of European cooperation. As tensions simmered within Northern Ireland, the Republic of Ireland embarked on its own journey of closer ties with its European neighbors, seeking to leverage integration as a means to transcend historical divisions and foster prosperity. This subchapter delves into the intertwined narratives of the Troubles in Northern Ireland and the European integration process of Ireland during the tumultuous decade of the 1970s. It explores the complex dynamics between domestic conflict and international cooperation, examining how events in Northern Ireland influenced Ireland's approach to European integration, and vice versa. By unpacking these interconnected strands, we gain a deeper understanding of how historical circumstances shape the trajectory of nations within the broader context of regional and global dynamics.

The 1970s saw an escalation of violence in Northern Ireland, known as "The Troubles." The Irish government faced challenges in dealing with the conflict while maintaining peace and stability within its own borders. Throughout the 1970s, the landscape of Northern Ireland was marred by an alarming escalation of violence, a dark chapter etched in history as "The

[156] See: Department of Foreign Affairs, *Ireland and the EU: A History*, https://www.dfa.ie/media/dfa/alldfawebsitemedia/ourrolesandpolicies/irelandintheeu/ireland-in-the-eu-history.pdf.

Troubles." This protracted period of conflict was characterized by sectarian tensions, paramilitary activity, and political upheaval, leaving scars deeply ingrained in the social fabric of the region. As the turmoil unfolded, the Irish government found itself confronted with the daunting task of addressing the complex dynamics of the conflict while simultaneously safeguarding peace and stability within its own borders. Balancing the imperatives of diplomacy, security, and domestic tranquility, policymakers navigated a treacherous terrain, seeking elusive pathways toward resolution amidst the relentless cycle of violence and discord. The challenges posed by "The Troubles" tested the resilience of Ireland's leadership and the nation's commitment to peace, underscoring the imperative of finding sustainable solutions to entrenched conflicts within and beyond its borders.[157]

The Irish government faced challenges in dealing with the conflict while maintaining peace and stability within its own borders. Throughout the 1970s, the landscape of Northern Ireland was marred by an alarming escalation of violence, a dark chapter etched in history as "The Troubles." This protracted period of conflict was characterized by sectarian tensions, paramilitary activity, and political upheaval, leaving scars deeply ingrained in the social fabric of the region. As the turmoil unfolded, the Irish government found itself confronted with the daunting task of addressing the complex dynamics of the conflict while simultaneously safeguarding peace and stability within its own borders.

Balancing the imperatives of diplomacy, security, and domestic tranquility, policymakers in the Republic of Ireland navigated a treacherous terrain, seeking elusive pathways toward resolution amidst the relentless cycle of violence and discord. The Irish government, under leaders such as Jack Lynch and later Liam Cosgrave, took a cautious approach, emphasizing the need for political solutions while condemning violence. They worked to support peace initiatives, such as the Sunningdale Agreement of 1973, which aimed to establish a power-sharing executive and a cross-border Council of Ireland. Although the agreement ultimately failed due to opposition from unionists and a loyalist general strike, it represented a significant effort to address the underlying political issues.

---

157 See: A. Guelke, *The International System and the Northern Ireland Peace Process*, Working Papers in British-Irish Studies No. 21, 2002 Institute for British-Irish Studies University College, pp. 1–14.

Simultaneously, the Republic of Ireland pursued a broader strategy of economic and political integration with Europe, joining the European Economic Community (EEC) in 1973.[158] This move was driven by a desire to foster economic growth and stability, but it also had profound implications for the nation's identity and international relationships. European integration offered Ireland a platform to transcend its insular conflicts and align with a broader, cooperative framework that emphasized shared prosperity and peace. The accession to the EEC marked a pivotal shift, providing Ireland with economic aid and access to larger markets, which contributed to modernization and development.

The dual focus on addressing the Northern Ireland conflict and pursuing European integration reflected a multifaceted approach to national policy. On one hand, the Irish government remained deeply engaged in efforts to mediate and resolve the Troubles, advocating for peaceful solutions and engaging in diplomatic negotiations. On the other hand, the European integration process provided a counterbalance, offering a vision of progress and stability that contrasted sharply with the violent strife to the north.

The challenges posed by "The Troubles" tested the resilience of Ireland's leadership and the nation's commitment to peace, underscoring the imperative of finding sustainable solutions to entrenched conflicts within and beyond its borders. By engaging with Europe, Ireland sought not only economic benefits but also a strategic reorientation that could help mitigate the impact of the Troubles. This period thus highlights the interplay between domestic conflict and international cooperation, illustrating how a nation can navigate internal turmoil while seeking broader alliances to secure its future. The 1970s were a transformative decade for Ireland, marked by the convergence of crisis and opportunity, conflict and integration, shaping the trajectory of the nation's development in profound ways.[159]

---

[158] On May 10, 1972, 70 % of Irish voters went to the polls to vote on the ratification of the Treaty of Accession.
The result of the referendum was no surprise: 81 % of the Irish supported entry into the European Economic Community (EEC), the European Atomic Energy Community (EAEC or Euratom) and the European Coal and Steel Community (ECSC). https://www.cvce.eu/en/obj/ireland_s_accession-en-c6c28822-886f-4009-908a-980482c94817.html [accessed 22.05.2024].

[159] See more: M. Mulholland, *The Longest War: Northern Ireland's Troubled History*, Oxford 2004.

To sum up, The 1970s were a turbulent period for Northern Ireland, experiencing intense violence known as "The Troubles," characterized by bombings, shootings, and riots involving nationalist/republican groups seeking unification with the Republic of Ireland and unionist/loyalist groups wanting to remain part of the UK. The British military presence exacerbated tensions. Amid this conflict, the Republic of Ireland sought closer ties with Europe, joining the European Economic Community (EEC) in 1973 to foster economic growth and stability. Irish leaders like Jack Lynch and Liam Cosgrave emphasized political solutions, supporting peace initiatives such as the Sunningdale Agreement, despite its ultimate failure due to unionist opposition. This dual approach of addressing domestic conflict and pursuing European integration highlighted Ireland's strategy to navigate internal turmoil while aligning with broader cooperative frameworks. This period underscored the resilience of Ireland's leadership and its commitment to peace, marking a transformative decade that shaped the nation's development through a blend of crisis management and international collaboration.

As forementioned before, following the resignation of French President Charles de Gaulle on April 28, 1969, the path to European Community enlargement was reopened, providing Ireland with a renewed opportunity to seek membership. De Gaulle's departure removed a substantial obstacle, as he had previously vetoed the accession of the United Kingdom and other countries, including Ireland, due to his vision of a more limited European integration. Despite this opening, Irish Ambassador to the European Communities Seán Morrissey cautioned that there was no overwhelming sense of euphoria in Brussels regarding the enlargement. His observation underscored the pragmatic and cautious approach that would characterize Ireland's diplomatic efforts during this period.

In Ireland, the general election in June 1969 brought Patrick Hillery to the forefront of the country's foreign policy as the new Minister for External Affairs, succeeding Frank Aiken. Aiken had focused largely on the United Nations, but Hillery's appointment was a clear signal of Dublin's renewed determination to secure EC membership. Under Hillery's leadership, Ireland's foreign policy pivoted toward Europe with greater vigor and focus.

Throughout the summer of 1969, Hillery and other senior Irish officials embarked on a series of ministerial visits to the European Commission in Brussels and to the capitals of the Six founding EC member states—Belgium, France, Germany, Italy, Luxembourg, and the Netherlands. These visits were part of a concerted diplomatic campaign to foster a positive image of Ireland and to build support for its membership bid. The Irish delegation sought to emphasize Ireland's commitment to the European project, its readiness to meet the economic and political criteria for membership, and its potential contributions to the Community.[160] These efforts were instrumental in changing perceptions and garnering support among the member states. The strategic diplomacy conducted by Hillery and his team laid the groundwork for Ireland's successful application and eventual accession to the EC.

This period marked a shift in Irish foreign policy from a broader international focus to a concentrated effort on European integration, reflecting the country's recognition of the economic and political benefits of EC membership. Ultimately, the signing of the Treaty of Accession and the subsequent ratification by referendum in May 1972, followed by Ireland's official entry into the EC on January 1, 1973, represented the culmination of years of diplomatic effort and strategic planning. This move not only aligned Ireland more closely with its European neighbors but also signified a major step in the country's economic and social development, heralding a new era of engagement with Europe.[161] Worth seeing this Ireland's European journey through these triumphs and trials, exploring the dynamic interplay of political agreements, economic transformations, and the resilience of a nation navigating its path in an ever-evolving global landscape. From the collaborative spirit of the Anglo-Irish Agreement to the economic surge of the Celtic Tiger, and from the peace and stability fostered by the Good Friday Agreement to the challenges posed by the global financial crisis, Ireland's recent history is a testament to its enduring strength and adaptability.[162]

---

160 See: *Ireland in the EU*, https://www.ireland.ie/en/eu50/history-of-ireland-in-the-eu/ [accessed 22.05.2024].

161 See more: P. Hession, *Riding three horses at once: Ireland's EU membership as a national development strategy*, 2019, "Renewal," 27:2, pp. 64–74.

162 See: M. FitzGerald, *Ireland's Relations With the EEC: From the Treaties of Rome to Membership*, "Journal of European Integration History," 2001, 7(1), pp. 11–24.

United Kingdom and Ireland, European Union and Northern Ireland Peace Process (1973–2016)

3.1. UK and Ireland in the EEC (1973–1991)

The period from 1973 to 1991 was a transformative era for both the United Kingdom (UK) and Ireland as they joined the European Economic Community (EEC), the precursor to the European Union (EU). This marked the EEC's first enlargement beyond its six founding members: Belgium, France, Italy, Luxembourg, the Netherlands, and West Germany. Both the UK and Ireland sought economic benefits from EEC membership, aiming for access to a larger market and potential growth. While the UK had a more contentious and ambivalent relationship with the EEC, Ireland generally viewed membership as a positive force for economic and social development. The experiences of both countries during this time laid the groundwork for their future interactions with the European Union.

For the UK, it was also a strategic move to bolster its declining global influence post-World War II, while Ireland viewed it as a path to modernization and economic development. The economic impact was mixed for the UK; the initial years were challenging due to high inflation and unemployment exacerbated by the global oil crisis of the 1970s. However, by the 1980s, the UK reaped significant benefits from the single market, becoming one of Europe's leading economies. Ireland experienced substantial economic growth, benefiting from EEC structural funds that modernized its infrastructure and agriculture, transforming its economy from agrarian to more diversified with increased foreign investment.

Politically, the UK held a referendum in 1975, with 67 % voting to remain in the EEC, indicating a broad consensus despite notable dissent within major political parties. Prime Minister Margaret Thatcher, in office from 1979 to 1990, had a complex relationship with the EEC; she supported the single market but was critical of increased political integration and secured a rebate on the UK's financial contributions. Ireland, maintaining its policy of neutrality, was cautious about political and defense commitments but fully engaged in economic integration, which accelerated social and political changes, including economic liberalization and the adoption of European norms in policies from agriculture to women's rights. Both countries were significantly influenced by the Common Agricultural Policy (CAP), with the UK often critical of its costs while Ireland benefited from agricultural subsidies. The Single European Act of 1986, aimed at creating a single market, further integrated their economies. Toward the Maastricht Treaty, the UK was skeptical about further integration, opting out of the social chapter, while Ireland supported the treaty, seeing it as beneficial for further economic integration. This era laid the groundwork for their future interactions with the EU, with the UK maintaining a contentious and ambivalent relationship and Ireland viewing membership positively for its economic and social development.[163]

Discover the transformative decades from the 1980s to the present, a period marked by significant milestones in Ireland's history. The Anglo-Irish Agreement of 1985 laid the groundwork for collaboration amidst the enduring conflict in Northern Ireland, demonstrating a commitment to peace and cooperation. Moving into the 1990s, Ireland witnessed the remarkable rise of the Celtic Tiger, a period of unprecedented economic prosperity driven by substantial foreign investment and robust support from the European Union. This era of economic growth transformed Ireland into a beacon of success and modernity on the global stage.

The peace dividends of the Good Friday Agreement in 1998 further solidified Ireland's path toward stability and cooperation. This landmark accord not only brought an end to decades of sectarian violence but also fostered a new era of political and social harmony in Northern Ireland. As Ireland continued to grow and develop, it faced the looming specter of the 2008 global financial crisis, which posed significant challenges to the nation's economic stability and growth. Throughout these decades, one pivotal moment stands out in

[163] See: A. Jackson, op. cit, p. 338.

Irish foreign policy: the signing of the Treaty of Accession in 1972, marking Ireland's determined and strategic effort to join the European Communities (EEC). This momentous event, set against a backdrop of significant political changes within both Ireland and Europe, represented a decisive step in Ireland's integration into the European economic and political framework. The accession to the EEC not only provided Ireland with substantial economic benefits but also positioned the country as a proactive and influential member of the European community.

Ireland's entry into the European Economic Community (EEC) in the 1970s marked a transformative chapter in the nation's history, driving profound economic, social, and political changes. The decision to join the EEC was overwhelmingly supported by the Irish people in a referendum held in May 1972, where more than 83 % of voters endorsed membership. This decisive mandate reflected the country's aspirations for modernization and economic development. Officially joining the EEC in January 1973, Ireland sought to break free from its historical dependence on the United Kingdom and to establish itself as an active participant in the broader European project.

From the outset, Ireland's membership in the EEC brought new responsibilities and opportunities. In January 1975, Ireland assumed the presidency of the EEC Council of Ministers for the first time. Over the six-month term, Ireland demonstrated its ability to manage European affairs and contribute to shaping the policy agenda of the community. This role was an early indication of Ireland's ambition to be a proactive and influential member of the EEC. The social landscape of Ireland also began to shift during this period, influenced in part by the country's alignment with European norms. A significant milestone came in June 1977 with the abolition of the marriage bar, a policy that had prevented married women from working in the public sector. This reform, influenced by EEC commitments to gender equality, marked a turning point for women's rights in Ireland, signaling the country's gradual embrace of modern European social policies.

Ireland's growing engagement with European institutions was further demonstrated in October 1977, when Michael N. Murphy became the first President of the European Court of Auditors. This was a prestigious appointment for Ireland and underscored the country's contribution to the governance and oversight of European financial policies. Around the same time, Ireland also became the home of Eurofound, the European Foundation for the Improvement of Living and Working Conditions. The Eurofound office, which officially opened in Dublin in October 1978, was a clear recognition of Ireland's strategic role within the EEC, particularly in areas such as labor policy and social welfare.

Economic integration was another cornerstone of Ireland's membership in the EEC. In March 1979, Ireland joined the European Monetary System (EMS), aligning its currency with the European Exchange Rate Mechanism. This move aimed to stabilize Ireland's economy, reduce its dependence on the British pound, and strengthen its economic ties with other EEC member states. The decision to join the EMS reflected Ireland's broader commitment to becoming a fully integrated member of the European economic framework, even as it faced challenges in managing inflation and unemployment.

In the same year, Ireland participated in the first direct elections to the European Parliament in June 1979. This democratic process gave Irish citizens the opportunity to elect their representatives to the European Parliament for the first time, deepening Ireland's engagement with European governance and fostering a stronger connection between Irish citizens and European institutions. Shortly after, Ireland took on its second presidency of the EEC Council of Ministers from July to December 1979. This was another opportunity for Ireland to shape the EEC's agenda, particularly in areas such as agricultural policy and economic coordination, which were of vital importance to the country.

Environmental policies also began to play a more prominent role during this period, reflecting the influence of European directives. In April 1981, the Bird Directive, one of the EEC's key pieces of environmental legislation, came into effect. This directive underscored the EEC's commitment to wildlife conservation and required member states, including Ireland, to implement measures to protect native bird species and their habitats. The directive was one of the first indications of how EEC membership would shape Ireland's environmental policies, laying the groundwork for future conservation efforts.

The period from 1973 to 1981 was transformative for Ireland. Economically, EEC membership facilitated access to structural funds that modernized infrastructure and agriculture, helping Ireland shift from a largely agrarian economy to a more diversified one with increased foreign investment. The Common Agricultural Policy (CAP) provided subsidies that were crucial for Irish farmers, boosting rural development and reducing poverty in the countryside. These funds, combined with Ireland's growing role in European institutions, positioned the country as a beneficiary of European solidarity and cooperation. Socially and politically, the changes were equally significant. Membership in the EEC helped accelerate Ireland's modernization, promoting reforms in areas such as gender equality and labor rights. It also marked a shift in Ireland's international identity, as the country moved away from its traditional focus on relations with the UK and embraced its role as a European nation. Over time, this alignment with European norms and values would contribute to Ireland's economic liberalization and the adoption of more progressive social policies.

Ireland's first decade in the EEC laid the foundation for its continued integration into Europe. The benefits of membership were increasingly evident, not only in economic terms but also in the country's growing confidence on the European stage. By embracing the opportunities presented by the EEC, Ireland positioned itself as a forward-looking and outward-oriented nation, ready to play a full part in the evolving European project.[164]

From 1982 to 1992, Ireland deepened its engagement with the European Economic Community (EEC), navigating significant political and legal milestones that shaped its role in the evolving European project. In June 1984, Ireland participated in its second European Parliament elections, allowing its citizens to directly elect representatives to the European Parliament. These elections underscored Ireland's growing integration into European institutions and highlighted the increasing influence of the EEC on Irish political and economic life. Shortly afterward, from July to December 1984, Ireland held its third presidency of the EEC Council. Under the leadership of Taoiseach Garret FitzGerald, the Irish presidency facilitated dialogue among member states, focusing on advancing European integration and addressing economic challenges, with key emphasis on agricultural policy and preparations for the Single European Act.

March 1985 saw a pivotal moment in Ireland's contribution to the European project when James Dooge, a prominent Irish politician, chaired

---

[164] See: CSO Report, *Ireland and the EU 1973–2003 Economic and Social Change*, https://www.cso.ie/en/media/csoie/releasespublications/documents/statisticalyearbook/2004/ireland&theeu.pdf

the Dooge Committee, tasked with exploring ways to strengthen European cooperation. The committee's recommendations laid the foundation for the Single European Act (SEA), a landmark treaty that expanded the EEC's powers in areas such as the single market, environmental policy, and regional development. The SEA, signed in 1986, marked a major step toward deeper integration, and Ireland played a central role in shaping its provisions.

This period also brought significant legal and constitutional developments. In April 1987, the Irish Supreme Court delivered a landmark ruling in *Crotty v. An Taoiseach*, in which political activist Raymond Crotty challenged the government's authority to ratify the SEA without a referendum. The court ruled that such significant changes to EEC treaties required public approval through a constitutional referendum, reinforcing the principle that sovereignty ultimately lay with the Irish people. Following this decision, a referendum was held in May 1987, in which voters approved the SEA, demonstrating strong public support for European integration and enabling Ireland to fully participate in its initiatives, particularly the completion of the single market.

June 1987 marked another milestone with the launch of the Erasmus Programme, a flagship EEC initiative aimed at promoting educational and cultural exchange across Europe. For Ireland, the programme opened opportunities for students to study at European universities, enriching their academic experiences and strengthening Ireland's cultural ties with other member states.

Ireland's engagement with European democracy continued with the third European Parliament elections in June 1989. These elections reflected growing public interest in European matters as integration deepened, particularly in light of the significant changes on the horizon, such as the Maastricht Treaty. Ireland assumed its fourth presidency of the EEC Council in the first half of 1990, under Taoiseach Charles Haughey. This presidency occurred during a critical period marked by the end of the Cold War and intensified preparations for further European integration. Ireland prioritized the acceleration of the single market and contributed to discussions that paved the way for the Treaty of Maastricht. This demonstrated the country's diplomatic skill and commitment to fostering European unity during a transformative period for the continent.

The decade culminated with the June 1992 referendum on the Treaty of Maastricht, which established the European Union (EU) and introduced significant new areas of cooperation, including a common foreign and security policy and the foundation of the Economic and Monetary Union. Irish voters approved the treaty, reaffirming their support for European integration and Ireland's active role in shaping the EU's future. This moment solidified Ireland's position as a committed and influential member of the European project, capping a decade of profound political, legal, and societal engagement with the EEC.[165]

3.2. UK and Ireland in the EU (1992–2016)

Ireland's economic transformation in the 1990s is a remarkable example of how a combination of strategic policy choices and external factors can drive rapid economic growth. During this period, Ireland emerged as one of the fastest-growing economies in the European Union (EU) and among the OECD countries. This transformation was underpinned by a multifaceted policy approach that integrated industrial policy, macroeconomic stabilization, European integration, and a novel model of social partnership. Each of these elements played a crucial role in shaping Ireland's path to economic success.

Ireland adopted an outward-looking industrial strategy focused on attracting foreign direct investment (FDI), particularly in high-value sectors like technology, pharmaceuticals, and financial services. By offering competitive corporate tax rates, skilled labor, and access to the EU market, Ireland became a hub for multinational corporations. This influx of investment not only created jobs but also boosted productivity and exports, driving economic growth. Simultaneously, Ireland faced a severe economic crisis in the 1980s, characterized by high unemployment, massive public debt, and fiscal imbalances. To stabilize the economy, the government implemented stringent fiscal policies aimed at reducing the budget deficit and restoring investor confidence. While these measures were painful in the short term, they laid the foundation for sustainable growth by controlling inflation and reducing fiscal imbalances, ultimately stabilizing the economy.

---

[165] J. Brennan, *Ireland and the European Union: Mapping Domestic Modes of Adaptation and Contestation*, https://mural.maynoothuniversity.ie/id/eprint/2919/1/JOB_Ireland_and_the_European.pdf

Membership in the EU was a transformative factor for Ireland, as it benefited significantly from EU structural funds, which were used to modernize infrastructure and invest in education and training. Access to the single European market also opened up new opportunities for trade and investment, further integrating Ireland into the global economy. European integration influenced domestic policies, as Ireland aligned its regulatory framework with EU standards, enhancing its attractiveness as a destination for FDI. This integration reinforced the country's economic growth by providing greater access to international markets and encouraging policy reforms aligned with European norms.

A critical element of Ireland's economic recovery and growth was the adoption of a social partnership model in 1987, which brought together key economic, political, and social stakeholders—government, employers, trade unions, and community organizations—to negotiate and agree on a cohesive strategy for addressing economic and social challenges. Social partnership agreements focused on wage moderation, labor market reforms, and social cohesion, creating an environment of stability and cooperation. This collaborative approach fostered a shared vision among stakeholders and ensured the implementation of coherent and sustainable policies. The model emphasized deliberation, problem-solving, and pragmatic consensus-building rather than rigid organizational frameworks typically associated with neocorporatism. It allowed for flexibility and adaptability, enabling Ireland to respond effectively to changing domestic and international conditions. This unique approach, based on trust and mutual understanding, facilitated the mediation of competing interests, reduced industrial disputes, and ensured broad support for critical reforms.

The 1980s represented a period of deep economic, social, and political crisis for Ireland, marked by high unemployment, emigration, rising inequality, and fiscal instability, which created widespread disillusionment. This crisis highlighted the limitations of previous policy approaches and prompted a critical reassessment by policymakers and social actors. From this challenging period emerged a new perspective on Ireland's economic strategy and governance, one that recognized the interdependence between domestic policy and the broader European context. It marked a shift from traditional, insular policymaking toward a more integrated and outward-focused strategy, which acknowledged that Ireland's small, open economy required adaptive and innovative solutions to compete globally.

Ireland's transformation was shaped by a complex interplay between domestic policy choices and international influences. On the domestic front, the willingness of stakeholders to cooperate and innovate was crucial. On the international stage, European integration provided the resources, market access, and regulatory framework necessary for Ireland to succeed. While the social partnership model was not without its critiques, particularly from neo-liberal and orthodox economists who questioned its long-term sustainability, it delivered significant benefits. Critics raised concerns about potential inefficiencies and the risk of stifling competition, yet the partnership approach succeeded in mediating interests, ensuring economic stability, and enabling Ireland to capitalize on emerging global opportunities.

Between 1993 and 2014, Ireland's relationship with the European Union (EU) evolved through a period of significant political and economic changes, reflecting both national and European developments. A key milestone came in January 1993 with the establishment of the EU's Single Market, which effectively removed the customs border between Ireland and Northern Ireland. This was a vital step in facilitating trade and travel between the two regions and significantly improved Ireland's integration within the EU. Following this, Ireland played an active role in the European Parliament elections, with the Fourth European Parliament Elections taking place in June 1994, signaling the country's continued engagement in EU governance. This was a period of optimism, further bolstered by the July 1995 launch of the PEACE Programme, which provided EU funding aimed at promoting peace and reconciliation in Northern Ireland.

In the late 1990s, Ireland continued its prominent role within the EU. The country held its Fifth EU Presidency between July and December 1996, which underscored Ireland's growing diplomatic presence within the Union. In 1998, Ireland hosted a referendum on the Treaty of Amsterdam, further demonstrating the nation's influence on EU treaties. The end of the century saw the first woman from Ireland, Fidelma Macken, appointed to the European Court of Justice in October 1999, marking a historic achievement for gender representation in EU institutions. Around the same time, David

O'Sullivan was appointed Secretary General of the European Commission in June 2000, continuing Ireland's strong presence at the heart of EU governance.

The early 2000s saw a series of major events for Ireland within the EU. In January 2002, the introduction of the Euro currency marked a new chapter in Ireland's economic development, further integrating it into the EU's financial framework. Later that year, Irish MEP Pat Cox became President of the European Parliament, reflecting Ireland's growing political influence. The country's involvement in major treaty changes continued with the 2001 and 2002 referendums on the Treaty of Nice, followed by Ireland's Sixth EU Presidency in January 2004. The EU also witnessed the historic decision to make Irish an official EU language in January 2007, a significant cultural milestone for the country.

Ireland's role within the EU continued to evolve through the economic and political challenges of the 2000s and early 2010s. The Irish financial crisis culminated in the country entering the EU-IMF financial assistance programme in November 2010, a key moment in Ireland's economic history. Despite these challenges, Ireland maintained its influence within the Union, as evidenced by the successful completion of its Seventh EU Presidency in 2013 and the reform of the Common Fisheries Policy in 2013. Ireland also participated in the European Parliament elections of 2009 and 2014, reflecting the country's active engagement in shaping EU policies. During this period, Ireland's importance in the EU remained steady, with figures such as Professor Michael O'Flaherty representing the country in key EU institutions, cementing Ireland's role in the development of European fundamental rights and governance.[166]

In conclusion, Ireland's experience demonstrates the power of combining internal consensus with external alignment. By leveraging the opportunities of European integration and fostering a culture of partnership and problem-solving, Ireland achieved a remarkable economic turnaround and set an example for other small, open economies.[167]

---

[166] See: *50 Steps*, "Ireland and European Integration," Vol. 1–5.

[167] R. O'Donnell, *Ireland's Economic Transformation Industrial policy, European Integration and Social Partnership*, https://aei.pitt.edu/27/1/Odonnell.pdf

3.3. UK and Ireland peace process (1968–1998)

It is worth examining why Sinn Féin and the IRA strongly opposed English rule during The Troubles. To do this, one must thoroughly trace the history. During the Second World War period, Sinn Féin also faced significant financial problems. In 1943, a legal case began against the then leadership of Sinn Féin, who were accused of misappropriating nearly 9,000 British pounds from the party's funds from before 1926. This trial, known as the "Sinn Féin Funds Case," concluded in 1948. The case was widely publicized across Ireland due to the involvement of the prominent Éire figure, Éamon de Valera, who believed that the Sinn Féin funds from before 1926 legally did not belong to the accused party leadership. M. Buckley argued that the money held by Sinn Féin before the 1926 split rightfully belonged to her party, not to Fianna Fáil as de Valera contended, since Sinn Féin after 1926 was the legitimate successor of those assets.

The verdict delivered in 1948 was significant for both financial and moral reasons. The presiding judge, K. Moore, in a Solomon-like decision, declared: "[...] the members of the Sinn Féin leadership in 1942 unlawfully appropriated money from 1924 (£8,610), but the Sinn Féin funds after 1926 (approximately £24,000) legally belong to the Sinn Féin party of 1942, as it is the legal heir of those assets post-1926 [...]." This ruling was indeed a Pyrrhic victory for Sinn Féin. On one hand, the judge acknowledged that the Sinn Féin of 1948 was the same organization as in 1923, yet the continuity of the party before 1923 was questioned. On the other hand, Sinn Féin lost the case of misappropriation and was burdened with legal costs, leading the party to the brink of bankruptcy by the late 1940s. This was also because in 1947, a year before the verdict, the Dáil passed the "Sinn Féin Funds Bill," which, under the informal influence of de Valera, de facto and de jure confiscated the entire sum of money awarded post-factum to Sinn Féin (£24,000) for social purposes.[168]

The only success for Sinn Féin after the verdict was a moral victory, in the form of recognizing the then members of the party as rightful heirs to the ideological legacy of Sinn Féin after 1926. In 1949, after the declaration of the Republic of Ireland in the 26 southern counties, Sinn Féin once again

[168] About "Sinn Féin funds" case see further in: B. Feeney, op. cit., pp. 179–181.

became a focus of interest for the IRA, which, after unsuccessful attempts at collaboration with Germany during World War II, sought to rebuild its political base. The supreme formal body of the Army, the IRA Convention, passed a resolution allowing the IRA to infiltrate and control the Sinn Féin party. According to this resolution, IRA members began to join Sinn Féin *en masse* in the early 1950s, gradually dictating its terms of operation. By 1950, Patrick McLogan, associated with the IRA, became the new chairman of Sinn Féin.

The IRA Convention's decision to infiltrate Sinn Féin led to new members, already part of the IRA, joining the party. According to J. Bowyer Bell, a historian of the republican movement in Ireland, Sinn Féin after 1950, was the civilian wing of the IRA. The first test of strength for the new iteration of Sinn Féin was its participation in the May 1955 elections to the British House of Commons and the March 1957 general elections to the Dáil. Sinn Féin continued to uphold the principle of abstentionism, so the results of these elections were only symbolic. Sinn Féin fielded 19 candidates in the 1957 Dáil elections, receiving over 65,000 votes, amounting to 5.3 % of the national vote, translating into four seats. The IRA conducted a sabotage campaign codenamed "Harvest Operation" from December 1956 to the end of February 1962. This action did not gain supporters in Ireland, and its radical nature resulted in Sinn Féin receiving only 3 % of the vote in the October 1961 Dáil elections. This was a clear indication of the Irish public's disapproval of both the IRA and Sinn Féin republicans' actions.[169]

From 1962 to 1969, Sinn Féin and the IRA struggled for a new identity. A significant factor here was the long-standing informal division within the party and the Army into a left-wing faction, opposing armed struggle, mainly associated with the South of the island, and a more traditional, republican "Northern" faction, advocating for the continuation of this struggle. By the late 1960s, these factions clashed for supremacy in leading Sinn Féin and the IRA. In 1962, McLogan was succeeded as Sinn Féin chairman by the left-leaning politician Tomás MacGiolla.[170] The IRA's chief of staff at the time was also a left-wing figure, Cathal Goulding. MacGiolla believed that Ireland needed a strictly leftist party. In a country of deep poverty and

169 See more: Bell J. Bowyer, *The Secret Army: A History of the I.R.A.*, London 1972, passim.
170 E. Moloney, *A Secret History of the IRA*, New York 2003, p. 538.

severe unemployment, MacGiolla thought there was room for a new image of Sinn Féin. The party then planned to abandon abstentionism regarding local elections in the South while maintaining this principle at the Dáil, Stormont (Northern Ireland Parliament), and Westminster levels.

In the late 1960s, the IRA witnessed a clash between supporters of Goulding's left-wing policies and proponents of armed struggle and more traditional republicanism from the North. The former wanted to abandon violence in IRA activities, while the latter, largely due to the consequences of the tragic events in Northern Ireland in the late 1960s, believed that maintaining armed tactics was necessary to protect the Catholic minority in the British part of Ulster. In February 1967, the Northern Ireland Civil Rights Association (NICRA) was formed to oppose the discrimination of the Catholic minority by Protestants in Northern Ireland. This initial attempt to combat social inequalities affecting Northern Catholics was met with disapproval from unionist organizations. Many NICRA members were accused, often unjustly, of belonging to the IRA and engaging in subversive activities. On October 9, 1968, students from Queen's University Belfast associated with NICRA founded the more radical "People's Democracy," a socialist-Trotskyist organization.

On January 4, 1969, "People's Democracy" organized a march from Belfast to Londonderry (Derry) in defense of Catholic civil rights. The peaceful march was inadequately secured by the Royal Ulster Constabulary (RUC). Protestant residents attacked the demonstrators just before Londonderry (Derry). Riots ensued in the city, and that evening the RUC and its special units, "B-Specials," stormed the Catholic part of Londonderry, Bogside. In retaliation, Catholic residents of Bogside barricaded themselves and formed the so-called "Free Derry" district. The events in Londonderry (Derry) compromised the Northern Ireland government of Terence O'Neill. In April 1969, O'Neill was replaced by James Chichester-Clark. By August of that year, violence again escalated in Londonderry. On August 12, during the loyalist "Apprentice Boys" parade, Catholic residents of Derry, who did not want RUC units to enter the Bogside district, clashed with the police. The riots, lasting nearly three days, ended on August 14, 1969, with the arrival of British military units. The toll was 145 injured and 10 civilians killed, and 4 policemen wounded. Throughout 1969, riots also occurred in Belfast, and there were many bombings and sabotage activities carried out by both the

IRA and loyalist militias. Northern Ireland's Catholic residents, no longer trusting either the RUC or the British army, gradually placed themselves under the "protection" of the Irish Republican Army (IRA).[171]

The confrontation between Goulding's left-wing faction and the "Northern" faction occurred during a secret IRA convention in December 1969 in Dublin. The left-wing faction submitted a motion to abandon armed struggle and abstentionism, as well as to recognize the existence of separate parliaments and governments in the South and North. The motion was passed by a vote of 39 to 12. A group of opponents, led by Seán MacStiofáin, refused to comply with the convention's decision and left the assembly. In protest, this group decided to form a Provisional Army Council and issued a statement reaffirming allegiance to the Republic proclaimed on Easter 1916 and pledging to fight for the reunification of the island. In Irish historiography, MacStiofáin's secessionist faction is referred to as the "Provisional IRA," while Goulding's faction, remaining after the Army split, is called the "Official IRA." The "Official IRA" declared a ceasefire in May 1972, so from that point on, the abbreviation "IRA" will mainly refer to the "Provisional" wing.

The split in the IRA had consequences in the form of a similar event during the Sinn Féin convention on January 10–11, 1970, in Dublin. At the convention, an identical motion to the previously mentioned IRA convention resolution was put to a vote. The anti-abstentionists won the vote by 153 to 104 (the resolution needed 18–19 more votes to pass). The abstentionists, mainly from the North, did not accept the will of the majority and left the assembly. The gathered—later (on January 11)—together with the group "Provisional IRA" led by MacStiofáin in the Kevin Barry Hall at Charles S. Parnell Square in Dublin, announced the formation of the Sinn Féin Caretaker Executive and declared obedience to the Provisional Army Council. The split in Sinn Féin also became a fact. Thus, two groups emerged: "Official Sinn Féin"—subordinated to the "Official IRA" and operating under this name for only 7 years, and "Provisional Sinn Féin." From the perspective of this study, the

---

[171] See: M. Farrell, *Reflections on the Northern Ireland Civil Rights Movement: Fifty Years On*, Paper for conference at George Mitchell Institute, Queen's University, and Belfast: Human Rights Futures: The Agenda for the next 50 Years, Belfast, 12th December 2018, pp. 4–6.

"provisional" wing of the party, which included abstentionists associated with the North of the island, will now be the focus.[172]

"Provisional Sinn Féin" (from 1977, without the additional adjective) faced enormous challenges after the split, given the escalation of the conflict in Northern Ireland in the late 1960s and early 1970s. Members of "Provisional Sinn Féin," mostly residing in the six northern counties of Ulster, were more determined than the rest of the republican movement to fight for the unification of the divided parts of the island. Thus, the split in Sinn Féin was inevitable. At the turn of the 1960s and 1970s, the broader radical republican camp faced the dramatic question of the future: How far could this movement shift toward revolutionary leftism without losing its republican idealism?

Members of "Provisional Sinn Féin" did not want the republican movement to lose its original nationalist momentum. The status of Northern Ireland within the United Kingdom was the most pressing issue at the time. The division of Ireland under the Anglo-Irish Treaty of 1921 still seemed to be the source of conflict. For the "Provisionals," it was Britain—in their view, the eternal, greatest enemy of Ireland—that was fully responsible for the escalation of violence in the North. This stemmed from the traditional nationalist view that Britain was an occupier of Ireland and needed to be removed from the island by any means necessary. Hence, the confirmed need for armed struggle tactics, which was then an axiom for the "Provisionals." The "Officials," by gradually abandoning violence in favor of strictly political activity and adopting a radically leftist course, became schismatics in the eyes of the "Provisionals" within the entire republican movement. W. Konarski states that "the entire 'provisional' faction in the republican movement, apart from emphasizing the necessity of armed struggle to unite Ireland, also claimed the right to their own interpretation of concepts they considered usurped by the 'official' faction (e.g., the concept of socialism)." Throughout the 1960s and 1970s, a struggle ensued within the republican camp over the right to be heirs of the entire nationalist-republican legacy. The ceasefire declared by the "official" faction in 1972 and the gradual abandonment of the traditional name by "Official Sinn Féin" allowed the "Provisionals" to be the sole "guardians" of their tradition. Members of the Provisional IRA

[172] E. Moloney, op. cit., p. 538.

and Sinn Féin were fully aware of the gravity of their situation at the time. For several decades, the connections of prominent Sinn Féin politicians with the structures of the Army would be a focal point for British intelligence services, the Ulster police (RUC), and journalists.

Numerous conspiracy theories regarding these activists and their connections with the IRA would emerge. Sinn Féin activists themselves could not or did not want to hide their undemocratic maneuvers, simultaneously operating within the party and the Army (IRA). The Sinn Féin party seemed heavily infiltrated by IRA radicals at that time. The party and Army structures were intertwined. Politicians of the party did not hide that they had or could have influence over the actions of IRA paramilitaries, as they often co-directed it. B. Feeney mentions one conspiracy theory regarding the interconnections among the "Provisionals." According to this theory, the moderate republican Fianna Fáil, dominant on the southern Irish political scene for several decades, was behind the formation of the "Provisional" faction in the IRA and Sinn Féin. The alleged actions of Fianna Fáil to cause the split in Sinn Féin and the IRA were motivated by the fear of Fianna members that the radical republican movement's leftist-Marxist face, adapting to democratic action, could become a serious threat to their dominant position in the future. This thesis seems quite implausible, judging by the effectiveness of the actions of the "official" faction of leftist republicans, who for the next several years could not handle their difficult political situation, gradually moving to the margins of public life in Ireland.

The specificity of the second faction of Sinn Féin can be synthetically described as a gradual shift from doctrinaire rhetoric to conciliatory argumentation.' This process, started in the 1970s, intensified when Gerry (Gerard) Adams took over the party leadership in 1983. However, it should be noted that Sinn Féin had already tried to reassess certain concepts and shift its vision of a future united Ireland in the 1970s. The process of democratizing Sinn Féin's actions "did not correspond with an increase in its credibility as a factor influencing the calming of the situation in Northern Ireland." The issue was primarily the party's connections with IRA structures. Sinn Féin chairmen from 1970 to 1983, Ruairí Ó Brádaigh and his deputy Dáithí Ó Conaill, "were listed in the information circulation as high-ranking members of the illegal Provisional IRA." The current party leader Gerry Adams and his deputy Martin McGuinness are accused of being IRA chiefs while holding party positions. The years 1970–1975 were marked by a broad military campaign by the IRA, resulting in the highest number of casualties in the Northern Ireland conflict. In the worst year, 1972, 470 people were killed, including 17 policemen, 131 British soldiers, and 322 civilians. 1972 was also significant due to the change in Northern Ireland's legal status. On March 24, 1972, due to the very difficult situation, direct rule by London over the province was announced.

In March 1972, Sinn Féin presented its program proposal for the future of Ireland titled Éire Nua (New Ireland). This concept was closely associated with the personas of both chairmen: R. Ó Brádaigh and D. Ó Conaill. The starting point was the idea of creating a federation encompassing the entire island of Ireland. The system of the future Ireland would consist of four levels: local, regional, provincial, and national. At the local level, county councils would be established, while regional authorities would be responsible for promoting and coordinating economic, social, and cultural initiatives. At the provincial level, there would be "four democratically elected provincial parliaments based on Ireland's four historical provinces—Ulster, Leinster, Connacht, and Munster." The parliament in Ulster (Dáil Uladh) would be appointed for all nine historical counties, thus eliminating the internal border between the southern and northern parts of the island. The Éire Nua program rejected the possibility of restoring Stormont (parliament for the six counties of British Northern Ireland). A sine qua non condition for the implementation of the "New Ireland" program was the requirement for the British to give a definitive date for withdrawing all military units from Northern Ireland.[173]

This program became a very important project for Sinn Féin in the 1970s. However, it should be noted that the proposals contained in it seemed almost impossible to achieve. The most difficult issue to implement was the possibility of "enforcing the British to give a date for the withdrawal of troops." The debate on the future of the republican movement, which was taking place within Sinn Féin at that time, became increasingly heated. The discussion also concerned the possibility of rejecting the tactic of abstentionism and renouncing armed struggle. However, it should be noted that by the late

---

173 "Éire Nua" document, Dublin 1972, passim. See:https://cain.ulster.ac.uk/issues/politics/docs/sf/sinnfein79.htm

1970s, Sinn Féin was almost entirely controlled by the IRA's paramilitary structures. An IRA staff document, essentially a report on Sinn Féin's role in the republican movement, assumed "even greater IRA control over the party and recommended even greater radicalization of Sinn Féin." Peter Taylor believes that "the system of IRA links with Sinn Féin has not significantly changed to this day [...]." Meanwhile, Sinn Féin, as the civilian equivalent of the radical republican movement, was then under the complete control of its main paramilitary representative.

At the Sinn Féin convention in 1980, a resolution was passed demanding an immediate response from the British regarding the date for withdrawing troops from Northern Ireland. The lack of a British response led to discussions in 1981 about abandoning the Éire Nua concept. The difference of opinion between supporters of this concept (Ó Brádaigh's and Ó Conaill's group) and supporters of creating a new one (Adams' and McGuinness' group) grew increasingly larger. At the 1981 convention, it was also decided to pursue the election campaign for Sinn Féin more seriously. The plan of future actions, especially among the Northern electorate, was given a catchy slogan: "an Armalite and a ballot paper in each hand." This idea marked the political strategy of the republican party in the 1980s and 1990s.[174]

It is worth considering how British forces coped with the activities of the IRA and other paramilitary groups during the Troubles in Northern Ireland. Their main task was to contain violence. During the Troubles in Northern Ireland, which spanned from 1969 to 1998, British intelligence agencies and the army were deeply involved in monitoring and combating the activities of the Irish Republican Army (IRA) and other paramilitary groups. Central to their efforts was the gathering of intelligence through a variety of means, including human intelligence (HUMINT), signals intelligence (SIGINT), and open-source intelligence (OSINT). MI5, the domestic intelligence agency, and MI6, the foreign intelligence agency, played key roles in this intelligence gathering, employing agents and technical resources to infiltrate IRA cells, intercept communications, and collect information on individuals involved in paramilitary activities.

---

[174] See more: S. Hopkins, *Sinn Féin, the Past and Political Strategy: The Provisional Irish Republican Movement and the Politics of 'Reconciliation,'* "Irish Political Studies," no 30(1), January 2015, passim.

The British Army, alongside specialized units like the Special Air Service (SAS) and the Special Reconnaissance Regiment (SRR), conducted extensive surveillance operations targeting IRA members and suspected terrorists. These operations involved monitoring movements, intercepting communications, and gathering evidence for potential arrests or military operations. This surveillance was crucial for understanding the IRA's organizational structure, tactics, and objectives, allowing for informed decision-making within the intelligence community and military leadership.

Counterinsurgency operations formed another significant aspect of the British response to the IRA during the Troubles. The British Army conducted patrols, raids, and targeted arrests of suspected terrorists, aiming to disrupt IRA activities and reduce its capabilities. Tactics such as vehicle checkpoints and searches were also employed to disrupt IRA logistics and operations, contributing to the overall security efforts in Northern Ireland. Collaboration with the Royal Ulster Constabulary (RUC) and later the Police Service of Northern Ireland (PSNI) was essential, with intelligence agencies sharing information and coordinating operations to enhance the effectiveness of counterterrorism efforts.

In addition to overt operations, British intelligence agencies occasionally conducted covert operations aimed at disrupting IRA activities or gathering intelligence. These operations, often conducted by MI6 and involving undercover agents and specialized units, were vital in penetrating IRA networks and gathering valuable information behind enemy lines. Technical surveillance also played a crucial role, with advanced technologies deployed to monitor IRA communications and activities. Listening devices, CCTV cameras, and other technical means were used to gather intelligence on the IRA's movements and plans, providing valuable insights for ongoing operations.

Despite their efforts, the British intelligence community and army faced criticism for their tactics, which were often seen as heavy-handed and led to allegations of human rights abuses. However, from the perspective of the British government, these measures were deemed necessary to maintain security and stability in Northern Ireland and to combat the threat posed by the IRA during the Troubles.[175]

---

175 See more: P. Taylor, *Brits. The War Against the IRA*, London 2005, passim.

The origins of the peace process in Northern Ireland can be traced back to when Gerry Adams took over the leadership of Sinn Féin in November 1983. Under Adams' leadership, the party began to gain increasing independence from the Irish Republican Army (IRA). This shift was primarily due to the strategies and policies introduced by the new chairman. The takeover of the party leadership by Adams and his associates initiated a cautious process of change in the mutual relations between the IRA and Sinn Féin in favor of the latter. During the party conference held on November 13, 1983, Adams, immediately after being elected as the new chairman, stated that "armed struggle is a necessary and morally justified form of resistance in the 'Six Counties' (a nationalist term for Northern Ireland) against a government (the United Kingdom) whose presence is rejected by the vast majority of the people of Ireland." At that time, the majority of party members agreed with Adams' view. For Adams, this statement was an attempt to stabilize the party by assuring the delegates of the continued necessity of armed struggle, while simultaneously advocating for active participation in elections. This marked a continuation of the Sinn Féin strategy of "Armalite and Ballot Box," developed in the early 1980s by Adams' close associate, Danny Morrison.[176]

Gerry Adams, along with his deputy Martin McGuinness, planned to dramatically change Sinn Féin's political isolation by gradually moving the party away from the principle of abstentionism in favor of full political participation in the political life of both Northern Ireland and the Republic of Ireland. Adams' plan also aimed to equalize Sinn Féin's position with the IRA, so that the party would have increasing influence over the actions of the Army. It is noteworthy that McGuinness remained a member of the IRA Army Council during this time. By 1984, thanks to the influence of Sinn Féin politicians on the IRA, the number of civilians killed by the Army had significantly decreased. Adams even began to consider the possibility of a ceasefire by the IRA, which he discussed in the press.

These speculations coincided with an open conflict between a significant portion of the IRA Belfast Brigade, led by Ivor Bell, and the Sinn Féin leadership regarding IRA funds intended not for the Army's armed struggle but for the party's election campaigns. Bell and his associates opposed this solution.

[176] See: J. Tonge, *Northern Ireland: Conflict and Change*, New York 2002, pp. 153–168.

However, due to the influence of Adams and particularly McGuinness within the IRA, Ivor Bell and his supporters were expelled from the Army in May 1985. In May 1984, the Social Democratic and Labour Party (SDLP), founded in 1970 and primarily active in Northern Ireland, published the "New Ireland Forum" report. This report asserted that "the unification of Ireland can only occur through peaceful means... and any changes in the status of Northern Ireland require the consent of the majority of its residents." Despite the groundbreaking nature of these provisions, it should be noted that "the firm opposition of Margaret Thatcher (the then British Prime Minister) to the Forum's findings diminished their significance." Most unionist circles, as well as Sinn Féin, were quite skeptical of the Forum's outcomes. Furthermore, "the involvement of the SDLP and John Hume (the SDLP chairman) in the Forum's work, followed by their full support of its recommendations, was seen by Sinn Féin as futile and overly conciliatory."[177]

On October 12, 1984, the IRA carried out an attack at the Grand Hotel in Brighton during the annual conference of the British Conservative Party, resulting in five deaths and over 30 injuries. Margaret Thatcher, the primary target and British Prime Minister, narrowly escaped harm. This event deeply shocked both British and Irish public opinion. In a statement published in Time on October 22, 1984, the IRA declared, "Thatcher now realizes that Britain cannot occupy our country, torture prisoners, and shoot people on their own streets, and expect to get away with it. Today we were unlucky. But remember, we only have to be lucky once; you will have to be lucky always."[178]

This event demonstrated that the path to peace in Northern Ireland was still very long, and the influence of Sinn Féin over IRA actions was still insufficient. In 1984, the IRA formalized an agreement with the Libyan government under Colonel Muammar Gaddafi for the supply of arms (including AK-47 rifles, 5.56-mm M-16 assault rifles, rocket launchers, and flamethrowers) and explosives (mainly Semtex). By 1985, approximately 17 tons of weapons had been smuggled into Ireland from Libya in two voyages by the ship

---

[177] B. Feeney, op. cit., pp. 326–331.

[178] See: A. Nogacz, *The IRA and Sinn Féin during the Troubles: two faces of the same organization*, British Columbia 2012, passim; T. Hennessey, *The Northern Ireland Peace Process: Ending the Troubles?*, Dublin 2000, p. 36.

Casamara.[179] This agreement was facilitated by very good contacts between the IRA staff (negotiated by the current IRA chief of staff, Tom "Slab" Murphy, and another IRA member, later an opponent of Adams' peace strategy, Micky McKevitt) and the Libyan special services.

By the end of 1984, despite the IRA's terror campaign, there were emerging proposals within the broader nationalist camp for a peaceful resolution of the conflict in Northern Ireland. Ed Moloney identified three potential solutions discussed among republican circles. The first was to "replace IRA violence with the creation of a platform (alliance) of the entire nationalist camp in the fight for the unification of Ireland." The second solution was the "idea of creating a pan-Irish conference that would take into account the opinions and ideas of the entire nationalist-republican political scene on the island, which would force the British to respond accordingly." The third proposal was to "pressure the British to declare neutrality towards Northern Ireland and agree to negotiations regarding the future of the northern part of the island without their involvement." This last proposal seemed the least realistic at the time.

In November 1984, Gerry Adams addressed the idea of Irish pan-nationalism at the Sinn Féin convention, calling for "a lasting and solid agreement among all nationalist parties and communities in Ireland to break the unionist veto on the concept of reunification of the island, which would create a new situation in which future agreements concerning the North would be created for the first time in negotiations." In his political plans, Adams went further, and in February 1985, he appealed to SDLP leader John Hume on a Belfast radio program to "begin talks aimed at establishing a united nationalist platform in Ireland." The following month, in March 1985, he officially reiterated this idea, limiting it only to Northern Ireland. This was a clear gesture toward the SDLP. Adams needed cooperation with this party to break out of political isolation. To this end, he also began collaborating with the hierarchy of the Roman Catholic Church in Ireland. His close associate in peace talks, with the approval of the Catholic Primate of Ireland, Cardinal Ó Fiaich, was Father Alec Reid. Cardinal Ó Fiaich repeatedly expressed concern about the situation in the North in the 1980s. In 1985 alone, he appealed to

[179] See: A. R. Oppenheimer, *IRA, the bombs and the bullets: a history of deadly ingenuity*, Dublin 2018, p. 74.

the British three times, suggesting that "Their rule in Northern Ireland may not last forever if they do not try to ease the situation between Protestants and Catholics by using their excellent political institutions."[180]

On November 15, 1985, at Hillsborough Castle near Belfast, an agreement was signed between the government of the United Kingdom (signed by Prime Minister Margaret Thatcher) and the government of the Republic of Ireland (signed by Prime Minister Garret FitzGerald), known as the Anglo-Irish Agreement. This agreement, a result of months of intergovernmental negotiations, granted the Republic of Ireland the right, while respecting the consent principle of the Northern Irish, to "present views and proposals" on governance and administration in the North, particularly concerning prison security, law and order, specific prisoners' issues, and the establishment and role of the Police Complaints Board and police authorities in Northern Ireland. The agreement also established an advisory body in the form of the "Intergovernmental Anglo-Irish Conference," which held its first meetings on December 11, 1985. The signing of the Anglo-Irish Agreement met with significant criticism from republican circles. In the opinion of nationalists, this agreement was largely inspired by the British, further entrenching the island's division. A seemingly friendly gesture toward the Republic of Ireland only revealed the true intentions of the British side. Gerry Adams stated that "Mrs. Thatcher has repeatedly shown how little respect the British administration has for Dublin... on the other hand, for the British, there was no reason to respect the government of a divided Ireland, which repeatedly displayed subservience to Great Britain." Martin McGuinness added that "the only talks that could have any significance and hope for Ireland would be those involving republicans and discussing two categories of issues: the complete withdrawal of Britain from our country and the national self-determination of the Irish."[181]

According to Sinn Féin leaders, both London and Dublin were very concerned about the growing influence of the republican movement in Ireland, viewing it as a threat to their position. These actions, in their view, were aimed at isolating republicans on the political stage in Ireland. Both leaders

---

[180] P. Crutchley, IRA ceasefire 20 years on: The priest who brokered the peace, "BBC News" 31st of August 2014, https://www.bbc.com/news/uk-28812366 [accessed 21.08.2024].

[181] T. Hennessey, op. cit., pp. 72–75.

believed that only breaking with the doctrine of abstentionism, rebuilding Irish national pride, and further cooperation with the SDLP and the Catholic Church for peace could pull the party out of political isolation and revive social support for the republican movement in both Northern and Southern Ireland. The first step toward this goal was to submit a motion to abandon the principle of abstentionism at the level of elections to the Dáil for a vote at the Ard Fheis (Sinn Féin party conference). The main opponents of electoral renewal within the party were dogmatic supporters of abstentionism, such as former Sinn Féin leaders R. Ó Brádaigh and D. Ó Conaill. This confrontation was won by the new Adams-McGuinness pair, heralding further breakthroughs in Sinn Féin's political strategy.

The triumph of the anti-abstentionists at the November 1986 convention was highly significant: since Ó Brádaigh's departure, no one in Sinn Féin has emerged capable of challenging Adams's leadership, thus affirming the increasing prominence of pragmatism within the party's actions. This pragmatic shift first manifested in the publication of the party's program titled "A Scenario for Peace" during the Sinn Féin Ard Chomhairle in May 1987. The initial assertion of this document was the recognition that the island known as Ireland has always been viewed as a whole throughout its history. Emphasizing the unity and indivisibility of Ireland as a historical and geographical entity aimed to demonstrate the futility of maintaining the island's artificial division. Another crucial assertion within the document was that "the Irish people have never ceased to demand the right to self-determination." The document also recognized that "the main obstacle to independence is British colonial interference." Konarski comments, "Such a hierarchy of priorities clearly identified who the republicans considered the primary source of Ireland's troubles, demonstrating that for republicans, it was not the loyalists, termed 'a national minority in Ireland.'"[182] Consequently, Sinn Féin proposed drafting a new constitution that would grant "loyalists, along with all other citizens, reliable guarantees of their religious and civil liberties." The authors of the program asserted that "ending the division, ceasing British interference in Ireland, and restoring

---

[182] W. Konarski, op. cit., p. 277.

the right to self-determination to the Irish nation remains the only way to conclude the British colonial conflict in Ireland."[183]

The Sinn Féin leadership believed that the first condition for the success of their proposed solution was for the British government to adopt a strategy of decolonization. This strategy involved revoking the Government of Ireland Act and publicly declaring that Northern Ireland was no longer part of the United Kingdom. They also believed that Britain should announce that its military forces and political administration would remain in Northern Ireland only as long as necessary. Once these conditions were met, the path would be clear to establish constitutional, economic, social, and political agreements for a new Irish state through the creation of an all-Ireland Constitutional Conference. This conference, composed of representatives of the Irish nation, would be tasked with drafting a new constitution for a future united Ireland. The proposal to convene this conference indicated that Sinn Féin intended to reassure the loyalists that Catholics and Protestants would coexist in a future unified state. However, the Irish and British public reacted indifferently to this proposal, with the SDLP refusing to comment substantively on the "Scenario for Peace," and the unionists largely ignoring its existence. The "Scenario for Peace" reflected Sinn Féin's perspective of negotiating with the British on the timeline for their withdrawal from Northern Ireland, a stance that deeply unsettled the unionists. While Sinn Féin expressed willingness to assist those unionists who wished to leave, they also made it clear that those who wanted to stay could do so. This approach revealed the underlying motives of Sinn Féin in formulating the "Scenario for Peace." Between 1987 and 1989, Sinn Féin, aside from presenting its ideas for resolving the conflict in Northern Ireland, attempted to engage in electoral politics. In both the 1987 and 1989 local elections in Northern Ireland and elections to the Dáil, the party received 11.4 % and 1.9 % (1987) and 11.1 % and 1.2 % (1989) of the vote, respectively. These results, particularly poor in the South, indicated that Sinn Féin still had a long way to go before achieving significant political success. The prolonged absence from general elections to the Dáil resulted in the party being relatively unknown in the South, as

183 See more: R. Wiepking, *The Path to Peace: Conflict Theory and Northern Ireland's Troubles (1968–1998)*, San Francisco 2011, Master's Theses. 13, https://repository.usfca.edu/thes/13 [accessed 21.08.2024].

feared by M. McGuinness. According to the Sinn Féin vice-chairman, the long-standing abstentionist tactic had resulted in low electoral support, particularly in the Republic of Ireland.[184]

Recognizing the risk of political isolation due to close ties with the violent IRA, Sinn Féin leaders attempted to collaborate with the largest Catholic minority party in Northern Ireland, the SDLP. In January 1988, the first meeting took place between the leaders of both parties: Gerry Adams and John Hume of the SDLP. Adams presented Hume with his party's peace proposals contained in the "Scenario for Peace" and the early 1988 "Sinn Féin Policy" document. Sinn Féin believed that SDLP's acceptance of the "Anglo-Irish Agreement" was a key goal of the British government's strategy, which aimed to stabilize its interests in the "Six Counties" by introducing symbolic and inherently limited reforms, making the North more acceptable to some nationalist circles and international public opinion. In response to Sinn Féin's position, Hume prepared an alternative vision of the situation in Northern Ireland. In a 1988 letter to Adams, he identified the methods of the Republican Movement (implying Sinn Féin and the IRA) solely with the violent campaigns of the "Provisionals." He added that "the price of these campaigns is evident to everyone: people on the streets lose their lives, young people lose their youth in prisons, causing enormous damage to the economy destroying (through violence) the future and hope of many young people, devaluing the idea of Ireland." Believing that violence could not achieve the unification of Ireland, Hume rhetorically asked Adams in his letter: "does anyone in Ireland, even among IRA supporters, believe that the current British Government will accede to IRA demands through its terrorist activities? Does this not mean that the entire country and IRA members and their families have suffered for decades of conflict without any guarantee of achieving the desired goal? Is it not now the appropriate moment for the entire Provisional Republican Movement to seriously reconsider the validity and purpose of its methods, at a time when these methods have become more sacred than the goal?" Hume proposed another way to resolve the conflict in Northern Ireland without escalating violence, calling on Adams to persuade prominent IRA leaders to unconditionally cease hostilities. In Hume's opinion, "the political

[184] See the results: https://cain.ulster.ac.uk/issues/abstentionism/chron.htm [accessed 21.08.2024].

path is the only possible way to ensure lasting peace in Ireland.[185] For the SDLP, for Ireland, the priority is the people, with territory being secondary, because territory without inhabitants is just another place on Earth, but it is the Irish people who have the right to national self-determination, it is the Irish people who have the right to sovereignty, and it is the search for an agreement among the Irish people on how they can exercise their rights that is the true pursuit of peace and stability in Ireland."

Hume also criticized Sinn Féin's superficial treatment of the term "national self-determination," which, according to the SDLP, should not be reduced to "[…] abstract requirements, such as whether the British have the right to stay in Ireland, because the Irish will always answer that they do not, and the British will say otherwise." According to Hume, Sinn Féin misplaces the fundamental premise of its arguments, which should not be "How to get the British to leave Ireland?" but rather "Is there anything preventing us from convincing the British to pursue a more pro-Irish policy?" This misplaced emphasis in Sinn Féin's peace program was the main criticism against Adams and his party. Thomas Hennessey notes that the talks (in 1988) between the SDLP and Sinn Féin revealed how fundamentally different nationalist interpretations of the Northern Ireland problem could be. Adams and Sinn Féin viewed British strategic, economic, and political interests as the root cause of the conflict. Hume (and the SDLP), on the other hand, believed that the content of Article 1(c) of the "Anglo-Irish Agreement" was a British declaration that they had no interests in staying in Ireland longer-term. In short, the SDLP leader maintained that the British Government (original spelling) was from that point "neutral in the conflict and no longer pro-unionist," so nothing stood in the way of it becoming more pro-Irish. The SDLP's task was to achieve this. Hennessey identifies three main lines of divergence between the SDLP and Sinn Féin programs: firstly, the issue of Irish people's self-determination; secondly, the British role in Ireland; and thirdly, the issue of violence. Meetings between the leaders of both parties, initiated in January 1988, continued for another six months. According to B. Feeney, these talks were crucial for the peace process in Ireland because: "firstly, the SDLP's willingness to cooperate with the republicans was already

[185] See more on Hume – Adams talks in: B. Feeney, op. cit., pp. 351–357.

a significant success for Sinn Féin. Secondly, Hume took Adams's party seriously, responding in detail by letter to Sinn Féin's program. Thirdly, the SDLP agreed to immediate talks even the then-current events on the streets (of Northern Irish cities) could easily have led Hume to walk away from the negotiations."[186]

Indeed, the situation in Northern Ireland was very tense during this period. In mid-1987, the anticipated Libyan arms deal for the IRA fell through, with the ship "Eksund" carrying weapons intercepted by British forces. On November 8, 1987, an IRA bomb killed 11 Protestants in Enniskillen, County Fermanagh. This attack was in retaliation for the killing of eight IRA members by British special forces (SAS) on May 8, 1987, in Loughgall, County Armagh. The IRA escalated further, killing the head of the loyalist paramilitary UDA ("Ulster Defence Association"), John McMichael, in Belfast on December 22, 1987. On the date of the next Hume-Adams meeting, March 6, 1988, news came from Gibraltar about the SAS killing three unarmed IRA staff members: Mairéad Farrell, Seán Savage, and Danny McCann, under unclear circumstances. A few days later, during the funeral of the "Gibraltar Three" at Milltown Cemetery in Belfast, UDA sniper Michael Stone opened fire on the crowd around the coffins, killing three and injuring about 60 people. In response to these tragic events, on August 20, 1988, the IRA bombed and killed eight British soldiers from the Light Infantry Regiment, injuring 19. Ten days later, on August 30, the SAS retaliated by killing three IRA members. The cycle of violence seemed endless during this period. Under such conditions, on September 5, 1988, after more than half a year of meetings, talks, and exchanges of positions and documents, the SDLP decided to end the dialogue with Sinn Féin. In a joint statement, the leaders of the SDLP and Sinn Féin stated that "the talks did not lead to an agreement or significant conclusions and that generally, they could be considered a failure."[187]

According to B. Feeney, "Sinn Féin was very keen to cooperate with the SDLP and the Dublin government at that time. Most proposals in Sinn Féin's programs suggested cooperation to present them jointly to the British diplomatically. In other words, the idea that the IRA could fight alone to get the

---

186 A. Jackson, op. cit., p. 435.
187 E. Moloney, op. cit., p. 546.

British out of Ireland was no longer relevant." For Hume, it was clear that before key meetings and peace negotiations could take place, IRA violence had to stop immediately. Gerry Adams understood the SDLP leader's concerns well. In his statement on talks with the SDLP from the second half of 1988, he significantly changed his opinion about the earlier effects of these talks, writing that "in the course of our discussions, we concluded that we share the same view on the national self-determination of the Irish people. In our common, democratic stance, we believe that the basis for resolving the conflict in Northern Ireland should be the pursuit of a lasting and peaceful agreement that also considers the views and opinions of Northern Protestants." Feeney asserts that at this time, Sinn Féin leaders "gradually modified the party's program so that the republican movement could completely abandon violence in political struggle. Over several years from 1989, they became convinced that the use of violence was completely inadequate to the situation, and that this process was a milestone in the party's development, similar to the gradual abandonment of abstentionism."[188] Feeney's reasoning suggests that the departure of the IRA and Sinn Féin from the path of terror was only a matter of time. Adams knew that only cooperation with the SDLP could lift his party from political marginalization, which he was very keen on. On the other hand, this process was, as it would turn out, very difficult and protracted. However, it must be acknowledged that the first steps toward peace on the island were taken.

The years 1989–1991 did not bring a breakthrough in peace negotiations. These were years of behind-the-scenes efforts for peace by Sinn Féin leader Gerry Adams and years of crisis within the IRA, which continued its entirely ineffective terror tactics. In 1990, the then British Secretary of State for Northern Ireland, Peter Brooke, reiterated that Britain no longer had strategic interests in the North. In 1990–1991, secret negotiations also took place between the IRA leadership and British intelligence (MI6) regarding the former's ceasefire. The negotiations did not yield the desired results for the British, and the IRA continued its violence. Consequently, in 1991, shortly after M. Thatcher resigned as British Prime Minister, Sinn Féin officially announced that it no longer took responsibility for IRA actions.

---

[188] B. Feeney, op. cit., pp. 358–359.

This step, although radical, was difficult to be considered credible. It should be remembered that the then and current vice-leader of Sinn Féin, Martin McGuinness, still remained the chairman of the IRA Army Council. A double game continued between Sinn Féin and the IRA and the British side. It was decidedly a game of appearances, stemming from mutual distrust of the opponent. Gerry Adams continued secret talks with John Hume of the SDLP between 1988 and 1992, despite the public being unaware of these talks until early 1993. Adams used this period to prepare a new Sinn Féin document on the peaceful resolution of the Northern Ireland conflict. This document was intended to replace or supplement the theses contained in the earlier "Scenario for Peace," while also convincing the IRA of the need to pursue peace.[189]

At the beginning of 1992, elections to the British House of Commons were held, in which Sinn Féin received only 10 % of the vote in Northern Ireland, and Gerry Adams lost his parliamentary seat for West Belfast (still unoccupied at this stage of the party's strategy). In 1992, Sinn Féin published a program titled "Towards a Lasting Peace in Ireland." According to Konarski, "what stands out during the reading of this document is not so much the conciliatory tone towards the loyalists (or unionists), but the extensive historical and legal background of the proposals contained therein. This allows for theses that demonstrate the republican movement's conclusions from its past experiences." In the introduction to the document, the authors state that "ending the conflict does not necessarily lead to lasting peace. The peace process leading to lasting peace must eradicate the symptomatic causes of this conflict." According to Sinn Féin, the cause is "British policy in Ireland, which opposes the idea of national self-determination (of the Irish people) and thus violates this internationally recognized right of nations." They further state: "Peace is not just the absence of war, but also the creation of conditions that ensure its permanence. That means allowing us (the Irish) national self-determination, which lies at the foundation of justice, democracy, and equality, and these are prerequisites for freedom and lasting peace." Sinn Féin believed that the search for conflict solutions should be the responsibility of "people associated with the governments: in London and Dublin" and added

[189] See: E. Moloney, op. cit., p. 545.

that "it is also the responsibility of the international community." Konarski notes that an important aspect of this document is "a specific concession from the entire radical republicanism, stating that armed struggle is an ultimate option for republicans. This had no precedent and indicated re-evaluations within the IRA, confirming its agreement with Sinn Féin's strategy of the 'ballot and the gun,' with an emphasis on the former." This concession from the republican side soon became a driving force for the intensified process of peace stabilization in Northern Ireland. The shift in Sinn Féin's policy focus could not go unnoticed by the British and unionist sides.[190]

The interactions between the Irish republican movement and the British government, initiated in the early 1990s, continued into 1993. On March 19, 1993, the British government issued a significant document to the republican community, addressing the ongoing violence in Northern Ireland. The document emphasized that no one has a monopoly on suffering and highlighted the urgent need for healing the situation. This communication underscored the British government's readiness for peace negotiations and political stabilization in Northern Ireland. However, the British conditioned their willingness to engage in talks on the cessation of armed conflict by the Irish Republican Army (IRA). Sinn Féin and the IRA responded with considerable caution. Although republicans hoped that John Major, the newly appointed British Prime Minister and conservative successor to Margaret Thatcher, would exhibit greater flexibility on Northern Ireland than his predecessor, they remained skeptical about the sincerity of his intentions. Major swiftly dispelled any doubts Sinn Féin might have had by dismissing the republican leaders' responses to the British appeal as deceitful and propagandistic.[191]

The core issue at this stage, as analyzed by historians like T. Hennessey, was a profound mutual misunderstanding of the parties' intentions. The British government demanded a permanent cessation of violence, while it was clear that the republicans could, at most, offer only a temporary ceasefire, given the ongoing electoral-military dual strategy. With no further signals from the British, the republican movement turned its focus closer to home, seeking renewed cooperation with the Social Democratic and Labour Party (SDLP)

---

190 See quote: W. Konarski, op. cit., p. 277.

191 See: E. O'Kane, *Anglo–Irish Relations and the Northern Ireland Peace Process: From Exclusion to Inclusion*, "Contemporary British History," 18:1, 2004, pp. 78–99.

and its leader, John Hume. This cooperation, which had already begun to strengthen in the early months of 1993, was based on Hume's persistent belief that the republican movement could be persuaded to renounce violence, despite the failure of previous talks between the SDLP and Sinn Féin in 1988.

After several months of negotiations, Hume and Gerry Adams, the leader of Sinn Féin, issued a joint statement on April 24, 1993. The statement emphasized their shared belief in the Irish people's right to national self-determination. They acknowledged that while the majority on the island supported this view, it was not universally accepted. The statement highlighted the need for consensus among the Irish people on this matter. However, they also recognized that there was little divergence of opinion within their respective parties.

On September 25, 1993, Hume and Adams reached what became known as the "Hume-Adams Agreement." According to Adams, the essence of this agreement could be summarized in seven key points:

1. The Irish people as a whole have the right to national self-determination.
2. An internal Northern Ireland settlement is not a solution.
3. National self-determination is a matter of agreement.
4. Unionist engagement in the peace process is essential for lasting peace.
5. Unionists should not have a veto over British policy toward Ireland.
6. The British government must assist in persuading unionists of the need for talks.
7. The governments in London and Dublin bear the primary responsibility for securing the peace process.[192]

Although the Hume-Adams Agreement was expected to be well-received by republican circles, the IRA was not prepared to renounce violence. Adams attempted to persuade the IRA Army Council to agree to a ceasefire and engage in negotiations with the British. However, this effort failed, leading to continued violence on the streets of Northern Ireland. For instance, on October 23, 1993, a bomb planted by the IRA in a fish shop on Shankill Road, a Protestant area in Belfast, killed ten people. In retaliation, loyalists

[192] See: J. Ingraham, *The Irish Peace Process*, https://cain.ulster.ac.uk/events/peace/talks.htm [accessed 30.12.2024].

killed ten Catholics in a bar in Londonderry (Derry) a week later. Adams and Hume quickly condemned these incidents in a joint statement on November 20, 1993.

In the latter part of 1993, on December 15, the Prime Ministers of the Republic of Ireland, Albert Reynolds, and the United Kingdom, John Major, issued a joint declaration known as the "Downing Street Declaration." This declaration affirmed that both governments would respect the wishes of the majority in Northern Ireland regarding their support for either the union with Britain or a sovereign, united Ireland. This was a clear signal to the IRA and Sinn Féin to declare a ceasefire. The first point of the Hume-Adams Agreement, concerning the alignment of London and Dublin, seemed to be fulfilled at this stage. While the SDLP was ready for talks, the republican movement was internally divided. Within the IRA, a strong faction opposed Sinn Féin's peace program and Adams' leadership.

In early 1994, the IRA Army Council initially rejected the Downing Street Declaration, citing suspicions about the sincerity of its authors. Adams continued to argue that a ceasefire was necessary for initiating peace talks. However, key figures such as Sinn Féin's deputy leader Martin McGuinness, IRA Chief of Staff Kevin McKenna, and Tom Murphy, who would later succeed McKenna, opposed this stance. When the IRA's mini-convention in the first half of 1994 rejected peace, it seemed that nothing could compel the IRA to agree to a ceasefire and allow Sinn Féin to join negotiations.

On June 2, 1994, the IRA launched a rocket attack on a Royal Air Force (RAF) helicopter at Mull of Kintyre, resulting in the deaths of 25 SAS members. Although the IRA never confirmed its involvement, the British were convinced of their culpability. This attack prompted Sinn Féin's working group, led by Adams and including J. Gibney, to develop a new strategy known as the "Totally Un-Armed Strategy" (TUAS) during the summer of 1994. This strategy was eventually accepted by the IRA Army Council, including McGuinness, who had by then changed his position. On August 31, 1994, the IRA declared its first ceasefire as part of TUAS.

Sinn Féin's "Totally Un-Armed Strategy" (TUAS) was based on the premise of renouncing violence for political purposes. It acknowledged that the republican movement's ultimate goal of a united Ireland could be achieved through peaceful means. This marked a significant shift in the movement's thinking, from revolutionary idealism to a more conciliatory pragmatism.

TUAS emphasized increased political cooperation among the Irish government, the SDLP, and Sinn Féin within a framework described as the "Irish nationalist consensus." Sinn Féin affirmed its commitment to establishing a united, democratic socialist republic comprising all 32 counties of Ireland. The strategy also underscored the need for a unified national stance on Northern Ireland and the importance of international support, particularly from the United States and the European Union, in the peace process.

Sinn Féin outlined nine principles that formed the basis of their peacebuilding strategy:

1. The partition of Ireland has failed.
2. The political structures in Ireland must be reformed.
3. A solution confined to Northern Ireland alone is untenable.
4. British policy must accommodate the possibility of Irish national self-determination.
5. The Irish people have an inalienable right to national self-determination.
6. The recognition of this right depends primarily on the governments in Dublin and London and all political parties on both islands.
7. Unionists should not have a veto over the outcomes of peace negotiations.
8. Resolving the issue requires political and constitutional changes in Ireland.
9. A united, independent Ireland is the aspiration of all republicans; however, this unity must be achieved with the consent of the majority of its inhabitants.[193]

Sinn Féin's explicit commitment to nonviolent political activity was largely motivated by their electoral successes. This assertion seems credible, as the party's decision to abandon its abstentionist strategy led to a steady increase in its political influence throughout the 1980s and 1990s. Throughout 1995, maintaining the IRA's ceasefire was a constant challenge. In contrast, the Combined Loyalist Military Command, representing various loyalist paramilitary groups, maintained its ceasefire without interruption since October 13, 1994. However, there were indications from the IRA leadership that the

[193] See: CAIN Web Service, https://cain.ulster.ac.uk/othelem/organ/ira/tuas94.htm [accessed 20.08.2024].

ceasefire was only temporary and contingent on the progress of negotiations. In mid-1995, the British government proposed peace talks with

Sinn Féin, which were conditional on the IRA's disarmament. Sinn Féin, while acknowledging its influence over the IRA, insisted that all weapons, including those held by security forces, should be decommissioned, and that the IRA would not disarm unilaterally. They also demanded amnesty for imprisoned IRA members, the transfer of prisoners from Britain to Northern Ireland, the disbandment of the Royal Ulster Constabulary (RUC), the withdrawal of the British army to barracks, and the initiation of talks involving all parties. In a show of goodwill, the British government withdrew military patrols from Londonderry in November 1994 and removed security barriers and military barracks in Belfast by July 1995. Many of the redeployed British military units returned to the United Kingdom. John Bruton, who succeeded Albert Reynolds as the Prime Minister of the Republic of Ireland, along with John Major, presented a plan for Northern Ireland on February 22, 1995, titled "Framework for the Future." This plan proposed a Northern Ireland Assembly with legislative and executive powers, elected on a proportional basis. However, the two largest unionist parties, the moderate Ulster Unionist Party (UUP) led by John Trimble, and the radical Democratic Unionist Party (DUP) led by Reverend Ian Paisley, rejected the "Framework for the Future" until the IRA fully disarmed. Sinn Féin and the IRA responded by refusing to disarm and demanding the commencement of talks with all parties without preconditions.

IRA rejected a face-saving compromise offered by Sir Patrick Mayhew, the then British Secretary of State for Northern Ireland, who proposed that the British government would not demand full IRA disarmament before negotiations but would require a commitment to gradually hand over its weapons. Consequently, the British government did not take steps to initiate direct talks. The tense situation in Northern Ireland continued throughout 1995, with both sides experiencing growing frustration and political uncertainty.

The events of late 1995 and early 1996 reflect the intense debate within the republican movement regarding the future of their cause in Ireland. Meanwhile, the governments of the United Kingdom and the Republic of Ireland, in collaboration with the United States, sought to break the deadlock over disarmament. To persuade all paramilitary groups in Northern Ireland to lay down their arms and ensure an independent assessment of disarmament, an international three-member commission was established, chaired by U.S. Senator George Mitchell. The other members were Harri Holkeri, former Prime Minister of Finland, and General John de Chastelain, Chief of the Canadian Defence Staff. Over the next 22 months, they engaged in talks with various parties. Their primary task was to evaluate and advise on how to achieve complete and credible disarmament and determine whether those possessing illegal weapons were committed to disarmament.

When it became clear that the negotiations between Sinn Féin and the British government during 1994–1995 had failed, the IRA decided in early 1996 to end the nearly eighteen-month "first" ceasefire. On February 9, 1996, an IRA-planted bomb exploded in the Canary Wharf area of London, killing two people and injuring approximately 100 others, with material damage estimated at around £100 million. IRA actions, informally supported by Sinn Féin, continued throughout 1996 in both Britain and Ireland. According to O'Beirne Ranelagh, these actions were part of a primitive strategy to see how many concessions could be gained before these organizations (IRA and Sinn Féin) engaged in democratic processes.[194]

On May 30, 1996, elections were held for the Northern Ireland Forum, as previously outlined in the "Framework for the Future" program. The Ulster Unionist Party (UUP) won with 24.2 % of the vote and secured 30 seats in the Forum, while Sinn Féin received 15.5 % of the vote, a relatively good result that earned it 17 seats in the Forum. However, it should be noted that Sinn Féin was unable to participate in the Forum's work or subsequent interparty talks on the future of the province until the IRA disarmed in accordance with the recommendations of the Mitchell Commission.[195] A lively debate resumed within the ranks of the IRA and Sinn Féin regarding the conditions for republicans to enter talks. After heated discussions, on July 19, 1997, the IRA decided to reinstate the ceasefire and accept the "Mitchell Principles" on disarmament. A faction within the IRA, opposed to peace talks with the

---

[194] See more: D. Morrow, *Transformation or Truce? Tracing the Decline of "Reconciliation" and Its Consequences for Northern Ireland Since 1998*, "Treatises and Documents Journal of Ethnic Studies" [Razprave in Gradivo Revija za Narodnostna Vpršanja] , nr 90/2023, pp. 45–61.

[195] See more: O. Gay, B. Morgan, *Northern Ireland: political developments since 1972*, House of Commons, "Research Paper," 98/57, p. 50.

British government, broke away to form the "Real IRA," which was later responsible for several acts of terror, including the Omagh bombing on August 15, 1998, which killed nearly 30 people.

Two significant factors aided the IRA and Sinn Féin in making this decision. First, the change in British politics—in May 1997, the Labour Party won the House of Commons elections, breaking the long-standing dominance of the Conservative Party, which had been strongly supportive of the unionists. The new Prime Minister was Labour leader Tony Blair. Second, Sinn Féin's strong performance in the aforementioned House of Commons elections, where the party received 16.1 % of the vote, provided a powerful bargaining chip in negotiations with the British government.

By September, Sinn Féin was already participating in multiparty peace talks. However, acts of violence occurred between the "Real IRA" and loyalist paramilitaries who did not recognize the ceasefire at the end of 1997. As a result of these events, Ian Paisley's Democratic Unionist Party (DUP), which was indirectly involved in loyalist terror activities, withdrew from the talks. In early 1998, Sinn Féin was excluded from the multiparty talks due to alleged breaches of the ceasefire by the IRA. At that point, the DUP rejoined the negotiations with voting rights. However, the Royal Ulster Constabulary (RUC) determined that the IRA was not involved in violating the ceasefire, allowing Sinn Féin to return to the talks, cleared of allegations of supporting terrorism. Upon Sinn Féin's return to the negotiating table, the DUP and the United Kingdom Unionist Party (UKUP) withdrew from the talks again. The final round of negotiations was conducted without the participation of these two parties, but with significant involvement from Sinn Féin.

The peace agreement reached during the multiparty talks in Northern Ireland at the turn of 1997–1998 was signed on April 10, 1998, known as the Good Friday Agreement. The talks and negotiations were chaired by George Mitchell, with British Prime Minister Tony Blair participating in the final round of negotiations. According to J. O'Beirne Ranelagh, the Good Friday Agreement was a balanced compromise for all parties involved. The foundation of the agreement was based on elements presented in the "Framework for the Future." W. Konarski believes that the agreement "formally, and later materially, confirmed the significant changes that had occurred in the previously idealistic or even doctrinaire strand of Irish nationalism."

Referendums on the adoption of the provisions of the Good Friday Agreement were held on May 22, 1998, simultaneously in the Republic of Ireland and Northern Ireland. In both parts of Ireland, the agreement, which aimed to end nearly 30 years of terror in the North, was positively received, with 94 % support in the South and 71 % in the North. This was irrefutable evidence that the majority of residents in both divided parts of the island wanted to live together in peace again.[196]

3.4. UK and Ireland after GFA (1998): Northern Ireland peace process

The cultural landscape of Northern Ireland has been significantly shaped by its tumultuous history and the political events surrounding the Good Friday Agreement in 1998. While the Agreement marked a formal end to decades of violent conflict, it has also given rise to a persistent cultural divide that continues to manifest in various social and political contexts. Participants in the peace process recognized the sensitivity of cultural symbols and emblems, emphasizing the need to use them in ways that promote mutual respect rather than division

The Good Friday Agreement (GFA), signed in 1998, is a pivotal political framework aimed at ending decades of conflict known as "The Troubles" in Northern Ireland, characterized by violence between nationalist/republican groups seeking unification with the Republic of Ireland and unionist/loyalist factions wishing to remain part of the United Kingdom.[197] The agreement marked a significant milestone in Northern Irish history, establishing a power-sharing government and promoting reconciliation through various institutional frameworks. Despite its political successes, the GFA has faced criticism for inadequately addressing deep-rooted social issues, leading to ongoing tensions and divisions within communities. While the GFA effectively curtailed overt paramilitary violence, it has been criticized for fostering a superficial peace that lacks genuine reconciliation. The legacy of the

[196] See: NI Assembly, *After the agreement*, https://education.niassembly.gov.uk/post-16/snapshots-devolution/belfastgood-friday-agreement/after-agreement [accessed 20.08.2024].

[197] See more: Rory O'Connell et al., *The Belfast/Good Friday Agreement and Transformative Change: Promise, Power and Solidarity*, "Israel Law Review" (2023), pp. 1–33.

conflict remains evident in persistent socio-economic disparities, cultural divisions, and sectarianism, culminating in what some refer to as a "culture war." Issues such as contentious parades and the symbolic use of flags have reignited sectarian tensions, highlighting the need for continued dialogue and trust-building initiatives to bridge the divides. Furthermore, the rise of Sinn Féin as the largest party in the 2022 Assembly election reflects shifting political dynamics, yet raises questions about governance and community integration in a complex and fragile political landscape. The impact of Brexit has further complicated the peace process, as discussions surrounding the avoidance of a hard border and the status of Northern Ireland's relationship with the EU have introduced new challenges to the GFA's implementation. Critics argue that unresolved grievances and the lack of a clear framework for mutual respect and civil rights have left many societal issues unaddressed, perpetuating a status quo that can easily revert to conflict under stress. As such, the ongoing quest for reconciliation emphasizes that lasting peace requires more than political agreements; it necessitates a deep, sustained commitment to addressing historical grievances.

The Good Friday Agreement established various institutional frameworks to facilitate cooperation between Northern Ireland and the Republic of Ireland, as well as between Ireland and Great Britain. Strand 3 of the Agreement focused on "east-west" issues, creating several institutions, including the British-Irish Intergovernmental Conference, the British-Irish Council, and an expanded British–Irish Interparliamentary Body. The British–Irish Intergovernmental Conference replaced the Anglo-Irish Intergovernmental Council and the Intergovernmental Conference from the 1985 Anglo-Irish Agreement. Additionally, the North/South Ministerial Council was formed to foster consultation and cooperation in 12 areas of mutual interest, aiming to develop common policies that could be implemented in both jurisdictions.[198]

The Agreement also set forth plans for an independent consultative forum to represent civil society, with the aim of ensuring that expert opinions were included in discussions on social, cultural, and economic issues. This forum was subsequently established in 2006 with the support of the Northern Ireland Executive. The Agreement included specific provisions related to rights,

---

[198] See: H. Roberts, *Sound Stupidity: The British Party System and the Northern Ireland Question*, "Government and Opposition," vol. 22, no. 4, Oct. 1987, p. 315.

safeguards, and equality of opportunity, which were intended to prevent any reduction in these rights following the UK's exit from the EU. The UK is mandated to uphold these rights, which are now also enforced through the EU's agreements with the UK, making them legally binding in both international and domestic contexts. Despite these frameworks, critics argue that the Agreement lacks sufficient clarity regarding how mutual respect for civil rights and religious liberties should be operationalized, leaving room for ongoing tensions and disputes related to cultural markers and communal symbols While the Good Friday Agreement successfully ended decades of violence, it has been criticized for inadequately addressing the social and cultural divides that persist in Northern Ireland. The power-sharing arrangements may encourage some cross-community cooperation, but deeper societal issues remain unresolved. The cultural protections embedded in the Agreement have often been seen as exacerbating divisions rather than bridging them, as evidenced by ongoing controversies surrounding flags and parades.

The implementation of the Agreement is viewed by some as part of a longer transitional process that may take generations to fully solidify, emphasizing that peace is not merely a result of political agreements but also requires significant societal change. This has led to a situation where tensions are managed rather than resolved, resulting in what has been described as "unembedded peace" where the potential for renewed conflict remains present. The aftermath of the Good Friday Agreement has revealed significant challenges and setbacks in achieving lasting peace in Northern Ireland. Despite the initial success in curbing paramilitary violence and establishing a power-sharing government, underlying issues have persisted, leading to a social stalemate characterized by negative peace rather than genuine reconciliation. High levels of deprivation in surrounding areas have made it difficult to attract jobs and investment, contributing to community tension and a sense of alienation among residents. This economic stagnation has hampered local efforts aimed at regeneration and conflict resolution.

While organizations strive to empower local communities through training and support, the disconnect between community relations initiatives and the socio-economic realities faced by many has been apparent. The prioritization of cross-community engagement often neglects the immediate needs of individuals who are not yet ready to engage with the "other side" due to their own struggles with poverty and violence. In the years following the peace agreement, the emergence of "culture wars" has highlighted the persistent divisions within Northern Irish society. While overt paramilitary violence has diminished, the schisms between communities remain deep, with manifestations of sectarianism resurfacing in the form of murals and cultural expressions that reinforce in-group identities. These developments indicate a shift from physical violence to more subtle forms of cultural division, suggesting that while violence may have decreased, the underlying tensions have not been resolved.

The formal end of direct rule by London over Northern Ireland on December 1, 1999, coincided with the formation of a cross-party provincial government the following day, although this was accompanied by some serious political disruptions. This government, led by John Trimble of the UUP, represented the practical implementation of one of the most significant devolutionary provisions of the Good Friday Agreement. W. Konarski asserts that: "The formation of the government, while creating hope for the smooth functioning of the Province under new constitutional and political conditions, did not eliminate the threats that could still disrupt the process of transformation initiated by the April Agreement."

Regarding the main threats to the political stabilization process in Northern Ireland between 1999 and 2005, the first issue to be mentioned is the lack of full and consistent agreement by the IRA to disarm, which was meant to ensure the maintenance of peace in the Province. The second significant problem was the clashes and conflicts caused by loyalist paramilitaries, rooted in their refusal to accept the implementation of the Agreement's provisions, a stance skillfully fueled by the loyalist-populist DUP party, the largest opponent of the April Agreement. Finally, the third major threat to peace in the Province was the renewed polarization and radicalization of the Northern Irish political scene, which can be traced by analyzing the election results in Northern Ireland from 2001 to 2005. This aforementioned polarization and radicalization of views, both on the unionist (loyalist) and nationalist (republican) sides, primarily stemmed from the fatigue of both communities with what they perceived as the weak outcomes of implementing the Good Friday Agreement's provisions.[199]

[199] See more: M. McGlinchey, *Irish Nationalist and Republican Attitudes to the Good Friday Agreement: Sell-Out or Steppingstone?*, "Treatises and Documents Journal of Ethnic Studies" [Razprave in Gradivo Revija za Narodnostna Vpršanja], nr 90/2023, pp. 79–95.

These factors led to a short-term suspension of the Northern Irish executive's activities from February to May 2000. The restoration of the executive in 2000 did not halt the escalation of violence in the Province, primarily driven by loyalist groups. On June 7, 2001, elections were held for the British House of Commons, in which Northern Ireland was allocated 18 seats. Simultaneously, elections were held for local elective bodies (to 26 District Councils). As a result of the elections to the House of Commons, the UUP received 26.8 % of the vote (gaining 6 seats—losing three seats compared to the 1997 election), the DUP won 22.5 % of the vote (5 seats), the SDLP gained 21% of the vote (3 seats—maintaining its previous standing), and Sinn Féin obtained 21.7 % of the vote (4 seats—marking the party's first representation in the House of Commons, signaling a final abandonment of the abstentionist policy). The Alliance Party (APNI) received 3.6 % of the vote but did not win any seats.

In the local elections, out of a total of 582 seats in 26 District Councils, the UUP won 154 seats (22.9 % of the vote), the DUP was second with 131 seats (21.4 % of the vote), the SDLP won 117 seats (despite coming fourth in terms of vote share: 19.4 % of the vote), Sinn Féin secured 108 seats (despite coming third in vote share: 21.7 % of the vote), the APNI took 28 seats (5.1 % of the vote), while other political groups (mainly from the fragmented unionist movement) won a total of 12 seats and 14.5 % of the Province-wide vote. The election results, both for the House of Commons and especially for the local councils, showed the beginning of a gradual process of polarization of public life in Northern Ireland and "the loss of control over most local bodies by both centrist parties (UUP, SDLP)."

It should be noted that this trend, analyzing the subsequent election results in the Province from 2002–2005, became even more pronounced. On July 1, 2001, David Trimble resigned as the First Minister of the Northern Irish Executive and called on the British government to suspend the functioning of the Northern Ireland Assembly and halt the implementation of the Good Friday Agreement. Trimble's decision was driven by his inability to reach an agreement with the majority of influential members of his UUP party, the IRA's refusal to disarm, and a renewed wave of violence by extreme loyalists. The government crisis coincided with riots caused by loyalist extremists who attacked Catholic populations during the annual Orange Order parades in July 2001. The challenges in calming the tense situation in Northern Ireland persisted until the fall of 2001. During this period, the Northern Irish self-government was suspended twice, each time for one day (on August 10 and September 20, 2001), to stabilize the political situation in the Province and appoint an executive with a new First Minister.

The several-month vacancy in the position of the Northern Irish government head lasted until November 6, 2001, when David Trimble was reappointed as First Minister, with Mark Durkan, the new leader of the SDLP, chosen as his deputy. Durkan replaced John Hume in this role on November 10. On April 5, 2002, the first recruitment to the new policing body in Northern Ireland (Police Service for Northern Ireland, PSNI) took place, based on the principle of recruiting 50 % Protestants and 50 % Catholics.

Thanks to the influence of Sinn Féin and the Independent International Commission on Decommissioning (IICD—a body established under the April 1998 Agreement), it was possible, despite initial complications, to achieve partial, two-phase disarmament of the IRA (on October 23, 2001, and April 8, 2002). However, it should be noted that by early 2005, the IRA had not agreed to surrender its entire arsenal of weapons. The growing political importance of Sinn Féin was evident in the elections in the Republic of Ireland on May 17, 2002. The republicans received 6.5 % of the vote, translating into 5 seats in the Dáil. This was the best result for the party in the South since its abandonment of the abstentionist doctrine.

The year 2003 was significant for Sinn Féin and other Northern Irish parties because the second elections to the Northern Ireland Assembly were held, in which Sinn Féin achieved a very strong result: 23.5 % of the vote, securing second place after the DUP (25.6 %, a total of 33 seats) and 24 seats. For the first time in its electoral history in the North, Sinn Féin won a higher percentage of votes than the UUP, which obtained only 22.7 % (almost 1 % less than Sinn Féin). The SDLP, which came in fourth in the election, suffered a significant defeat, garnering only 17 % of the vote and securing just 18 seats in the Assembly. Comparing these results to the already mentioned results of the first Assembly elections in 1998, it should be noted that the proportions of votes within the nationalist-republican electorate in Northern Ireland have perfectly reversed in favor of Sinn Féin (in 1998: Sinn

Féin—18 seats, and the SDLP—24 seats; while in 2003: Sinn Féin—24 seats, and the SDLP only 18 seats).

The trends indicating the hardening of attitudes within both communities (unionist and nationalist) regarding their distinct visions for the Province's development are most evident in the election results from 2004–2005. In 2004, elections were held in Northern Ireland for the European Parliament (with the Province allocated 3 seats).[200] The decisive winners of these elections were the radical parties: the loyalist DUP and the republican Sinn Féin, gaining 32% and 26.3% of the vote, respectively, resulting in one seat each in the European Parliament (for Sinn Féin, this was the first seat won at the European level in its hundred-year history). The third seat in these elections was won by the UUP, narrowly defeating the SDLP (by only 0.7 % of the vote).

These confrontational trends were ultimately confirmed in the elections to the House of Commons and local councils in Northern Ireland the following year, on May 5, 2005. The DUP achieved a decisive victory in both elections (33.7 % of the vote and 9 seats in the House of Commons, as well as 29.6 % of the vote and 182 seats in local councils). Sinn Féin secured the second-highest result in both elections, despite facing difficulties due to accusations from some parts of the Province's public opinion about the revitalization of extremist positions by the IRA, gaining 24.3 % of the vote and 5 seats in the House of Commons (an increase of 2.6 % and one additional seat compared to the 2001 elections) and 23.2 % of the vote and 126 seats in local councils (18 more seats than before). The moderate parties, UUP and SDLP, suffered significant losses in these elections. The UUP lost as many as 5 seats in the House of Commons compared to the previous elections (it had 6 seats in 2001) and almost 40 seats in local councils. The SDLP maintained its representation in the House of Commons (3 seats) but lost over 15 seats in the 26 district councils. The Alliance Party (APNI) retained fifth place (3.9 % of the vote) but did not win any seats in the House of Commons, while it gained two more seats in local councils than in 2001. Other groups in the local council elections received a total of 6.8 % of the vote and 28 seats, and 5.1 % of the vote in the House of Commons election.

---

[200] See more: R. Mac Ginty et al., *No War, No Peace: Northern Ireland after the Agreement*, "Political Psychology," Vol. 28, No. 1, 2007, pp. 1–11.

Based on the analysis of the political events of 2001–2005 in Northern Ireland, it should be noted that the key factors shaping the process of political transformation in this region of the United Kingdom during this period were the incomplete disarmament of the IRA, the rise in importance of Sinn Féin (especially in the 2003 and 2004 elections), the leadership crisis within the UUP, the radicalization of unionist views (as evidenced by the 2003–2005 election results), and the polarization of political positions on both sides (unionist-loyalist and nationalist-republican) of the Northern Irish political scene. This polarization of attitudes, stemming primarily from disillusionment with the effectiveness of implementing the Good Friday Agreement's provisions, as well as the ongoing (albeit smaller than in the 1990s) incidents of violence in the Province, have been the most significant threats to the continuation of the stabilization process in Northern Ireland initiated in April 1998.[201] On October 14, 2002, Parliament was suspended and Northern Ireland returned to being governed directly by Westminster. This was the second major suspension; the first occurred between February and May 2000. It lasted until May 8, 2007. It was resumed in October 2006 after an agreement was reached in St. Andrews, Scotland. The UUP and SDLP were the main negotiators of the 1998 Good Friday Agreement. This time in St. Andrews it was the Democratic Unionist Party and Sinn Féin. They emerged as the largest parties in the second parliamentary election on November 26, 2003. The negotiations in St. Andrews covered issues such as Sinn Féin's support for policing and the running of the institutions created under the 1998 agreement. The Democratic Unionist Party wanted Sinn Féin to support the Socialist Party and called for changes to the way Parliament was run. Sinn Féin wanted to ensure that all parties were fully involved in the power-sharing committee and to maintain the shared nature of the position of First Minister.[202]

---

201 See further: L. Drong, *Doing justice to the troubles: Imaginary reconciliations and restorative memory in post-agreement Northern Ireland*, "Arts & Cultural Studies Review," 2018, Issue 3 (37), pp. 409–425.

202 See: NI Assembly, *The St Andrews Agreement (2006) and St Andrews Agreement Act (2007)*, https://education.niassembly.gov.uk/post-16/snapshots-devolution/st-andrews-agreement-2006-and-st-andrews-agreement-act-2007 [accessed 20.08.2024].

However, these issues did not result in the abandonment of the transformation process in Northern Ireland, as evidenced by Sinn Féin's decision on July 28, 2005, to definitively disarm the IRA and the announcement by the Irish Republican Army's General Staff to abandon all forms of illegal and paramilitary activities. These actions represent an important breakthrough in the process of implementing the Agreement, especially since the situation is now in the hands of the radical party Sinn Féin, whose presence in the Province's political life is still unwelcome to a large part of the Protestant population. The next decades will be crucial in the implementation of the Agreement's provisions and determining whether the disarmament of the IRA will lead to the end of violence in Northern Ireland.

In the early twenty-first century, Northern Ireland experienced significant political and social changes following the signing of the Good Friday Agreement (GFA) in 1998. The GFA marked a milestone in the peace process, aiming to end decades of conflict known as "the Troubles." Despite the agreement, the period that followed was marked by challenges in implementing the accord, ongoing tensions between unionist and nationalist communities, and the complex dynamics of Irish-British relations.[203]

The GFA established a devolved government in Northern Ireland, with a power-sharing Executive that included both unionist and nationalist parties. The principle of consent, which stated that any change in Northern Ireland's status could only occur with the majority's agreement, was central to the agreement. This was intended to balance the aspirations of unionists, who wanted to remain part of the UK, and nationalists, who desired a united Ireland. However, the implementation of the GFA was fraught with difficulties. Issues such as the decommissioning of paramilitary weapons, police reforms, and human rights remained contentious. The power-sharing arrangement was often unstable, reflecting the deep-seated distrust between the communities. For years, the devolved government faced periods of suspension and crises due to disagreements between the leading parties, particularly the Democratic Unionist Party (DUP) and Sinn Féin.

---

[203] See: E. Tannam, *The Future of UK-Irish Relations*, "European Journal of Legal Studies," 2019, Vol. 12, SI, pp. 275–304, Special Issue on "The Brexit negotiations and the May government"; Published online: October 29, 2019.

Sinn Féin played a crucial role in this period. The party's strategic shift from militant radicalism to mainstream politics was pivotal. Historically associated with the Irish Republican Army (IRA), Sinn Féin began to focus on electoral politics, distancing itself from its violent past. This transition was crucial for gaining broader support among the electorate, particularly as the IRA began to decommission its weapons and reduce its influence. The party's political strategies led to significant electoral success throughout the early twenty-first century. Sinn Féin increased its representation in both Northern Ireland and the Republic of Ireland, gradually becoming a dominant force in Irish politics. The leadership change in 2018, with Mary Lou McDonald succeeding Gerry Adams, further modernized the party's image and helped it to continue expanding its influence. Sinn Féin's emphasis on policies addressing everyday issues, such as health, education, and the economy, resonated with voters, contributing to their growing success.

On the unionist side, the DUP emerged as the leading party, often taking a hardline stance on issues related to the GFA's implementation. The DUP's focus was on maintaining Northern Ireland's status within the UK and resisting any moves that might lead to Irish unification. The party's reluctance to compromise on certain issues, such as police reform and the decommissioning of IRA weapons, often led to tensions with Sinn Féin and periods of political deadlock. While the GFA led to a significant reduction in violence, loyalist paramilitary groups remained active, particularly in working-class Protestant areas. These groups were often involved in criminal activities and maintained a presence in certain communities, perpetuating sectarian divisions. The threat of dissident republican violence also persisted, although it was much reduced compared to the peak of the Troubles.

The relationship between Northern Ireland, the Republic of Ireland, and the UK was further complicated by the Brexit referendum in 2016. The issue of the border between Northern Ireland and the Republic of Ireland became a central point of contention in Brexit negotiations. Many in Northern Ireland, particularly nationalists, were concerned about the potential for a hard border, which could undermine the peace process and economic stability. Brexit also reignited debates about Northern Ireland's future status. Sinn Féin capitalized on the uncertainty by advocating for a border poll—a referendum on Irish unification—arguing that Brexit fundamentally altered the political landscape. On the other hand, unionists, particularly the DUP, were strongly pro-Brexit, seeing it as a way to strengthen Northern Ireland's ties to the UK, despite the potential risks.

In summary, the early twenty-first century in Northern Ireland was a time of both progress and ongoing challenges. While the Good Friday Agreement laid the foundation for peace, the years that followed were marked by political instability, the evolving roles of Sinn Féin and unionist parties, and the broader implications of Brexit. The period underscored the complexity of Northern Ireland's identity and its relationship with both the UK and the Republic of Ireland.[204]

The aftermath of the Good Friday Agreement has led to what some observers describe as a "culture war" in Northern Ireland. This schism is particularly evident in ongoing sectarian tensions, as illustrated by annual events such as the July Twelfth parades and associated bonfires. These events have often served as flashpoints for sectarian conflict, with a significant percentage of bonfires incorporating contentious symbols such as the Irish flag, which many interpret as acts of aggression or hate crimes. In response to the enduring divisions, various non-governmental organizations (NGOs) have adopted strategic approaches to foster inter-community relations. These include cross-community initiatives aimed at encouraging dialogue and collaboration between Protestant and Catholic communities, as well as inter-community efforts focused on addressing shared socio-economic interests. Despite the challenges, there are indications that grassroots initiatives focused on socio-emotional reconciliation may offer pathways toward a more cohesive society. Research suggests that local, decentralized efforts could effectively address the remnants of division by fostering positive inter-community contact and building relationships based on mutual understanding. Ultimately, the cultural impact of the Good Friday Agreement remains a complex interplay of historical narratives, social dynamics, and ongoing efforts toward reconciliation in Northern Ireland.

---

[204] See: C. Landow, J. McBride, *Moving Past the Troubles: The Future of Northern Ireland Peace*, "CFR Reports—Backgrounder," https://www.cfr.org/backgrounder/moving-past-troubles-future-northern-ireland-peace; "Congress Research Service Report," *Northern Ireland Peace Process: Background and Challenges* 2019–2024, updated: https://www.everycrsreport.com/reports/RS21333.html [accessed 29.08.2024].

The political landscape remains fraught with challenges as well. The commitment of local politicians and community leaders toward genuine rapprochement has been questioned, as some groups feel alienated from the political process. Moreover, the legacy of the agreement has revealed that the deal often rewarded former combatants, raising concerns about the lack of fundamental reappraisal among ex-prisoners regarding their past actions. Many contentious issues left unresolved by the Good Friday Agreement have continued to fester, reinforcing a status quo that hinders progress. Initiatives designed to address sensitive topics, such as parades and cultural expressions, have often met with resistance from both communities, demonstrating the entrenched nature of division. The failure to adequately address these divisive issues reflects both the challenges of the peace process and the limitations of the agreement itself, which aimed for a peaceful coexistence without fully addressing the underlying grievances that fueled conflict.

Since the signing of the Good Friday Agreement (GFA) in 1998, Northern Ireland has experienced significant economic growth, with Gross Domestic Product (GDP) more than doubling from £19.8 billion to £43.7 billion by 2020. Employment growth in Northern Ireland has been notably high outside London, and wages for the lowest paid have improved relative to the rest of the UK, although economic inactivity remains a concern. The tourism sector has also benefited from the peace dividend, with revenues peaking at £1 billion in 2019. However, the COVID-19 pandemic severely impacted this growth, prompting the implementation of a Tourism Recovery Plan. It is worth noting about the economic situation in the Republic that until the early 1990s, Ireland was one of the least developed member states of the European Union.[205] It suffered from serious structural problems, high unemployment, low exports, a large budget deficit and external debt. In the second half of the year, national macroeconomic indicators improved significantly and Ireland became one of the fastest-growing economies in the world. This was the result of a combination of factors, including the country's skillful use of EU funds and pro-growth government policies that encouraged increased business activity and foreign direct investment. The main goal of the EU's regional policy in Ireland was to achieve external convergence based on

[205] See more: A. M. Kowalski, *The Regional Policy of the European Union in Ireland* [*Polityka regionalna Unii Europejskiej w Irlandii*], "Gospodarka Narodowa," Nr 4/2005, pp. 73–98.

equalization of economic growth and income between Ireland and the rest of the EU. In connection with this approach, the economic boom deepened socio-economic differences between the country's various regions.

The combination of Brexit and the pandemic has presented significant challenges for the Northern Irish economy. Nevertheless, the Windsor Framework has helped maintain a special status for Northern Ireland within the UK, creating opportunities for sectors to leverage dual access to both UK and EU markets. Economic strategies have focused on priority sectors, including agri-food technology, sustainable energy, information and communications technology (ICT), and life and health sciences. Despite improvements, Northern Ireland's economy continues to grapple with legacies of conflict, including economic inequality and underdevelopment traps. The region's reliance on a historically weak private sector and large staple industries has hindered sustainable growth. Academic research indicates that while some sectors have seen positive effects from the peace dividend, the overall benefits have been variable and not substantial enough to overcome structural challenges

Efforts to empower local communities have been vital in addressing economic disparities and fostering social cohesion. Community development programs aim to enhance leadership skills among local activists, thereby helping communities better manage their own affairs and reduce tensions arising from deprivation. However, the emphasis on community relations can sometimes overshadow the immediate needs of local populations struggling with poverty and alienation. This underscores the necessity for tailored approaches that consider both community relations and developmental needs to effectively address the socio-economic issues at hand. In 1998, the Good Friday Agreement was ratified by majorities in simultaneous referendums in the north and south, marking the first time in more than a century, and perhaps the first time ever, that the political structure on the island of Ireland was widely recognized as legitimate. Part of the price of this recognition (including amendments to the Irish Constitution) was the creation of cross-border institutions and the formalization of the Irish government's advisory role in Northern Ireland. The border issue was ultimately resolved as it lost its economic, cultural, and military importance. Cross-border institutions are one of the least controversial aspects of the Good Friday Agreement.[206]

---

[206] See: N. Ó Dochartaigh, *Bounded by Violence: Institutionalizing Local Territories in the North of Ireland*, "Nationalism and Ethnic Politics," 19:1 (2013), pp. 119–139, and I.

The political landscape in Northern Ireland has undergone significant changes following the Good Friday Agreement, yet it remains complex and fraught with challenges.[207] The 2022 Assembly election marked a historic moment as Sinn Féin emerged as the largest party for the first time, symbolizing a shift in the political dynamics of the region, traditionally dominated by Unionist parties. This election outcome raised questions about governance, particularly regarding the role of the Democratic Unionist Party (DUP) and its refusal to join the power-sharing government, which many view as a regression to Unionist supremacy and a rejection of the agreement itself. Despite the political milestones, community relations remain fragile. Research indicates that while efforts to promote peace and community integration are endorsed at higher political levels, local initiatives often fall short in prioritizing these goal. Many in local communities continue to experience alienation and deprivation, which complicates efforts to foster unity and reconciliation. The prevailing attitudes toward "the other" are often influenced by contemporary events, suggesting that deeper structural issues persist beneath the surface. Furthermore, the political climate has been affected by Brexit, as post-Brexit arrangements have intensified tensions within Unionism, leading to the DUP's refusal to participate in the executive. This highlights ongoing concerns about the constitutional integrity of Northern Ireland and the complex interplay between national identity and governance in a post-conflict society. As political figures acknowledge, while progress has been made, significant work remains to address the historical grievances that continue to resonate within Northern Ireland's communities.

The 2019 negotiations regarding Britain's withdrawal from the EU brought renewed attention to the Good Friday Agreement, particularly concerning issues like the avoidance of a hard border, North-South cooperation, and the status of citizenship. The EU emphasized the need to uphold the rights and provisions established in the Agreement as essential to a successful Brexit process. Consequently, the UK was tasked with addressing these concerns

---

McBride, *The Tyranny of Majorities: Democracy, Brexit and the Northern Irish Border*, in: J. Mair, S. Mccabe, N. Fowler, L. Budd (eds), *Brexit and Northern Ireland: Bordering on Confusion?*, Goring-By-Sea 2019, passim.

207 On the complexity and specificity of the Northern Irish conflict see more in: Sh. O'Neill, *Critical Theory and Ethno-National Conflict: Assessing Northern Ireland's Peace Process as a Model of Conflict Resolution*, "Irish Political Studies," 22:4, 2007, pp. 411–431.

to progress to subsequent stages of negotiations. Despite the challenges, the Agreement remains a cornerstone of peace in Northern Ireland, and its implementation continues to evolve in response to changing political landscapes and societal needs.

To summarize, it can be stated that the process of political stabilization in Northern Ireland, culminating in the signing of the Good Friday Agreement on April 10, 1998, was a groundbreaking event in the over eighty-year history of this province. The fact that both communities, Catholic and Protestant, can once again live together in relative peace can be seen as a significant success of this process. This, of course, does not mean that the conflict between these communities has been completely resolved. The results of the elections in Northern Ireland from 2001–2024, which show a gradual rise in radical sentiments among the electorate, both from nationalist-republican circles (with a significant increase in public support for the Sinn Féin party) and unionist-loyalist circles (with an increase in support for the DUP party), are indicative of this. A serious threat to the future of Northern Ireland may soon arise from the cessation of political dialogue between these two communities and their political representatives, that is, the Northern Irish parties. Another challenge for the peace process in the Province is to achieve successful and complete disarmament of the IRA, as well as loyalist paramilitary organizations.[208]

As for the role played by Sinn Féin in the process of political stabilization in the North, it can be considered crucial. Sinn Féin, by abandoning the doctrine of abstentionism and supporting the armed struggle tactics led by the IRA, has in recent years become the political voice of a large portion of the nationalist electorate in the Province. Thanks to its active participation in the political life of both Northern Ireland and the Republic of Ireland, Sinn Féin has become a significant player in current political events in both parts of the island. By shifting its stance from a radical and doctrinaire one to a pragmatic and conciliatory approach, Sinn Féin contributed, among other things, to the signing of the critically important Good Friday Agreement in 1998, while leaving the most important point of its political program—Irish unification—still an open issue. The change in Sinn Féin's position between

[208] D. Mitchell, E. Tannam, S. Wallace, *The Agreement's impact on political cooperation*, "Irish Political Studies," 33:3, (2018), pp. 283–310.

1983 and 2005 is inextricably linked to its leader, Gerry Adams. This former IRA Chief of Staff understood that greater constitutional changes could be achieved through political compromise rather than through the use of terror and violence. Thanks to Adams—the architect of Sinn Féin's peaceful program from 1983–2005—his party is now the leading representative of Irish nationalism in the North (clearly outpacing the SDLP in recent years). This fact must be recognized as a major political success for Adams. It is also hoped that Sinn Féin's electoral successes in recent years (2001–2024) will be properly utilized to achieve political stabilization and consolidate peace in Northern Ireland. Only through this path can the main goal of Irish nationalist and republican policy, the unification of the island, be realized.

Brexit presents a certain opportunity for the Irish republican movement; however, the question remains whether the leadership of women—Michelle O'Neill and Mary Lou McDonald—will fulfill the over 100-year-old dream of a 32-county republic. Sinn Féin, a significant political party in both Northern Ireland and the Republic of Ireland, has played a pivotal role in the evolving political landscape of Northern Ireland since the onset of the peace process in the 1990s. Following the 1994 IRA ceasefire, the party embraced a strategy of political engagement that culminated in the 1998 Good Friday Agreement, which established a framework for power-sharing and emphasized the importance of consent in determining Northern Ireland's status. As a result, Sinn Féin has transformed from a party historically associated with armed struggle into a key player in the pursuit of social justice, equality, and the potential for Irish reunification. In the twenty-first century, Sinn Féin has achieved remarkable electoral success, notably securing the highest number of first-preference votes in the 2020 Irish general election and winning the most seats in the 2022 Northern Ireland Assembly elections. However, the party grapples with a complex array of challenges, including ongoing sectarian tensions, the implications of Brexit on Northern Ireland's identity and governance, and public disillusionment with the perceived efficacy of local representatives. Moreover, issues such as housing and economic inequality have become focal points in Sinn Féin's political agenda, reflecting the party's commitment to addressing pressing social concerns while navigating the historical divisions that still influence community relations in the region. Prominent controversies surrounding Sinn Féin include its historical ties to the IRA, which continue to shape public perceptions and political discourse.

Furthermore, the party faces criticism regarding its handling of local governance and the effectiveness of its representatives, particularly as it seeks to solidify its influence in a rapidly changing political environment. The tensions surrounding Brexit and the Northern Ireland Protocol have also reignited debates about identity, governance, and the potential for a united Ireland, making Sinn Féin's role in contemporary Northern Irish politics both significant and contentious. As the party navigates these challenges, its capacity to build inclusive community relations and address the aspirations of diverse constituencies will be crucial for its future success.[209]

[209] See more: L. Cahillane, D. K. Coffey, *The Centenary of the Irish Free State Constitution, Constituting a Polity?*, Dublin 2024, passim.

Brexit and British-Irish Political and Economic Relations after Brexit (2016–2025)

4.1. Road to Brexit (2016): UK Euroscepticism versus Ireland EU enthusiasm

The journey toward Brexit marked a transformative period for British-Irish relations, revealing the deep divides between the United Kingdom's historically Eurosceptic stance and Ireland's strong pro-European sentiment. Both countries had joined the European Economic Community (EEC) in 1973, but their relationship with European integration diverged significantly over time. While the UK maintained an often ambivalent, sometimes antagonistic attitude toward the European Union (EU), Ireland embraced EU membership as an essential component of its economic and political renewal. Brexit, the decision by UK voters on June 23, 2016 to leave the EU, further magnified these contrasting outlooks. Ireland, as a long-time EU member, found itself in a precarious position. As the UK triggered Article 50 of the Treaty on European Union in March 2017 and began negotiating its exit terms, Ireland became deeply concerned about the potential impact of Brexit, particularly regarding Northern Ireland, trade, and the broader stability of its relationship with the UK.

For the UK, the vote was a culmination of decades of Euroscepticism and political discontent. From the earliest days of its EU membership, the UK had viewed its participation through a pragmatic lens, focusing on economic benefits and often questioning the political integration of Europe. Over time, this attitude hardened into full-scale opposition, especially with the rise of parties like UKIP, which championed the "Better Off Out" rhetoric. The 2016 referendum crystallized these sentiments, revealing deep divisions in public opinion about EU membership, exacerbated by concerns over immigration, sovereignty, and the economic direction of Europe.

In contrast, Ireland's position on Brexit was unequivocally pro-EU. The Irish government, alongside its citizens, viewed EU membership as a core element of its post-Troubles identity and economic transformation. Ireland had long benefited from EU membership, which had helped modernize its economy and provided significant access to the European Single Market. The prospect of a British exit presented major challenges, particularly given the unique position of Northern Ireland, which shares a border with the Republic of Ireland and had been part of the EU's single market and customs union. Ireland's concerns were further compounded by the potential return of a hard border, which would undo years of peacebuilding efforts in Northern Ireland, most notably the Good Friday Agreement.[210]

The UK's withdrawal process, formally initiated in 2017 and culminating in the end of the transition period in December 2020, was fraught with complexities, especially when it came to issues that directly affected Ireland. A key focus was ensuring that the delicate political and economic balance in Northern Ireland, which had been sustained by the EU's membership, would not be disrupted. The resulting *Withdrawal Agreement*, which came into force in February 2020, included the *Protocol on Ireland/Northern Ireland*. This Protocol was a critical component, designed to prevent the establishment of a hard border between the Republic of Ireland and Northern Ireland, while still maintaining the integrity of the EU's Single Market.

This Protocol became a focal point in the Brexit negotiations, particularly as it sought to balance Northern Ireland's status as part of the UK with its continued access to the EU market. The arrangement allowed Northern Ireland to remain within the UK customs territory, while simultaneously benefiting from the EU's Single Market for goods, thus avoiding physical checks and infrastructure along the Irish border. While the Protocol was lauded as a necessary and creative solution, its implementation proved complex, leading to ongoing friction between the UK and the EU, especially over issues like customs checks, agri-food regulations, and medicines.

The *Windsor Framework*, established in March 2023, sought to address many of these practical difficulties, offering a more streamlined system of checks for goods moving between Great Britain and Northern Ireland. The

[210] See: "PSA BLOG," https://www.psa.ac.uk/psa/news/whats-difference-british-and-irish-attitudes-towards-eu [accessed 24.01.2025].

introduction of green and red lanes for goods, along with the provision for trusted trader schemes, represented a significant step toward easing trade disruptions. However, despite these adjustments, Brexit's consequences were deeply felt across Ireland, from new customs checks on goods to changes in consumer rights and cross-border mobility. Ireland's continued support for the EU was reinforced by the financial assistance it received through the *Brexit Adjustment Reserve*, which allocated significant funds to mitigate the economic impact of the UK's exit. This funding, amounting to nearly €1 billion for Ireland, aimed to support businesses, sectors, and regions most affected by Brexit. Additionally, Ireland's position as an EU member state provided it with the leverage to continue shaping its relationship with the UK through multilateral negotiations, while also securing ongoing support for peace and reconciliation efforts in Northern Ireland, including the continuation of PEACE funding programs.[211]

Ultimately, the Brexit process highlighted the profound differences between the UK and Ireland's attitudes toward the EU. While the UK grappled with its complex, often contradictory views on European integration, Ireland stood firm in its commitment to the EU, seeking to preserve its economic and political stability through close cooperation with both the EU and the UK. The challenges of Brexit underscored the fragility of British-Irish relations, particularly in light of the unresolved status of Northern Ireland, which continues to be a central issue in British-Irish discourse.

Before the 2016 Brexit referendum, the UK's relationship with the European Union was deeply polarized, reflecting a complex mix of political, economic, and cultural factors. On one side, many Britons, particularly younger people, urban residents, and those in Scotland and Northern Ireland, supported EU membership. They valued the economic opportunities provided by access to the single market, the freedom to live and work across Europe, and the sense of being part of a broader European community. Political leaders from the Liberal Democrats, the Green Party, and factions within Labour and the Conservatives argued that EU membership enhanced the UK's global influence and promoted peace and cooperation. However, opposition to the

211 See: An official website of the European Union, https://ireland.representation.ec.europa.eu/strategy-and-priorities/key-eu-policies-ireland/impact-brexit-ireland_en [accessed 24.01.2025].

EU was equally strong, particularly among older voters, rural communities, and Eurosceptic politicians. Critics, including a significant portion of the Conservative Party and UKIP, focused on issues like immigration, sovereignty, and bureaucracy, arguing that the UK should reclaim control over its laws, borders, and trade policies.[212]

In contrast to the growing Euroscepticism in the UK, Ireland maintained a much more enthusiastic attitude toward the EU. For Ireland, the EU represented a vital partner in its economic development and a counterbalance to its historically complex relationship with the UK. EU membership had helped transform Ireland into a thriving economy, attracting foreign investment and providing access to vital funding and markets. Politically, Ireland's leaders and the majority of its citizens saw the EU as a force for stability and progress, particularly in the context of the peace process in Northern Ireland. While the UK debated its future in the EU, Ireland remained firmly committed to its role within the bloc, viewing it as essential to its national interests and identity.

The 2016 Brexit referendum campaign brought the UK's divisions to the forefront, with the "Remain" side warning of economic risks and the loss of global influence, while the "Leave" campaign emphasized sovereignty and immigration control. Media outlets played a significant role in shaping public opinion, with pro-EU newspapers like The Guardian highlighting the benefits of membership, while Eurosceptic publications like The Daily Telegraph and The Sun criticized the EU's perceived overreach. Ultimately, the narrow vote to leave the EU reflected the UK's deeply polarized attitudes, highlighting a nation torn between its European ties and its desire for sovereignty. Meanwhile, Ireland's steadfast support for the EU underscored the stark contrast between the two nations' perspectives, setting the stage for the complex negotiations and challenges that followed the Brexit decision.[213]

This chapter delves into the evolving British-Irish relationship during the Brexit process, examining how differing national attitudes toward the EU

---

[212] See: G. Petrakos, A. Sotiriou, *Grexit and Brexit: Incidents, accidents and wake-up calls on the bumpy road of European (dis)integration*, "European Urban and Regional Studies," 2021, Vol. 28(1), pp. 20–25.

[213] See more: "Irish News," *Ireland has the gloomiest view of Brexit*, Aug 9, 2016, https://www.independent.ie/irish-news/ireland-has-the-gloomiest-view-of-brexit/34950088.html

shaped the negotiation and implementation of the *Withdrawal Agreement* and the *Protocol on Ireland/Northern Ireland*. It explores the impact of Brexit on the political, economic, and social fabric of both countries, highlighting the complexities and challenges that defined British-Irish relations from 2016 to 2021. Through the lens of Northern Ireland's status, the chapter offers insights into the broader implications of Brexit for the future of the UK, Ireland, and their relationship with the European Union.

The road to Brexit was marked by starkly contrasting attitudes toward Europe on either side of the Irish Sea—a divide rooted in decades of differing political and economic experiences. While both the United Kingdom and Ireland joined the European Economic Community in 1973, their journeys with European integration evolved in divergent directions, setting the stage for the dramatic referendum of 2016.[214]

For the United Kingdom, membership in the European project was always a pragmatic arrangement, viewed largely through the lens of economic benefit rather than ideological commitment. Over the years, a growing current of Euroscepticism took hold among segments of the British public and political class. Figures and movements—most notably the rise of UKIP (after: Brexit Party, Reform UK)[215]—capitalized on concerns about immigration, national sovereignty, and the perceived overreach of Brussels. This skepticism ultimately culminated in the 2016 referendum, where the promise of reclaiming control over laws, borders, and trade resonated deeply with voters disillusioned by what they saw as an intrusive European bureaucracy.

In contrast, Ireland's experience with the European Union has been one of enthusiastic embrace. For a nation emerging from a history of political conflict and economic hardship, EU membership offered not only a gateway to modernizing its economy but also a means to secure political stability. The benefits were tangible: access to the Single Market, increased foreign investment, and substantial funding that supported the country's transformation. Furthermore, for Ireland, the EU became an essential partner in

---

214 See more: C. Grey, *Brexit Unfolded. How no one got what they wanted (and why they were never going to)*, London 2023, passim.

215 See: K. *Schlesinger, Partie skrajnie prawicowe w Unii Europejskiej wobec integracji europejskiej w latach 1992–2004* [Far-right parties in the European Union and European integration in 1992–2004], Warszawa 2024, pp. 258–261.

maintaining peace and stability on the island—especially in the context of the delicate situation in Northern Ireland, where the border had long been a symbol of reconciliation since the Good Friday Agreement.[216]

Brexit, therefore, did more than just signal the UK's departure from the EU—it accentuated the deep-rooted differences in how Britain and Ireland viewed their future in a European context. The ensuing negotiations, notably the Withdrawal Agreement and the Protocol on Ireland/Northern Ireland, were designed to protect the hard-won peace in Northern Ireland by avoiding a disruptive hard border. Yet, these arrangements also underscored the challenges inherent in reconciling Britain's desire for a reasserted national identity with Ireland's commitment to European integration.[217]

Subsequent adjustments, including the Windsor Framework, attempted to ease practical difficulties in trade and border management. However, the legacy of Brexit continues to influence both nations. In Ireland, initiatives like the Brexit Adjustment Reserve—allocating nearly €1 billion—highlight the ongoing economic and social ripple effects of the UK's departure from the EU. Ultimately, the journey to Brexit illustrates a defining moment where UK Euroscepticism collided with Irish EU enthusiasm, reshaping British-Irish relations and setting a course for a new, complex post-Brexit era.[218]

The road to Brexit revealed the stark contrast between the UK's long-standing Euroscepticism and Ireland's pro-European stance. While both the UK and Ireland joined the European Economic Community in 1973, the UK's relationship with Europe was often pragmatic and increasingly marked by opposition, culminating in the 2016 referendum where voters chose to leave the EU. The rise of movements like UKIP, emphasizing national sovereignty and concerns over immigration, reflected a growing sense of disillusionment with EU membership. In contrast, Ireland embraced EU membership as essential for its economic modernization, political stability, and peacebuilding, especially in relation to Northern Ireland. Ireland's commitment to the EU,

---

[216] See: E. Tannam, *British-Irish Relations in the Twenty-First Century: The Good Friday Agreement, Brexit, and the Totality of Relations*, Oxford 2024, pp. 1–27.

[217] See more: J. Story, *Brexit: a Certain Idea of Europe*, "politique étrangère," 2:2017, pp. 1–12.

[218] A. Głogowski, *The impact of Brexit on the security of Northern Ireland. A case study*, "International Journal of Humanities Social Science and Management (IJHSSM)," Volume 5, Issue 1, Jan.-Feb., 2025, pp. 841–851.

alongside its concerns about Brexit's potential impact, particularly regarding the border and the Good Friday Agreement, underscored the differing national perspectives that shaped the Brexit process.

As the UK triggered Article 50 and began its withdrawal negotiations, Ireland found itself facing significant challenges, especially with Northern Ireland's status and trade relations. The resulting Protocol on Ireland/Northern Ireland aimed to prevent a hard border by allowing Northern Ireland to remain in the UK customs territory while still participating in the EU's Single Market.[219] Despite this solution, the implementation proved complicated, leading to tensions between the UK and the EU. The Windsor Framework, introduced in 2023, sought to ease trade disruptions, but Brexit's economic and social impacts continued to be felt in Ireland, which received significant financial support through the Brexit Adjustment Reserve. Ultimately, Brexit highlighted the deep differences between the UK and Ireland's views on European integration, reshaping their relationship and leading to a new, complex post-Brexit era.

4.2. Brexit process: the EU and UK

Brexit is a phenomenon in the recent history of European integration. Never before has any country left the European Union structures. This process occurred in a democratic manner through the decision made by the British people in the nationwide referendum held in June 2016. The United Kingdom's exit from the European Union, supported by over half of the voters, meant a change in the rules regarding the movement of workers between the United Kingdom and the Community. Citizens remaining in the UK now live and work under British law, not EU law.[220]

---

[219] See more: CRG Murray, A. O'Donoghue, *Life after Brexit: Operationalising the Belfast/Good Friday Agreement's Principle of Consent*, "Dublin University Law Journal," (2019), vol 42(1), pp. 147–189.

[220] See: P. Biskup, *Brexit z perspektywy "długiego trwania": między suwerennością, federalizmem i równowagą siły* [Brexit from a "long-term" perspective: between sovereignty, federalism and the balance of power], in: S. Bachrynowski (ed.), *Brexit a francusko-niemiecka rywalizacja o przywództwo w Unii Europejskiej* [Brexit and the Franco-German rivalry for leadership in the European Union], Warszawa 2024, pp. 15–100.

The process of the UK's withdrawal from the European Union began on March 29, 2017, when the then British Prime Minister, Theresa May, signed the letter that triggered Article 50 of the EU Treaty. Prime Minister May's decision was directly influenced by the results of the referendum, in which the citizens of the UK voted for leaving the EU. The United Kingdom formally left the EU structures on January 31, 2020, starting an 11-month transition period, after which future diplomatic and trade relations were regulated under a new agreement between the UK and the European Union (i.e., the Trade and Cooperation Agreement). It is worth noting that by making this decision with a small majority of votes, the British people did not have the option to specify how the future relations between their country and the EU should look. It was the decisions of political elites that determined the further shape of the debate. Faced with a full set of possible models, the decision was made to interpret the referendum results as far-reaching. However, key players in British politics were not seeking close ties with the European Union.[221]

There is no single event or simple sequence of events that explains the origins of Brexit. British euroscepticism is a phenomenon with a long, at least half-century, tradition. The roots of the problems between the United Kingdom and the European Communities, and later the European Union, should be sought in historically shaped characteristics of the state and nation. The entire history of the UK's integration with the Communities has been marked by mutual ambivalence, which has resulted in tensions and conflicts. London's European policy was characterized by internal contradictions, remaining defensive and reactive. For this reason, the UK earned the reputation of being a "difficult foreign partner in Europe." These terms accurately reflect the incomplete and ambivalent engagement of the UK in the European integration process.

Paradoxically, from the moment the UK joined the integration process in 1973, it was a difficult and specific partner for the EU: it negotiated a special economic status, was outside the eurozone and Schengen Area, did not want to join the banking union, nor co-create the Common Foreign

---

[221] See: Simmons & Simmons, *Brexit: the transition period. The legal consequences of Brexit and their impact on UK businesses*, https://www.simmons-simmons.com/en/features/brexit/ckcbn0l3wl73z0a796j17rid3/brexit-regulatory-and-legislative/ck7gftn8p12ry-0a78e5qxsx86/brexit-brexit-the-transition-period [accessed 14.03.2025].

and Security Policy. It also benefited from special budgetary and financial privileges, such as the costly "British rebate," which exceeded an average of €5 billion per year. Additionally, in the early years of the UK's membership in the Communities, the most noticeable sign of its Eurosceptic stance was the British referendum in 1975 on continued membership in the EEC, just two years after joining the Communities. In this regard, the referendum of June 23, 2016, was not the first such vote in the UK.[222]

The 1975 referendum on the UK's continued membership in the European Economic Community took place on June 5. The question posed to voters was: "Do you think that the United Kingdom should remain in the European Economic Community?" Just over 67 % of those who voted supported remaining in the EEC, with a turnout of 65 %. England, Scotland, Wales, and Northern Ireland all supported continued integration of the UK with the other eight member states of the Communities. In contrast, the 2016 voting results differed dramatically, both regionally and in terms of party support for membership. Notably, the original advocates for the UK's exit from the EEC were the British Labour Party, whose euroscepticism was its official program until the late 1980s, while the opponent to leaving the EEC was the leader of the opposition and future prime minister, Margaret Thatcher.

In 2016, the referendum outcome was driven by the Eurosceptic wing of the ruling Conservative Party. After the Conservative victory in the May 2015 general election, David Cameron confirmed that he would renegotiate the terms of the UK's membership in the EU and then hold a referendum on continued membership. In the negotiations with Brussels, the British Prime Minister demanded, among other things, an increased role for non-eurozone countries within the EU, the protection of competitiveness, and restrictions on access to British welfare benefits for economic migrants from EU countries. During the EU summit in February 2016, Prime Minister Cameron reached an agreement with Brussels regarding changes to the terms of the UK's membership. The compromise, which the Conservative leader hoped would lead to a pro-European victory in the referendum, however, did not

---

[222] M. Musiał-Karg, *Operations Brexit. British referendums of 1975 and 2016 on EU membership*, "Acta Politica Polonica," 2016, 37 (3), pp. 5–18.

satisfy either side. The EU felt the agreement made too many concessions to Cameron, while eurosceptics saw it as a failure for the UK.[223]

Cameron set the date for the referendum on June 23, 2016. The question voters were asked was: "Should the United Kingdom remain a member of the European Union or leave the European Union?" The referendum ended with a victory for the pro-Brexit camp. According to official results, 51.9 % of British voters supported leaving the EU, while 48.1 % were against it. The voter turnout was 71.8 %, meaning over 30 million people voted out of 46.5 million eligible voters. Those in favor of remaining in the EU were in the majority in Northern Ireland (55.8 % for, 44.2 % against) and Scotland (62 % for, 38 % against). However, the pro-Brexit camp was victorious in England (53.4 % for, 46.6 % against) and Wales (52.5 % for, 47.5 % against), winning by over a million votes. The greatest opposition to continued UK membership in the EU came from supporters of the right-wing UK Independence Party (UKIP). Among voters who supported the Conservative Party, opinions on leaving the EU were roughly evenly divided, with a slight majority in favor of euroscepticism. Voters from other major political parties were mostly in favor of remaining in the EU. This vote initiated the lengthy Brexit process, which was formally completed on January 31, 2020. After prolonged negotiations, the Trade and Cooperation Agreement between the UK and the EU was signed on December 30, 2020, and came into force on May 1, 2021, after ratification.[224]

Brexit, understood both as the gradual process of the United Kingdom's exit from the EU and the actual departure from the EU structures, clearly affects the relationship between the UK and the EU, as well as the processes of European integration. The historical decision of the British to leave the EU should be viewed in two categories. First, as a manifestation of European disintegration, and second, as a factor of this disintegration. Both perspectives

---

[223] M. Matthijs, C. Toenshoff, *Brexit, British Politics and European Integration*, Political Science 2019, "Oxford Bibliographies,"https://sais.jhu.edu/sites/default/files/Brexit%2C%20British%20Politics%2C%20and%20European%20...itical%20Science%20-%20Oxford%20Bibliographies.pdf [accessed 14.03.2025].

[224] S. Hobolt, *The Brexit vote: a divided nation, a divided continent*, "Journal of European Public Policy," 23 (9), (2016), pp. 1259–1277.

on Brexit impact European integration, although definitively determining the direction of this influence is, at best, problematic.

In relation to the manifestation of European disintegration, the British decision to withdraw from the EU is a critical point in the culmination of processes that have been systematically and steadily increasing within the European Union. One must be aware that one of the reasons for the UK's accession to the EU was the need to rebuild a strong, imperial position for Britain after the radical decline of London's position and influence in world politics following the end of World War II. The UK's involvement in building the European Community was meant to serve as a way of reconstructing British imperial power, not on a global scale, but at a European level. Thus, one of the axioms behind the decision to join the Community was the desire for London to gain a leadership position. However, this aim was never realized. The UK's participation in integration processes never undermined the role of the Franco-German tandem in setting the direction of development and actions of the Communities.[225] Thus, in the perspective of over 40 years of membership in the Community, the UK never achieved one of the assumed priorities of its involvement in the European integration process. The UK also failed to achieve the second assumed priority, namely accelerated economic growth. Membership, obtained in 1973, coincided with a period of economic downturn caused, among other factors, by the oil crisis and the lack of structural reforms in the British economy, which was most visible during the decade of Prime Minister Margaret Thatcher's rule. Instead of the anticipated prosperity, the British experienced significant economic and social upheavals, which consequently led to the emergence of deep Euroscepticism. This was understood as a critique of the deepening European integration, and in the 1980s, it even gained the status of an official state agenda. In the 1990s, contentious issues between Brussels and London arose regarding subsequent revisions of the founding treaties, such as the Maastricht, Amsterdam, and Nice Treaties, which the UK perceived not only as unnecessary progress in integration processes but also as an assault on the sovereignty of member states. It is also important to note that tensions between London and Brussels were also evident in foreign policy. The natural

[225] See: S. Bachrynowski (ed.), *Shaping the Future of the European Union: Development After Brexit*, Warsaw 2025, passim.

pull of the UK toward Atlantic partnerships (USA, Canada), as well as differing interests, for example, in the Middle East, meant that problems within Europe were compounded by serious difficulties in aligning the interests of London, Paris, and Berlin outside Europe, which hindered the development of a single European (EU) foreign policy.[226]

The UK's far-reaching skepticism toward European integration was correlated with the perception of the UK as a troublesome partner and a brake on integration. Therefore, the decision regarding Brexit cannot be seen as a random, sudden, or, especially, unexpected act. The growing animosity between London and Brussels had, for a long time, been snowballing. Consequently, it should be stated that Brexit, as a manifestation of European disintegration, was associated with two main facts: the inability of London to overcome the hegemonic position of the Franco-German tandem and the processes of increasingly advanced integration, which envisioned the creation of a European superstate, at least a quasi-federal one, on the horizon.

Therefore, it should be pointed out that Brexit must be understood as a result of internal EU turbulence, which involves the pace of integration, its desired direction, and the role of member states within a single EU architecture. From this perspective, the discussion about the leading role of certain member states, whose actions may be perceived as exerting pressure on others and establishing a position of EU leadership, cannot be overlooked, as this may clash with the policies of other large and ambitious states.

The second aspect, Brexit as a factor of disintegration, stems from the fact that the UK's exit from the EU has significantly contributed to the emergence of new or the intensification of already existing disintegration factors within the entire Union. The departure of the UK from the EU should nominally strengthen the EU, but one must also consider a number of risks that could lead to the opposite effect, namely the weakening or even disintegration of the Union. First, Brexit creates a precedent that, by the domino effect, may encourage other member states to consider taking similar steps. This particularly concerns countries that are ambivalent about deepening European cooperation, primarily Denmark and Austria. Second, Brexit solidifies Germany's

---

[226] See more: D. Henig, *Negotiating Uncertainty in UK-EU Relations: Past, Present, and Future*, "ECIPE Policy Briefs," No. 17/202, 2024, pp. 1–20, https://ecipe.org/publications/negotiating-uncertainty-uk-eu-relations [accessed 14.03.2025].

dominance within the EU, irrespective of Germany's own will. The French are unable to independently balance the economic and political potential of Germany, something they managed tactically through alliances with the UK, entering episodic pragmatic partnerships. London played the role of the "maneuvering engine" in such alliances. Brexit has strengthened Berlin's power, and Paris must necessarily seek partners to balance its actions (which, paradoxically, may strengthen the role of countries like Poland). Third, Brexit brings the vision of a Europe of not different, but two speeds, closer to reality.

Before leaving the EU, the British government was preparing a proposal under which the model of European integration encapsulated in the slogan "Europe of different speeds" would become an official element of its policy within the Union. While Brexit has outdated this plan, the idea of a Europe of different speeds has returned in a new, much more dangerous form. This concept was raised by the founding "six" countries as a way to leap forward, leaving behind other member states that are unwilling to accept deeper integration. Therefore, one must consider that the acceleration and deepening of integration could take place within a smaller group of interested states (the first speed), with these countries not having to wait for others (the second speed). Fourth, the UK's departure from the EU could weaken the tendencies toward free-market policies and deregulation in Europe. This could herald the rise of protectionist tendencies within the economies of member states (as already occurred in France, for example, with actions detrimental to Poland and other Central European countries). It is worth noting that it was London that was the driving force behind the reform of the Common Agricultural Policy, which for decades absorbed a large portion of the Community's and later the EU's budget. It was also under the influence of the UK that the Single European Act was introduced, effectively eliminating non-tariff barriers to trade within the EU. The absence of such a strong center promoting the liberalization of the European economy could strengthen opposing tendencies, ultimately contributing to disintegration.

It is also important to note that Brexit did not have as significant an impact on individuals who were living in the United Kingdom as EU citizens and who had the right to legally work and registered with the UK's settlement system (the so-called UK Settlement Scheme) by the end of 2020. However, the situation changed for those who travel to the UK for a limited time, such as seasonal workers. There are also two significant changes for EU citizens, including Poles, living in the UK after Brexit. First, the British government now has the ability to suspend all social benefits for individuals who do not hold British citizenship. Second, Brexit has made it more difficult to find work for EU immigrants who were not previously registered. This is due to the changed rules introduced by the UK government after leaving the EU, which are much less favorable, especially for individuals running their own businesses in the UK, but also for employees.

The Trade and Cooperation Agreement between the EU and the UK, which came into force on May 1, 2021, is not just a simple free trade agreement; it includes preferential arrangements in many areas such as: trade in goods and services, digital trade, intellectual property, public procurement, aviation and road transport, energy, fisheries, social security coordination, law enforcement and justice cooperation in criminal matters, thematic cooperation, and participation in EU programs. The agreement is based on provisions ensuring a level playing field and respect for fundamental rights.[227]

The agreement includes, among other things, zero tariffs and zero quotas on all goods that meet the appropriate rules of origin. An important provision is that VAT will be due on imports to the EU according to the rate applicable to similar goods delivered within the EU. VAT will be paid to customs authorities at the time of import unless the importing member state allows for VAT registration in periodic VAT declarations.

Additionally, both parties to the agreement have committed to ensuring a level playing field by maintaining high standards of protection in areas such as environmental protection, climate change mitigation, and setting charges for greenhouse gas emissions, social and labor rights, tax transparency, state aid, and through the effective enforcement of these provisions at the national level, or the introduction of a binding dispute resolution mechanism and the provision of remedies for both parties.

In the field of transport, the agreement ensures permanent and sustainable air, road, rail, and maritime connections, although access to the market will be more limited than it was under the EU's single market. The agreement also includes provisions ensuring that competition in this field between the EU and the UK will be on a level playing field and will not adversely affect

[227] Document available here: https://commission.europa.eu/strategy-and-policy/relations-united-kingdom/eu-uk-trade-and-cooperation-agreement_en [accessed 14.03.2025].

passenger rights, workers' rights, and transport safety. This will allow the European transport industry to continue operating on the UK market. The provisions of the agreement are more favorable than the regulations arising from the so-called "emergency regulations" regarding road transport (Regulation No. 2020/2224) and air transport (Regulations No. 2020/2225 and 2020/2226) prepared in the event of no agreement between the EU and the UK.[228]

In the field of road freight transport, from January 1, 2021, European carriers can perform transport operations to/from the EU territory and to/from and through the UK territory without restrictions, based on a community license. Thanks to efforts made by Poland, transport companies based in one of the EU member states, including Poland, can perform two cabotage operations in the UK territory within 7 days. The main change from January 1, 2021, is the return to border controls and the implementation of new customs, phytosanitary procedures, as well as new rules for organizing traffic at the EU-UK external border.

In the field of bus and coach transport, EU carriers, including companies based in CEE and Poland, will be able to perform bus services to the UK. Regular and regular special services require permission, as was the case under EU law, issued by the appropriate authority in the relevant member state. The basis for performing transport operations is a community license. Polish driving licenses remain valid, and there will be no requirement to hold an international driving license. The introduction of such provisions, which effectively confirm the continuation of existing EU regulations, is also the result of persistent efforts by the Polish side, which raised this issue during the negotiations of the agreement. Thanks to the negotiated agreement, air connectivity between EU member states, including Poland, and the UK has been secured.[229]

The EU and the United Kingdom have agreed on new frameworks for joint management of fish stocks in EU and UK waters. These frameworks allow the UK to continue developing its fishing activities and ensure that

---

228 Documents available here: https://eur-lex.europa.eu/legal-content/EN/TXT/PDF/?uri=CELEX:32020R2224 [accessed 14.03.2025].

229 See: A. Chojan, *Brexit and ts Impact on Poland's Policy Towards Europe – An Attempt to Forecast*, "Studia Europejskie – Studies in European Affairs" 2020, nr 2, s. 94.

fishermen can maintain their operations and protect their livelihoods. At the same time, they also take into account the protection of natural resources. An important aspect of the agreement with significant social consequences is the coordination of social security for so-called "mobile workers," such as those temporarily assigned, for example, from Poland to the UK, who started work after January 1, 2021, when there was still the risk of a "hard Brexit" (i.e., the absence of agreements regulating relations in this area), which would have meant a lack of coordination rules and potentially resulted in double social security contributions or no insurance protection for these workers. However, this did not happen, and the new order in the field of social security coordination was ensured by the Trade and Cooperation Agreement. The agreement impacts individuals in cross-border situations, such as Polish employees working in the UK or employees and self-employed persons engaging in professional activities from the territory of multiple EU member states and the UK. A question arose regarding which national social security legislation they should be subject to.

In connection with the Trade and Cooperation Agreement and the attached Protocol on the Coordination of Social Security Systems, from January 1, 2021, individuals who found themselves in a cross-border situation after December 31, 2020 (e.g., starting work in the UK in 2021) will be subject to the legislation specified under the terms outlined in the Trade and Cooperation Agreement. With the entry into force of the agreement, the principle of paying social security and health insurance contributions only in one country remains in effect, which, as a general rule, will be the country of employment (either as an employee or self-employed).

However, several provisions have been introduced that provide exceptions to the above rule. First, in the case of workers assigned from an EU member state to the UK, or from the UK to EU member states, and provided certain conditions are met, it will be possible to maintain social security legislation (i.e., contributions) in the home country and be exempt from paying contributions in the country of employment for a period of 24 months of such assignment. To allow for the application of this exception for posted workers, individual EU member states were required to notify the European Commission and the UK within one month of the entry into force of the agreement. If a state does not decide to submit the notification, posted workers would be subject to social security contributions only in the country of employment (i.e., the country to which they are assigned), in accordance with the principle of one legislation.

Further specific rules are based on Regulation (EC) No. 883/2004 and its implementing provisions concerning workers employed in several EU countries and self-employed individuals. The application of these rules, however, does not require member states to submit a notification to the European Commission and the UK. Unlike the provisions of Regulation (EC) No. 883/2004, the rules concerning posted workers and workers employed in multiple countries apply only to EU member states and therefore do not apply to relations between the UK and Liechtenstein, Norway, Switzerland, and Iceland. Determining the applicable legislation in such cases will require an analysis of separate regulations.[230]

To provide greater legal certainty to businesses, consumers, and citizens, the agreement includes a specific chapter on governance that clarifies the operation and oversight of the Trade and Cooperation Agreement. The agreement also establishes a Joint Partnership Council, which will ensure the proper application and interpretation of the agreement and will address any emerging disputes. Binding enforcement mechanisms and dispute resolution procedures will ensure respect for the rights of businesses, consumers, and individuals. This means that businesses in the EU and the UK will compete on a level playing field. Furthermore, it allows for the avoidance of situations where either party could use its regulatory autonomy to grant unfair subsidies or distort competition. The agreement provides for the possibility of introducing balancing, remedial, compensatory, and protective measures. Both parties can take cross-sector retaliatory actions in the event of a breach of the Trade and Cooperation Agreement. These actions can take place in all areas of the economic partnership. In the event of a party failing to meet its obligations, specific clauses related to law enforcement cooperation and judicial cooperation are suspended.

The Trade and Cooperation Agreement establishes new frameworks for cooperation between law enforcement and justice authorities in criminal and civil matters. It acknowledges the need for close cooperation between national

---

[230] Document available here: https://eur-lex.europa.eu/eli/reg/2004/883/oj/eng [accessed 14.03.2025].

police forces and judicial bodies, especially in the context of combating and prosecuting cross-border crime and terrorism. It creates new operational capabilities, taking into account the fact that, as a non-Schengen state and no longer an EU member, the UK will not have the same opportunities in this regard as it did previously. Security cooperation can be suspended if the UK fails to comply with its obligation to continue adhering to the European Convention on Human Rights of the Council of Europe and to enforce it at the national level. Due to its length (1,400 pages), the agreement provides a solid foundation for continued cooperation and friendly relations between the EU and the UK, but its practical effectiveness will be verified by its application in practice.

Brexit represents a unique and unprecedented event in the history of European integration, as the United Kingdom became the first country to leave the European Union. This decision was made through a democratic process, with a nationwide referendum held in June 2016 in which a majority of British voters supported leaving the EU. The departure, which began with the triggering of Article 50 on March 29, 2017, led to the UK's formal exit from the EU on January 31, 2020. An 11-month transition period followed, during which future diplomatic and trade relations were to be regulated under a new agreement, the Trade and Cooperation Agreement. Despite the referendum's narrow victory for the Leave campaign, the specifics of the UK's future relationship with the EU were left to political elites to decide.

The roots of Brexit can be traced back to decades of British euroscepticism. The UK's relationship with European integration has been marked by ambivalence and contradictions, beginning with its initial membership in the European Economic Community (EEC) in 1973. While the UK engaged with the EEC, it negotiated special economic terms, opted out of key EU policies like the eurozone and the Schengen Area, and consistently expressed discomfort with deeper political integration. The British government also secured financial privileges, such as the "British rebate," which reduced its contributions to the EU budget by billions of euros each year. This cautious and often antagonistic stance led to a reputation of the UK being a "difficult partner" in European affairs.

Brexit did not emerge from a single event but was the culmination of a long-standing historical and political trend. The UK's reluctance to fully embrace European integration was evident as early as 1975, when a referendum was held on continued membership in the European Communities, just two years after joining. This early referendum foreshadowed the June 2016 vote, reinforcing the cyclical nature of Britain's uneasy relationship with Europe. Over time, the UK's defensive and reactive European policy only deepened divisions, with key political players advocating for a break from the EU rather than closer ties. The referendum of 2016 thus marked the latest chapter in the UK's complex and often ambivalent engagement with the European Union.

The UK-EU relationship, eight years after the Brexit referendum, remains one of the most complex and significant bilateral partnerships in the world. With a new UK government and European Commission in place, there is an opportunity to reset this relationship and move past previous obstructions. The relationship, which encompasses the world's second-largest trade flow and integrated neighborhood challenges, requires continuous negotiation and cooperation. Given the complexity involved, both sides must approach the partnership with a shared vision and roadmap to effectively manage the multiple issues that arise.

This broad and intricate relationship inevitably brings challenges and tensions, which can only be addressed through ongoing, senior-level dialogue. Regular meetings, including annual summits and discussions between UK ministers, EU commissioners, and experts, are essential for maintaining mutual understanding and resolving issues. The emotional aftermath of Brexit, with some hoping for a return to pre-Brexit conditions, adds complexity to negotiations. Nonetheless, these emotional dynamics must be managed carefully to ensure a constructive dialogue that allows both sides to move forward.

As the UK no longer fits neatly into the EU's existing frameworks, flexibility from the EU is necessary. The relationship cannot be constrained by previous models, and creative solutions must be found to address shared interests and specific needs. Informal negotiations should include businesses, civil society, local governments, and academics to ensure that the perspectives of all stakeholders are considered when shaping agreements. This broad engagement is key to creating mutually beneficial arrangements that account for the evolving needs of both parties.

The UK has had to adjust to its new status as a non-EU member, learning from past mistakes in negotiations, such as those seen in the Windsor

Framework.[231] Understanding the collaborative yet competitive nature of modern trade and the importance of trust and transparency in negotiations is crucial for future success. Moving forward, the UK and EU must prioritize these elements to build a stronger, more resilient relationship. Although there will be no perfect solution and the process will take time, both sides have strong incentives to pursue deeper, more robust arrangements. With ongoing engagement, flexibility, and patience, a stable and mutually beneficial partnership can be established.

4.3. Northern Ireland status: toward united Ireland after Brexit?

The status of Northern Ireland in relation to a potential united Ireland has become a particularly sensitive and contentious issue following Brexit. Prior to the United Kingdom's departure from the European Union, Northern Ireland, as part of the UK, benefited from the arrangements under the Good Friday Agreement of 1998,[232] which helped to bring peace to the region after decades of conflict known as "The Troubles." One key aspect of this agreement was the special status of Northern Ireland, which allowed for cooperation with the Republic of Ireland in various areas, including trade and political matters, while maintaining Northern Ireland's position within the UK. The shared EU membership of both the UK and Ireland further facilitated this cooperation, making the border between the two parts of the island virtually invisible.[233]

However, Brexit dramatically changed the dynamics of this arrangement. As the UK left the EU, Northern Ireland found itself in a unique position. The Northern Ireland Protocol, part of the Brexit deal, established a de facto customs border in the Irish Sea, creating an economic and political

231 See more: O. Svendsen, D. Ruy, *The Windsor Framework Heralds a Breakthrough in EU-UK Relations*, "CSIS Policy Paper," 6th of March 2024, https://www.csis.org/analysis/windsor-framework-heralds-breakthrough-eu-uk-relations [accessed 14.03.2025].

232 See: L. C. Whitten, *Brexit and Strand Three of the 1998 Agreement: The Three Faces of East-West*, "The Political Quarterly," Vol. 94, No. 1, January/March 2023, pp. 122–132.

233 See more: L. C. Whitten, *Post-Brexit dynamism: the dynamic regulatory alignment of Northern Ireland under the Protocol on Ireland/Northern Ireland*, "Northern Ireland Legal Quarterly," NI after Brexit, Vol. 73, No S2 (2022), pp. 37–64.

distinction between Northern Ireland and the rest of the UK. This arrangement, designed to avoid a hard border on the island of Ireland, has led to growing debates within Northern Ireland about its future. For many nationalists and republicans, Brexit has reignited calls for a united Ireland, arguing that the new post-Brexit reality, with its associated economic and political disruptions, is a compelling reason for reunification with the Republic of Ireland.

On the other hand, unionists, who wish to maintain Northern Ireland's place within the UK, have expressed dissatisfaction with the Protocol, seeing it as a threat to the union. The division over the issue is significant, as it touches on the broader themes of identity, sovereignty, and economic interests. While Brexit has certainly made the question of Irish unification more immediate, it has also highlighted the complexities of the situation. Public opinion in Northern Ireland remains divided, with surveys showing varying support for both unionism and nationalism, depending on the political and economic climate.

In this context, the issue of a united Ireland post-Brexit has moved from a theoretical debate to a more pressing political consideration. As tensions surrounding the Protocol continue to rise and as Northern Ireland's future relationship with both the UK and the EU evolves, the prospect of a united Ireland is becoming an increasingly prominent question in both Northern Irish and wider UK politics. The challenges of reconciling the competing desires of unionists and nationalists, along with the legal and economic implications of such a significant shift, make the future of Northern Ireland's status a highly complex and evolving issue.

The status of Northern Ireland in relation to the prospect of a united Ireland has become a prominent topic of debate, particularly in the wake of Brexit. Following the United Kingdom's departure from the European Union in 2020, discussions surrounding the future of Northern Ireland's governance and its potential unification with the Republic of Ireland have intensified, influenced by historical tensions rooted in sectarian divides and a complex political landscape established by the Good Friday Agreement of 1998. This agreement provided a framework for peace and self-determination, allowing the people of Northern Ireland to decide their constitutional future through democratic processes, particularly in light of changing public sentiment and political identities.

Brexit has reshaped the dynamics of Northern Ireland's political landscape, reawakening discussions about identity and unity. Polls indicate a rising support for reunification, particularly among younger voters and the Catholic community, although significant resistance remains within the Protestant population, with 81 % favoring continued association with the UK. Controversies surrounding the Northern Ireland Protocol, which maintains open trade with the EU while establishing customs checks with Great Britain, have further complicated these discussions, leading to fears of renewed sectarian tensions and economic uncertainty. Public opinion on a potential referendum for Irish unity reflects these complexities, with increasing calls for a vote tempered by concerns about economic implications and governance issues.[234] As of 2023, approximately 45 % of Northern Ireland's population believes unification is likely within the next two decades, indicating a shift in attitudes that could reshape the region's future.

However, the path to unification remains fraught with challenges, requiring careful navigation of political, economic, and social factors that have historically divided communities in the region. The status of Northern Ireland toward a united Ireland is characterized by a combination of historical grievances, evolving political identities, and the implications of Brexit. As the region grapples with these issues, the potential for a referendum on Irish unity continues to spark debate, reflecting deep-seated emotions and aspirations for the future among both nationalist and unionist communities.[235]

4.4. British-Irish relations during Brexit, and post-Brexit (2016–2025)

The relationship between Britain and Ireland has been shaped by centuries of complex history, but the period surrounding Brexit (2016–2025) brought new challenges and dynamics to this long-standing connection. The United

[234] J. Doyle, E. Connolly, *Brexit and the Future of Northern Ireland*, "DCU Brexit Institute" Working Paper, N. 1-2017, https://dcubrexitinstitute.eu/wp-content/uploads/2017/06/WP-2017-1-Doyle-Connolly-1.pdf [accessed 1.04.2025].

[235] S. Golden, *Towards a referendum for reunification in Ireland?*, "CIDOB opinion," no 791, February 2024, https://www.cidob.org/en/publications/towards-referendum-reunification-ireland [accessed 1.04.2025].

Kingdom's decision to leave the European Union in 2016 introduced a host of political, economic, and social uncertainties, particularly regarding the border between Northern Ireland (part of the UK) and the Republic of Ireland (an EU member state). The prospect of a hard border, which could disrupt the peace process established by the Good Friday Agreement (1998), became a focal point of discussions, with both sides emphasizing the importance of avoiding any physical infrastructure that could reignite tensions in the region.[236]

During the Brexit negotiations, the issue of the Irish border emerged as one of the most contentious and complex aspects. The UK government's desire to end freedom of movement within the EU clashed with the need to maintain an open border to preserve the peace and economic stability of Ireland. The European Union, particularly Ireland, insisted that any Brexit deal must respect the unique situation of Northern Ireland, which was caught between two divergent political and economic systems. This ultimately led to the introduction of the Northern Ireland Protocol, a mechanism designed to prevent a hard border by creating a de facto customs border in the Irish Sea, separating Northern Ireland from the rest of the UK.

For Ireland, Brexit posed significant challenges, especially in relation to its trade with the UK, which had been its largest trading partner prior to the referendum. The introduction of new barriers to trade, customs checks, and regulatory divergence required Ireland to adapt its economic strategies, seeking new markets and strengthening its position within the EU. Additionally, the political fallout from Brexit was felt on both sides of the Irish Sea, with the relationship between the UK and Ireland growing more strained at times, as each side navigated the delicate balance of their respective interests. From the Irish perspective, the importance of maintaining strong EU ties while ensuring peace and stability in Northern Ireland remained paramount.

A new chapter in Irish politics has begun, with a fresh coalition government taking office in Dublin, continuing the unprecedented partnership between Fianna Fáil and Fine Gael, now joined by independents. While the UK Labour government under Keir Starmer likely remained neutral during

[236] D. Benson, *A Divided Country: The Feasibility of a United Ireland*, "The Yale Review of International Studies: Yale's Undergraduate Global Affairs Journal" https://yris.yira.org/column/a-divided-country-the-feasibility-of-a-united-ireland [accessed 1.04.2025].

the Irish coalition talks, the resulting continuity and stability have been welcomed in London. In the wake of Labour's election victory in the UK, both governments made efforts to reset the British-Irish relationship, with warm statements and a commitment to annual prime ministerial summits starting in 2025. Simon Harris, who recently became Ireland's Minister for Foreign Affairs, has already met with Hilary Benn, the UK's new Northern Ireland Secretary, underscoring a renewed spirit of cooperation following years of post-Brexit turbulence.

The damage caused by Brexit to British-Irish relations and to the delicate political balance in Northern Ireland is still being reckoned with. The 2016 referendum campaign often ignored the implications for Northern Ireland and the Belfast/Good Friday Agreement, which had assumed EU membership as a foundational framework. Instead of engaging in joint British-Irish strategizing through the British-Irish Intergovernmental Conference (B-IIGC), both governments found themselves at odds. The UK pursued a hard Brexit that sidelined Irish concerns, while Dublin resorted to increasingly confrontational rhetoric. The resulting Northern Ireland Protocol and subsequent trade border angered unionists, and only with the Windsor Framework in 2023 and a follow-up deal in 2024 did efforts to stabilize the region gain traction.

Despite recent progress, the legacy of unilateral British actions from 2016 to 2022 continues to strain relations. One notable example is the UK's Legacy and Reconciliation Bill, which undermined a previous intergovernmental agreement and granted sweeping immunity for past crimes during the conflict. Its passage in 2024 led to a rare legal challenge by the Irish government at the European Court of Human Rights. Although the current Irish government's programme emphasizes cooperation, its vagueness on key 1998 Agreement structures—such as the B-IIGC and the North/South Ministerial Council—raises concerns about a weakening of formal bilateral mechanisms. Informal summits, while encouraging, cannot substitute the robust and institutionalized cooperation envisioned by the Agreement's architects.

Looking ahead, significant challenges remain. Even with goodwill on both sides, diverging national interests—exacerbated by the UK's departure from the EU—will persist. The Irish government is continuing its legal action over the Legacy Act, despite early signals of reform from the Labour government. Furthermore, potential constitutional questions, such as a future referendum on Irish unity, could reignite tensions if handled without structured dialogue.

While informal summits and new funding initiatives like the Shared Island Unit signal a desire to move forward, long-term stability will require recommitment to the formal institutions of the 1998 Agreement. Without this, British-Irish relations risk slipping back into reactive crisis management, rather than the proactive, treaty-based cooperation needed for lasting peace and progress.[237] By 2025, the full impact of Brexit on British-Irish relations is still unfolding, with both countries continuing to adjust to the new realities. While the Northern Ireland Protocol remains a source of tension, it also reflects a shared understanding of the need for cooperation to safeguard peace and economic interests. This era has tested not only political and economic ties but also the enduring connections of the people of Britain and Ireland, whose relationship remains shaped by history, geography, and the shared challenges of navigating a post-Brexit world.[238]

---

[237] See: C. J. Kelly, E. Tannam, More of the same or a new opportunity for British-Irish relations? "The Constitution Unit" blog, 5th of March 2025, https://constitution-unit.com/2025/03/05/more-of-the-same-or-a-new-opportunity-for-british-irish-relations/ [both accessed 1.04.2025].

[238] See: P. Diamond, B. Colfer, *Irish Unification After Brexit*, "CIRSD Horizons," Spring 2023, Issue no 23, https://www.cirsd.org/en/horizons/horizons-spring-2023---issue-no23/irish-unification-after-brexit and Institute for Government, *Irish reunification explainer*, https://www.instituteforgovernment.org.uk/explainer/irish-reunification [both accessed 15.04.2025].

The Future of British-Irish Relations in the Third Decade of the XXI Century

The political relationship between Britain and Ireland has been shaped by a long and often turbulent history, marked by centuries of shifting power dynamics, ideological conflict, and evolving national identities. However, the period surrounding Brexit—spanning from 2016 to 2025—has introduced new complexities and challenges, reshaping this historical relationship in profound ways. The United Kingdom's decision to leave the European Union in 2016 triggered political, economic, and social uncertainties, with the most contentious issue being the border between Northern Ireland, part of the UK, and the Republic of Ireland, an EU member state.

The prospect of a hard border—an imposition of physical infrastructure on the land border between Northern Ireland and the Republic—became a focal point in both public and political discourse. A hard border could have disrupted the peace process established by the Good Friday Agreement (GFA) of 1998, which had played a pivotal role in bringing stability to the region after decades of conflict. Both the UK and Ireland were acutely aware of the risks associated with any hardening of the border, not only for the peace process but also for the economic and social stability of the island.

The negotiations surrounding Brexit highlighted the tension between the UK government's desire to reclaim control over its borders and the European Union's insistence on respecting the unique situation of Northern Ireland, which exists between two political and economic systems. The result was the introduction of the Northern Ireland Protocol, a mechanism designed to prevent a hard border by creating a de facto customs border in the Irish Sea. This arrangement, while preventing a physical border on the island of Ireland, further complicated UK-Ireland relations and raised significant political, economic, and social challenges in Northern Ireland.

For Ireland, Brexit posed not only challenges regarding the status of Northern Ireland but also significant disruptions to its trade relationship with the UK, which had been its largest trading partner. The imposition of customs checks, regulatory divergence, and the introduction of new barriers to trade required Ireland to recalibrate its economic strategies, seeking new markets while strengthening its position within the EU. Politically, the fallout from Brexit created moments of tension between the UK and Ireland, particularly in the early years following the referendum. However, despite these challenges, Ireland's focus on preserving peace in Northern Ireland, while also maintaining strong ties to the EU, remained central to its diplomatic agenda.

A new chapter in Irish politics emerged with the formation of an unprecedented coalition government in Dublin between Fianna Fáil, Fine Gael, and independents, reflecting an ongoing commitment to stability and cooperation. This stability was welcomed by the UK government, particularly following the election of Labour leader Keir Starmer. The Labour government's neutral stance in the Irish coalition talks and the subsequent resumption of annual prime ministerial summits in 2025 underscored a renewed spirit of cooperation after years of post-Brexit turbulence. Yet, despite efforts to reset British-Irish relations, the legacy of the UK's unilateral actions between 2016 and 2022 continues to strain diplomatic relations, particularly in Northern Ireland.

One notable example of this ongoing tension is the UK's Legacy and Reconciliation Bill, which undermines previous intergovernmental agreements and grants broad immunity for past crimes related to the conflict in Northern Ireland. This bill, passed in 2024, led to a rare legal challenge by the Irish government at the European Court of Human Rights, highlighting the continued friction between the two governments. Moreover, while informal summits and new funding initiatives, such as Ireland's Shared Island Unit, indicate a desire to move forward, the vagueness in the Irish government's programme regarding key mechanisms of the 1998 Good Friday Agreement—such as the British-Irish Intergovernmental Conference (B-IIGC) and the North/South Ministerial Council—raises concerns about the weakening of formal bilateral structures. Informal diplomacy, while promising, cannot substitute for the robust and institutionalized cooperation originally envisioned by the Agreement's architects.

Looking ahead, several key challenges remain. Diverging national interests, compounded by the UK's departure from the EU, continue to shape the political landscape. The Irish government's ongoing legal action regarding the Legacy Bill, coupled with the potential for constitutional questions—such as a future referendum on Irish unity—could reignite tensions in the absence of structured dialogue. In this context, the importance of recommitting to the formal institutions of the Good Friday Agreement cannot be overstated. Without this recommitment, British-Irish relations risk slipping into a cycle of reactive crisis management, rather than proactive, treaty-based cooperation aimed at lasting peace and progress.

By 2025, the full impact of Brexit on British-Irish relations remains unfolding, with both countries continuing to adjust to the new realities. The Northern Ireland Protocol remains a source of tension, but it also reflects a shared understanding of the need for cooperation to preserve peace and economic stability. The Brexit era has tested not only political and economic ties but also the enduring connections between the peoples of Britain and Ireland, whose relationship continues to be shaped by history, geography, and the shared challenges of navigating a post-Brexit world.

Addressing the hypotheses

In relation to the scientific hypotheses proposed in the methodological preface, the conclusions of this study can provide valuable insights.

Hypothesis 1, which posits that the United Kingdom's withdrawal from the European Union has significantly disrupted the institutional architecture of British-Irish relations, is supported by the evidence presented throughout this work. Brexit has undeniably weakened key mechanisms of cooperation established under the Good Friday Agreement, particularly those related to intergovernmental coordination, such as the British-Irish Intergovernmental Conference (B-IIGC). The political and constitutional instability in Northern Ireland, exacerbated by the Brexit process, underscores the validity of this hypothesis, highlighting the challenges posed by Brexit to Northern Ireland's governance and its role within the broader UK-EU framework.

Hypothesis 2, which suggests that despite the dislocations caused by Brexit, new opportunities for pragmatic engagement and diplomatic recalibration have emerged, is also evident in the analysis. The introduction of the Northern Ireland Protocol, along with the Windsor Framework of 2023, demonstrates a willingness on both sides to find pragmatic solutions to the challenges posed by Brexit. The UK's and Ireland's continued dialogue, through mechanisms such as prime ministerial summits and cooperative initiatives like the Shared Island Unit, reflects a commitment to recalibrate diplomatic relations despite the tensions created by Brexit.

Hypothesis 3, which addresses the enduring influence of historical narratives and contested identities in British-Irish relations, remains relevant. The ongoing tensions in Northern Ireland, driven by nationalist and unionist identities, continue to complicate the political landscape, often impeding purely technocratic solutions. The legacy of the Troubles and the symbolic significance of Northern Ireland's constitutional status are persistent sources of friction, influencing political discourse and decision-making in both London and Dublin.

Hypothesis 4, which introduces the notion of growing asymmetry in diplomatic capacity and strategic positioning between Ireland and the UK in the post-Brexit period, is reflected in the analysis of the legal and diplomatic friction surrounding issues such as the Legacy and Reconciliation Bill. Ireland's increasing reliance on its EU membership and multilateral alliances, contrasted with the UK's more unilateral approach, underscores this asymmetry. As the UK navigates its post-Brexit identity and its role on the global stage, Ireland's strengthened position within the EU offers it a diplomatic leverage that the UK struggles to match in its dealings with Ireland.

In conclusion, the Brexit period has been a critical juncture in British-Irish relations, and its legacy will continue to shape the political landscape for years to come. While challenges remain, the ongoing efforts at diplomatic engagement and the renewed commitment to cooperative mechanisms suggest that there is still potential for a stable, mutually beneficial relationship between the two countries. However, long-term stability will depend on the strength of formal institutional mechanisms and a shared commitment to addressing the political, economic, and constitutional challenges that lie ahead.

The long-term trajectory of British-Irish relations in the wake of Brexit will likely hinge on the ability of both governments to institutionalize flexible yet resilient frameworks of cooperation. The weakening of formal mechanisms established under the Good Friday Agreement has underscored the fragility of intergovernmental trust in the absence of a shared EU context. Yet, the adaptability demonstrated through the negotiation of the Northern Ireland Protocol and later the Windsor Framework suggests that both the UK and Ireland remain committed to preserving peace and stability, even amid growing political divergence. These frameworks, however imperfect, have provided critical scaffolding for ongoing dialogue and may serve as prototypes for future UK-EU or bilateral arrangements.

Looking ahead, Northern Ireland's constitutional status remains one of the most significant variables in the evolving British-Irish relationship. Brexit has intensified discussion around Irish unification, particularly among nationalist communities who see EU membership as an anchor of political and economic stability. Demographic trends and shifting political attitudes suggest that the question of a border poll could gain greater political salience in the coming decade. Yet, unification remains a deeply complex and contested issue, and any movement in this direction would require extensive public consultation, North-South cooperation, and sustained cross-community dialogue. Conversely, if Northern Ireland remains within the UK, future British-Irish relations will need to contend with the ongoing need for constitutional innovation and institutional reform to ensure Northern Ireland's unique status is sustainably managed.

Brexit has also forced a strategic recalibration in Ireland's foreign policy orientation. Freed from the constraints of coordination within the UK-EU framework, Ireland has strengthened its profile as an EU member state, leveraging its alliances in Brussels to support its national interests and to amplify its voice on issues affecting the island of Ireland. This shift has, in turn, introduced a new dynamic into British-Irish relations, as Ireland increasingly acts within multilateral structures while the UK pursues a more unilateral or bilateral approach. This divergence in diplomatic posture may create frictions, but it could also incentivize more creative, issue-specific partnerships between Dublin and London, particularly in areas like trade, security, and climate policy.

In conclusion, the post-Brexit era marks a profound transformation in British-Irish relations, defined by both disruption and opportunity. While Brexit dismantled shared platforms that previously facilitated cooperation, it has also prompted both countries to confront unresolved historical and constitutional questions with renewed urgency. The future of Northern Ireland—whether as part of the UK, a united Ireland, or a region with increasing autonomy—will remain central to these developments. What emerges will depend not only on political decisions in Westminster and Dublin but also on the will of the people of Northern Ireland. In this context, sustained engagement, robust institutions, and a shared commitment to peace and democratic principles will be essential to navigating the complexities of the post-Brexit settlement.

Literature Annex

Documents

Act of Union (1707): https://www.parliament.uk/about/living-heritage/evolutionofparliament/legislativescrutiny/act-of-union-1707

Act of Union (1800): https://www.parliament.uk/about/living-heritage/evolutionofparliament/legislativescrutiny/parliamentandireland/collections/ireland/act-of-union-1800

Constitution of the Irish Free State (1922): https://www.irishstatutebook.ie/eli/1922/act/1/enacted/en/print

Declaration of Independence (1919): https://www.difp.ie/volume-1/1919/declaration-of-independence/1/#section-documentpage

Documents of Irish Foreign Policy (1932–1936): https://www.difp.ie/volume-4/1932/british-irish-relations/1505

'Éire Nua' document, Dublin (1972): https://cain.ulster.ac.uk/issues/politics/docs/sf/sinnfein79.htm

Government of Ireland Act (1914): https://www.parliament.uk/about/living-heritage/evolutionofparliament/legislativescrutiny/parliamentandireland/collections/home-rule-1914/gov-of-ireland-act-1914/

Irish Church Act (1869): https://www.legislation.gov.uk/ukpga/1869/42/contents/enacted

Poynings' Law (1494): https://www.parliament.uk/about/living-heritage/evolutionofparliament/legislativescrutiny/parliamentandireland/overview/poynings-law

St. Andrews Agreement (2006): https://www.legislation.gov.uk/ukpga/2006/53/contents

St. Andrews Agreement Act (2007): https://www.legislation.gov.uk/ukpga/2007/4/contents

Press

"BBC News," 31st of August 2014.
"Irish News," 9th Aug 2016.
"The Irish Times," 26th of June 2020.

Internet

https://www.irishpost.com/news/a-coveted-island-nine-times-ireland-has-been-invaded-conquered-and-occupied-104171
https://celt.ucc.ie/nation_kingship.html
https://www.newworldencyclopedia.org/entry/Norman_Ireland
https://www.britannica.com/place/Ireland/The-14th-and-15th-centuries
https://wiki.acervolima.com/norman-invasion-in-ireland
https://www.britannica.com/place/The-Pale
https://sites.google.com/site/sukirishculture/cli/normans
https://www.libraryireland.com/Atlas/XXVI-Anglo-Irish-Lords.php
https://www.wesleyjohnston.com/users/ireland/past/history/12501450.html
https://blog.nationalarchives.gov.uk/end-bruce-invasion-ireland-1318
https://www.tcd.ie/medieval-history/assets/pdf/bruceinvasion.pdf
https://cain.ulster.ac.uk/othelem/chron/ch1169-1799.htm
https://www.parliament.uk/about/living-heritage/evolutionofparliament/legislativescrutiny/parliamentandireland/overview/poynings-law
https://www.history.com/news/henry-viii-divorce-reformation-catholic-church
https://www.rmg.co.uk/stories/topics/why-did-henry-viii-break-rome
https://scholar.smu.edu/cgi/viewcontent.cgi?article=1003&context=weil_ura
https://www.cs.mcgill.ca/~rwest/wikispeedia/wpcd/wp/c/Church_of_Ireland.htm
https://www.irishchurches.org/members/church-of-ireland
https://study.com/academy/lesson/church-of-ireland-history-lesson-quiz.html
https://www.ireland.anglican.org/about/about-us
https://www.nidirect.gov.uk/publications/plantations-ulster-1600-1641
http://oro.open.ac.uk/71421/1/PhD%20-%20Developments%20in%20the%20Political%20Thought%20of%20Theobald%20Wolfe%20Tone%20July%202020%20K%20Lucas.pdf
https://www.theguardian.com/world/from-the-archive-blog/2020/apr/08/ireland-becomes-a-republic-april-1949
https://writingthetroublesweb.wordpress.com/2020/12/01/bobby-sands-mp-whose-idea-was-it

https://ugc.futurelearn.com/uploads/files/2b/80/2b80cfb1-f3b9-420d-b692-c11ab6bbcdd4/Wk1_Britain_and_Ireland.pdf
https://www.dfa.ie/irish-embassy/great-britain/about-us/ambassador/ambassador-blog-2017/february2017/three-great-irish-parliamentarians
https://www.irishtimes.com/news/ireland/irish-news/john-hume-has-place-in-pantheon-of-irish-nationalist-leaders-such-as-o-connell-parnell-and-redmond-1.4321156
https://www.forces.net/heritage/wwi/ireland-stage-1916-easter-rising
https://www.gov.ie/en/publication/583995-the-executed-leaders-of-the-1916-rising
https://encyclopedia.1914-1918-online.net/article/easter_rising_great_britain_and_ireland https://www.theirishstory.com/2011/04/22/the-easter-rising-%e2%80%93-a-brief-overview/#.ZFycsHZByUk
https://www.militaryarchives.ie/collections/online-collections/bureau-of-military-history-1913-1921/reels/bmh/BMH.WS1739.pdf
https://www.waterfordmuseum.ie/exhibit/web/Display/article/318/3/The_Irish_War_of_Independence_1919__21_The_Decies_Brigade__The_Flying_Column.html
https://www.ireland-information.com/articles/kevinbarry.htm
https://www.ucd.ie/t4cms/KBpanel2.pdf
https://www.dfa.ie/about-us/ourhistory/100years/1919-1929/1921
https://www.historyireland.com/massacre-west-cork-dunmanway-ballygorman-killings
https://sluggerotoole.com/2020/07/21/the-forgotten-troubles-1920-1922-the-mcmahon-murders
https://www.theirishstory.com/2013/07/28/making-sense-of-the-irish-civil-war-a-conversation-with-gavin-foster/#.ZFytLXZByUk
https://www.theirishstory.com/2020/05/26/fine-gael-and-fianna-fail-civil-war-parties
https://www.irishtimes.com/news/politics/coalition-or-political-crisis-verdict-of-ff-fg-and-green-members-to-be-revealed-this-evening-1.4288833
https://www.gale.com/binaries/content/assets/au-resources-in-product/northernireland_essay_ww2.pdf
https://www.ria.ie/news/documents-irish-foreign-policy/ireland-leaves-commonwealth-1949
https://www.europarl.europa.eu/RegData/etudes/BRIE/2022/698877/EPRS_BRI(2022)698877_EN.pdf
https://www.ireland.ie/en/eu50/history-of-ireland-in-the-eu

https://www.dfa.ie/media/dfa/alldfawebsitemedia/ourrolesandpolicies/irelandintheeu/ireland-in-the-eu-history.pdf
https://www.cvce.eu/en/obj/ireland_s_accession-en-c6c28822-886f-4009-908a-980482c94817.html
https://www.bbc.com/news/uk-28812366
https://www.ireland.ie/en/eu50/history-of-ireland-in-the-eu
https://www.cso.ie/en/media/csoie/releasespublications/documents/statisticalyearbook/2004/ireland&theeu.pdf
https://mural.maynoothuniversity.ie/id/eprint/2919/1/JOB_Ireland_and_the_European.pdf
https://aei.pitt.edu/27/1/Odonnell.pdf
https://repository.usfca.edu/thes/13
https://cain.ulster.ac.uk/issues/abstentionism/chron.htm
https://cain.ulster.ac.uk/events/peace/talks.htm
https://cain.ulster.ac.uk/othelem/organ/ira/tuas94.htm
https://education.niassembly.gov.uk/post-16/snapshots-devolution/belfastgood-friday-agreement/after-agreement
https://education.niassembly.gov.uk/post-16/snapshots-devolution/st-andrews-agreement-2006-and-st-andrews-agreement-act-2007
https://www.cfr.org/backgrounder/moving-past-troubles-future-northern-ireland-peace;
https://www.everycrsreport.com/reports/RS21333.html
https://www.psa.ac.uk/psa/news/whats-difference-british-and-irish-attitudes-towards-eu
https://ireland.representation.ec.europa.eu/strategy-and-priorities/key-eu-policies-ireland/impact-brexit-ireland_en
https://www.independent.ie/irish-news/ireland-has-the-gloomiest-view-of-brexit/34950088.html
https://www.simmons-simmons.com/en/features/brexit/ckcbn0l3wl73z0a796j17rid3/brexit-regulatory-and-legislative/ck7gftn8p12ry0a78e5qxsx86/brexit-brexit-the-transition-period
https://sais.jhu.edu/sites/default/files/Brexit%2C%20British%20Politics%2C%20and%20European%20...itical%20Science%20-%20Oxford%20Bibliographies.pdf
https://ecipe.org/publications/negotiating-uncertainty-uk-eu-relations
https://commission.europa.eu/strategy-and-policy/relations-united-kingdom/eu-uk-trade-and-cooperation-agreement_en
https://eur-lex.europa.eu/legal-content/EN/TXT/PDF/?uri=CELEX: 32020R2224
https://eur-lex.europa.eu/eli/reg/2004/883/oj/eng

https://www.csis.org/analysis/windsor-framework-heralds-breakthrough-eu-uk-relations
https://dcubrexitinstitute.eu/wp-content/uploads/2017/06/WP-2017-1-Doyle-Connolly-1.pdf
https://www.cidob.org/en/publications/towards-referendum-reunification-ireland
https://yris.yira.org/column/a-divided-country-the-feasibility-of-a-united-ireland
https://constitution-unit.com/2025/03/05/more-of-the-same-or-a-new-opportunity-for-british-irish-relations
https://www.instituteforgovernment.org.uk/explainer/irish-reunification

Books and articles

"Congress Research Service Report," *Northern Ireland Peace Process: Background and Challenges* 2019–2024, updated and published online.
50 Steps, *Ireland and European Integration*, Vol. 1–5, published online.
Ainsworth J., *The Black & Tans and Auxiliaries in Ireland, 1920–1921: Their Origins, Roles and Legacy*, A paper presented to the Annual Conference of the Queensland History, pp. 1–8.
Algernon Cecil C., *Queen Victoria and Her Prime Ministers*, Eyre and Spottiswode, 1953.
Allwood G., *Ireland On Stage – The 1916 Easter Rising*, published online.
Bachrynowski S. (ed.), *Shaping the Future of the European Union: Development After Brexit*, Warsaw 2025.
Bachrynowski S., *Między angielskim lwem a Irlandzką harfą. Myśl polityczna Irlandzkiego Ruchu Republikańskiego [The Political Thought of IRM – Irish Republican Movement]*, Kalisz 2009.
Bachrynowski S., "*Od centralizmu do autonomii. Problem ustanowienia i funkcjonowania samorządu w brytyjskiej prowincji Irlandii Północnej w latach 1921–1999 [From Centralism to Autonomy. The Problem of Establishing and Functioning of Self-Government in the British Province of Northern Ireland in 1921–1999]*," Annales UMCS, Sectio K, Politologia, Vol. XIII, 2006, pp. 47–49.
Bachrynowski S., *Od konfrontacji do koncyliacji – historia irlandzkiej partii Sinn Féin [From confrontation to conciliation – the history of the Irish Sinn Féin party]*, Kalisz 2010.
Bachrynowski S., *Sojusznicy i wrogowie Irlandii na arenie międzynarodowej w myśli politycznej irlandzkiego ruchu republikańskiego [Allies and Enemies*

of Ireland on International Scene in the Political Thought of Irish Republican Movement], "Facta Simonidis," 2008, nr 1 (1), pp. 121–139.
Bardon J., *The Plantation of Ulster: The British Colonisation of the North of Ireland in the Seventeenth Century*, Dublin 2011.
Barnard T. C., *A New Anatomy of Ireland: The Irish Protestants 1649–1770*, New Haven 2003.
Barnard T. C., *The Kingdom of Ireland, 1641–1760*, Basingstoke 2004.
Barry F., *Industry and Policy in Independent Ireland, 1922–1972*, Oxford, 2023.
Barry F., *Ireland – Politics, Institutions and Post-war Economic Growth*, "CESifo Forum" 1/2008, pp. 1–12.
Bartlett T., *Ireland during the Revolutionary and Napoleonic Wars, 1791–1815*, in: T. Bartlett (ed.), *Cambridge History of Ireland, vol. III…*, op. cit., pp. 74–95.
Benson D., *A Divided Country: The Feasibility of a United Ireland*, "The Yale Review of International Studies: Yale's Undergraduate Global Affairs Journal," published online.
Biagini E. F., *Home Rule for Ireland (1874–1914): the Great Missed Opportunity?*, "Études anglaises," 2018/3, Vol. 71, pp. 259–275.
Biskup P., *Brexit z perspektywy "długiego trwania": między suwerennością, federalizmem i równowagą siły* [Brexit from a 'long-term' perspective: between sovereignty, federalism and the balance of power], in: S. Bachrynowski (ed.), *Brexit a francusko-niemiecka rywalizacja o przywództwo w Unii Europejskiej* [Brexit and the Franco-German rivalry for leadership in the European Union], Warszawa 2024, pp. 15–100.
Bouyoux Barthélémy C., *The Role of Minor Political Parties in the Republic of Ireland*, "Nordic Irish Studies," Vol. 17, No. 2 (2018), pp. 167–184.
Bowyer Bell J., *The Secret Army: A History of the I.R.A.*, London 1972.
Brennan J., *Ireland and the European Union: Mapping Domestic Modes of Adaptation and Contestation*, published online.
Broin L., *Revolutionary Underground: The Story of the Irish Republican Brotherhood 1858–1924*, Dublin 1976.
Bruton J., *The Redmond Family in Parliamentary Politics*, "An Irish Quarterly Review," Vol. 107, No. 426, Summer 2018, pp. 176–184.
Cahillane L., Coffey D. K., *The Centenary of the Irish Free State Constitution, Constituting a Polity?*, Dublin 2024.
Campbell K. L., *Ireland's History: Prehistory to the Present*, Bloomsbury 2014.
Canning Paul P. M., *The impact of Éamon de Valera: domestic causes of the Anglo-Irish economic war*, "Albion," 15.3 (1983), pp. 179–205.

Chisholm H., (ed.), *Test Acts*, *"Encyclopædia Britannica,"* Vol. 26 (11th ed.) Cambridge University Press 1911.

Chojan A., *Brexit and its Impact on Poland's Policy Towards Europe – An Attempt to Forecast*, "Studia Europejskie – Studies in European Affairs" 2020, nr 2, s. 94.

Chubb B., *The Politics of the Irish constitution*, Dublin 1991.

Clark G., *Britain and Ireland: Ambiguities of Empire*, University of Exeter, published online.

Coffey D. K., *The Commonwealth and the Oath of Allegiance Crisis: A Study in Inter-War Commonwealth Relations*, "The Journal of Imperial and Commonwealth History," 2016, vol. 44, no. 3, pp. 492–512.

Connolly S. J., *Divided Kingdom: Ireland 1630–1800*, Oxford 2008.

Connolly S. J., *Religion, Law and Power: The Making of Protestant Ireland 1660–1760*, Oxford 1993

Corish P. J., The Cromwellian Regime, 1650–60, in: T. W. Moody, F. X. Martin and F. J. Byrne (ed.), *A New History of Ireland*, Oxford 1976, vol. 3.

Cosgrove A. (ed.), A New History of Ireland: Volume II, Medieval Ireland 1169–1534, Oxford 2008; B. Smith, T. Bartlett (eds.), *The Cambridge History of Ireland: Volume 1, 600–1550*, Cambridge 2018.

Cosgrove A. (ed.), *A New History of Ireland II: Medieval Ireland*, Oxford 1987.

Croinin D., *Early Medieval Ireland, 400–1200 (Longman History of Ireland)*, Harlow 1995.

Cronin J. J., Lenihan P., *Wars of Religion, 1641–1691*, in: J. Ohlmeyer (ed.), *Cambridge History of Ireland, Volume 1I: 1550 – 1730*, Cambridge 2018, pp. 246–272.

Crotty W., *The "Celtic Tiger": Economic Modernization and its Social and Political Ramifications in Ireland*, in: Catherine Maignant (ed.) *Le Tigre celtique en question L'Irlande contemporaine : économie, État, société*, Caen 1999, pp. 119–136.

Crowley A. E., *Law and the Irish Language / An dlí agus an Ghaeilge: ceachtanna staire. An tUltach*, Leeds 2014.

Cruise O'Brien C., *Parnell and His Party, 1880–1890*, Oxford 1964.

Crutchley P., *IRA Ceasefire 20 years On: The Priest Who Brokered the Peace*, "BBC News" 31st of August 2014.

CSO Report, *Ireland and the EU 1973–2003 Economic and Social Change*, published online.

Cullen L. M., *The Irish Diaspora of the Seventeenth and Eighteenth Centuries*, in: N. Canny (ed.), *Europeans on the Move: Studies on European Migration 1500–1800*, Oxford 1994.
Curtis E., *A History of Ireland: From Earliest Times to 1922*, London 2002.
Daly M. E., *The Irish Free State and the Great Depression of the 1930s: The Interaction of the Global and the Local*, "Irish Economic and Social History," Vol. 38 (2011), pp. 19–36.
Davies N., *The Isles. A History*, Oxford 1999.
Department of Foreign Affairs, *Ireland and the EU: A History*, published online.
Diamond P., Colfer B., *Irish Unification After Brexit*, "CIRSD Horizons," Spring 2023, Issue no 23, https://www.cirsd.org/en/horizons/horizons-spring-2023---issue-no23/irish-unification-after-brexit and Institute for Government, *Irish Reunification Explainer*, published online.
Dickson D., *New Foundations: Ireland 1660–1800*, Dublin 1987.
Dillon G., *The Irish Republican Brotherhood*, "University Review," Vol. 2, No. 8 (Winter, 1961), pp. 25–33.
Doherty M. A., *Kevin Barry and the Anglo-Irish Propaganda War*, "Irish Historical Studies," Vol. 32, No. 126 November 2000, pp. 217–223.
Dolan A., *Politics, Economy and Society in the Irish Free State, 1922– 1939*, in: T. Bartlett, (ed.), *Cambridge History of Ireland, Volume 1V:* from the 1880s to the present, Cambridge 2018, pp. 323–348.
Dorney J., *Peace after the Final Battle: The Story of the Irish Revolution, 1912–1924*, New Island 2014.
Dorney J., *The Civil War in Dublin: The Fight for the Irish Capital, 1922–1924*, Dublin 2017.
Doyle J., Connolly E., *Brexit and the Future of Northern Ireland*, "DCU Brexit Institute" Working Paper, N. 1-2017, published online.
Doyle O., Kenny D., McCrudden C., *The Constitutional Politics of a United Ireland*, in: O. Doyle, A. McHarg and J. Murkens (eds.), *The Brexit Challenge for Ireland and the United Kingdom: Constitutions under Pressure*, Cambridge 2021.
Drong L., *Doing justice to the troubles: Imaginary reconciliations and restorative memory in post-agreement Northern Ireland*, "Arts & Cultural Studies Review," 2018, Issue 3 (37), pp. 409–425.
Dryburgh P., *The End of the Bruce Invasion of Ireland*, 1318, online.
Dudley Edwards R., Moody T. W., *The History of Poynings' Law : Part I, 1494–1615*, "Irish Historical Studies," Volume 2 , Issue 8 , September 1941, pp. 415 – 424.

Duffy S. (ed.), *The World of the Galloglass: Kings, Warlords and Warriors in Ireland and Scotland 1200 – 1600*, Dublin 2007; "New World Encyclopedia."
Duffy S., *Ireland in the Middle Ages*, London 1997.
Duffy S., *Medieval Ireland: An Encyclopedia*, Routledge, London 2005.
Duffy S., *Narrative: 1169 and all that*, "History Ireland" Issue 3, May/June 2019, Volume 27.
Dunphy R., *The Making of Fianna Fáil Power in Ireland 1923–1948*, Oxford 1995, pp. 30–73.
Edwards D., *Beyond Reform: Martial Law & the Tudor reconquest of Ireland*, "History Ireland," Issue 2, Summer 1997, Volume 5.
Elton G. R., *The Tudor Revolution in Government*, Cambridge 1953.
English B., *William the Conqueror and Anglo-Norman Succession*, "Historical Research," Vol. LXIV, No. 155, October 1991, pp. 221–236.
English R., *Armed Struggle: The History of the IRA*, London 2003.
Fanning R., *Anglo-Irish Relations: Partition and the British Dimension in Historical Perspective*, "Irish Studies in International Affairs," Vol. 2, No. 1 (1985), pp. 1–20
Farrell M., *Fine Gael and Fianna Fáil: 'Civil War' Parties?* Published online.
Farrell M., *Reflections on the Northern Ireland Civil Rights Movement: Fifty Years On*, Paper.
Feeney B., *Sinn Féin. One Hundred Turbulent Years*, Dublin 2002.
Féron E., *Prisoners of History? British-Irish Relations and the Conflict in Northern Ireland*, "European Review of International Studies," Volume 1, Issue 3, 2014, pp. 3–15.
Ferriter D., *The Border: The Legacy of a Century of Anglo-Irish Politics*, London 2019.
FitzGerald M., *Ireland's Relations With the EEC: From the Treaties of Rome to Membership*, "Journal of European Integration History," 2001, 7(1), pp. 11–24.
Flanagan M. T., *Hiberno-Papal Relations in the Late Twelfth Century*, "Archivium Hibernicum," Vol. 34 (1977), pp. 55–70.
Flanagan M. T., *Irish Society, Anglo–Norman Settlers, Angevin Kingship*, Oxford 1989.
Flechner R., Meeder S. (eds.), *The Irish in Early Medieval Europe: Identity, Culture and Religion*, Montgomery 2016.
for conference at George Mitchell Institute, Queen's University, and Belfast: Human Rights.
Frame R., *Colonial Ireland, 1169–1369*, Dublin 1981.

Frame R., *'Les Engleys Nées en Irlande': The English Political Identity in Medieval Ireland*, "Transactions of the Royal Historical Society," Vol. 3 (193), pp. 83–103.

Frame R., *The Bruces in Ireland, 1315–18*, "Irish Historical Studies," Vol. 19, No. 73 (March, 1974), pp. 3–37.

Futures: The Agenda for the next 50 Years, Belfast, 12th December 2018, pp. 1—6.

Gay O., Morgan B., *Northern Ireland: political developments since 1972*, House of Commons, "Research Paper," 98/57.

Geoghegan P. M., *The Impact of O'Connell, 1815–1850*, in: T. Bartlett (ed.), *Cambridge History of Ireland, vol. III…*, op. cit., pp. 102–127.

George Boyce D., *Nationalism in Ireland*, Routledge, London 1995.

Gibney J., *Ireland leaves the Commonwealth, 1949*, in: "RIA Documents on Irish Foreign Policy," 18th April 2019, published online.

Gillespie R., *Colonial Ulster: The Settlement of East Ulster, 1600–1641*, Cork 1985.

Gillespie R., *Seventeenth-Century Ireland: Making Ireland Modern*, Dublin 2006.

Girvin B., *Nationalism and the Continuation of Political Conflict in Ireland*, in: B. Girvin (ed.), *Ireland North and South: Perspectives from Social Science*. Dublin 1999.

Girvin B., *Stability, Crisis and Change in Post- war Ireland 1945–1973*, in: T. Bartlett, (ed.), *Cambridge History of Ireland, Volume 1V: From the 1880s to the Present*, Cambridge 2018, pp. 381—406.

Głogowski A., *The impact of Brexit on the security of Northern Ireland. A case study*, "International Journal of Humanities Social Science and Management (IJHSSM)," Volume 5, Issue 1, Jan.–Feb., 2025, pp. 841–851.

Golden S., *Towards a referendum for reunification in Ireland?*, "CIDOB opinion," no 791, February 2024, published online.

Grey C., *Brexit Unfolded. How No One Got what They Wanted (and why They Were Never Going To)*, London 2023.

Guelke A., *The International System and the Northern Ireland Peace Process*, Working Papers in British-Irish Studies No. 21, 2002 Institute for British-Irish Studies University College, pp. 1–14.

Gurk J. J. N., *Ireland before the Norman Conquest*, "History Today," Volume 16, Issue 2, February 1966, "The Irish Post."

Harper-Bill C., van Houts E. (eds.), *A Companion to the Anglo-Norman World*, Suffolk 2003.

Heal F., *Reformation in Britain and Ireland*, Oxford 2005.
Henig D., *Negotiating Uncertainty in UK-EU Relations: Past, Present, and Future*, "ECIPE Policy Briefs," No. 17/202, 2024, pp. 1–20, published online.
Hennessey T., *The Northern Ireland Peace Process: Ending the Troubles?*, Dublin 2000.
Hession P., *Riding three horses at once: Ireland's EU membership as a national development strategy*, 2019, "Renewal," 27:2, pp. 64–74.
Hewitt M., *1798. The Year of Revolution*, Dublin 1998.
Hobolt S., *The Brexit vote: a divided nation, a divided continent*, "Journal of European Public Policy," 23 (9), (2016), pp. 1259–1277.
Holland M., *The synod of Kells in ms BL, Add. 4783*, "Peritia," Volume 19, pp. 164–172.
Hopkins S., *Sinn Féin, the Past and Political Strategy: The Provisional Irish Republican Movement and the Politics of 'Reconciliation,'* "Irish Political Studies," no 30(1), January 2015.
Hoppen K. T., Riding a Tiger: Daniel O'Connell, Reform, and. Popular Politics in Ireland, 1800–1847, in: T. Blanning and P. Wende (eds.), "Proceedings of British Academy," 1999, pp. 121–143.
Hoya E., *Provocation, Premeditation, and Pandemonium: The Irish Rebellion of 1641*, online.
Hunter R. J. (ed.), *Plantations in Ulster, 1600–41, A Collection of Documents*, Belfast 2019.
Ingraham J., *The Irish Peace Process*, published online CAIN website.
Jackson A., *Home Rule: An Irish History 1800–2000*, London 2003.
Jackson A., *The Two Unions: Ireland, Scotland and the Survival of the United Kingdom, 1707– 2007*, Oxford 2015.
Johnston W., *1300 – 1450: The Norman Decline, online.*
Joyce P. W., *Concise History of Ireland*, Dublin 1910, pp. 260–274.
Kautt W. H., *Militarising Policemen. The various members of the RIC and their response to IRA violence in Ireland, 1919–21*, Conference Paper, May 2003, pp. 1–17.
Kee R., *Ireland: A History*, London 1982.
Kelly C. J., Tannam E., More of the same or a new opportunity for British-Irish relations? "The Constitution Unit" blog, 5th of March 2025, published online.
Kelly J., *Poynings' Law and the Making of Law in Ireland, 1660–1800*, Dublin 2006.
Kelly J., *The Politics of Protestant Ascendancy, 1730– 1790*, in: T. Bartlett (ed.), *Cambridge History of Ireland, Volume 1II: 1730–1880*, pp. 48–73.

Kennedy M., *Irish Foreign Policy: 1919 to 1973*, in: T. Bartlett, (ed.), *Cambridge History of Ireland, Volume 1V: From the 1880s to the Present*, Cambridge 2018, pp. 611–621.

Keown G., *First of the Small Nations: The Beginnings of Irish Foreign Policy in the Inter-War Years*, 1919–1932, Oxford 2016.

Keown G., *Knocking on the Door: The Irish Presence at the Paris Peace Conference of 1919*, "Irish Studies in International Affairs," Vol. 30, 2019, pp. 41–57.

Kettle T. M., *A Note on Sinn Fein in Ireland*, "The North American Review," Vol. 187, No. 626, January 1908.

Kinealy Ch., *A Death-Dealing Famine: The Great Hunger in Ireland*, London 1997.

Knapp, *Church of Ireland Denomination*, online.

Knirck J., *Afterimage of the Revolution. Cumann na nGaedheal and Irish Politics, 1922–1932*, Madison 2014.

Konarski W., *Pragmatycy i idealiści. rodowód, typologia i ewolucja ugrupowań politycznych nacjonalizmu irlandzkiego w XX wieku* [*The origins, typology and evolution of the political parties of Irish nationalism in the 20th century*], Warszawa-Pułtusk, 2001.

Kowalski A. M., *The Regional Policy of the European Union in Ireland* [*Polityka regionalna Unii Europejskiej w Irlandii*], "Gospodarka Narodowa," Nr 4/2005, pp. 73–98.

Laffan M., *Resurrection of Ireland: The Sinn Féin Party 1916–23*, Cambridge 1999.

Landow C., McBride J., *Moving Past the Troubles: The Future of Northern Ireland Peace*, "CFR Reports – Backgrounder," published online.

Lawlor H. J., *A Fresh Authority for the Synod of Kells, 1152*, "Proceedings of the Royal Irish Academy: Archaeology, Culture, History, Literature," Vol. 36 (1921 – 1924), pp. 16–22.

Lowry D., *New Ireland, Old Empire and the Outside World, 1922–49: The Strange Evolution of a Dictionary Republic*, in: Cronin, M., Regan, J. M. (eds.), Ireland. The Politics of Independence, London 2000.

Lowry D., *The captive dominion: imperial realities behind Irish diplomacy, 1922–49*, "Irish Historical Studies," Volume XXXVI, No. 142, November 2008, pp. 202–226.

Lowry D., *The Neutral Dominion: Ireland and the British Empire in the Second World War*, "Global War Studies," Volume 7, Number 1, 2010, pp. 37–46.

Lucas K., *Developments in the Political Thought of Theobald Wolfe Tone*, PhD thesis The Open University 2020, pp. 258, published online.

Lydon J., *The Impact of the Bruce Invasion, 1315–27*, in: Art Cosgrove (ed.), *A New History of Ireland: Volume II, Medieval Ireland 1169–1534*, Dublin 2008.
Lydon J. F., *The Lordship of Ireland in the Middle Ages*, Toronto 1972, pp. 82–119.
Lyons F. S. L., *Charles Stewart Parnell*, Dublin 1977.
Lyons F. S. L., *Ireland since the Famine*, London 1981.
Mac Dermot F., *Theobald Wolfe Tone and His Times*, Dublin 1969.
Mac Ginty R. et al., *No War, No Peace: Northern Ireland after the Agreement*, "Political Psychology," Vol. 28, No. 1, 2007, pp. 1–11.
MacGarry F., *Easter Rising (Great Britain and Ireland)*, published online.
Maillot A., *The New Sinn Fein: Irish Republicanism in the Twenty-First Century*, New York 2004.
Maple J., *Anglo-Norman Conquest of Ireland and the Irish Economy: Stagnation or Stimulation?*, "The Historian," Vol. 52, No. 1, November 1989, p. 61.
Martin F. X., MacNeill E., *Eoin MacNeill on the 1916 Rising*, "Irish Historical Studies," Vol. 12, No. 47, March 1961, pp. 226–271.
Matthijs M. , Toenshoff C. , *Brexit, British Politics and European Integration*, Political Science 2019, "Oxford Bibliographies," published online.
Mc Garry F., *Revolution, 1916–1923*, in: T. Bartlett, (ed.), *Cambridge History of Ireland, Volume 1V:* from the 1880s to the present, Cambridge 2018, p. 258, and P. S. O'Hegarty, *The Victory of Sinn Féin* (new edn., University College Dublin Press) Dublin 2015.
McBride I., *The Tyranny of Majorities: Democracy, Brexit and the Northern Irish Border*, in: J. Mair, S. Mccabe, N. Fowler, L. Budd (eds), *Brexit and Northern Ireland: Bordering on Confusion?*, Goring-By-Sea 2019.
McCaffrey L. J., *The Irish Question: 1800–1922*, London 1968.
McCavitt J., *The Flight of the Earls, 1607*, "Irish Historical Studies," Vol. 29, No. 114 (Nov., 1994), pp. 159–173.
Mcconville S., *Irish Political Offenders, 1848–1922: Theatres of War*, New York 2002.
McCormick T., *Restoration Ireland, 1660–1688*, in: A. Jackson (ed.), *The Oxford Handbook of Modern Irish History*, Oxford 2014.
McDonough, T. (ed.), *Was Ireland a Colony? Economics, Politics and Culture in Nineteenth-Century Ireland*, Dublin 2005.
McGlinchey M., *Irish Nationalist and Republican Attitudes to the Good Friday Agreement: Sell-Out or Steppingstone?*, "Treatises and Documents Journal of Ethnic Studies" [Razprave in Gradivo Revija za Narodnostna Vpršanja], nr 90/2023, pp. 79–95.

McGraw S., Whelan K., *Daniel O'Connell in Comparative Perspective, 1800–50*, "Eire-Ireland; a journal of Irish studies," Number 40, 1 and 2(1), January 2005, pp. 60–89.
McNamee C., *The Wars of the Bruces: Scotland, England and Ireland 1306–1328*, Edinburgh 1997.
Mitchell D., Tannam E., Wallace S., *The Agreement's impact on political cooperation*, "Irish Political Studies," 33:3 (2018), pp. 283–310.
Mohr T., *British Imperial Statutes and Irish Sovereignty: Statutes Passed After the Creation of the Irish Free State*, "Journal of Legal History," nr 32 (1), 2011, pp. 61–85.
Mohr T., *The Statute of Westminster, 1931: An Irish Perspective*, "Law and History Review," 31 (4), 2013, pp. 749–791.
Moloney E., *A Secret History of the IRA*, New York 2003.
Morrow D., *Transformation or Truce? Tracing the Decline of "Reconciliation" and Its Consequences for Northern Ireland Since 1998*, "Treatises and Documents Journal of Ethnic Studies" [Razprave in Gradivo Revija za Narodnostna Vpršanja] , nr 90/2023, pp. 45–61.
Mulhall D., *Our History 1921 – London October-December 1921*, published online.
Mulhall D., *Three Great Irish Parliamentarians: O'Connell, Parnell and Redmond*, published online.
Mulholland M., *The Longest War: Northern Ireland's Troubled History*, Oxford 2004.
Murphy G., *A Measurement of the Extent of Our Sovereignty at the Moment': Sovereignty and the Question of Irish Entry to the EEC, New Evidence from the Archives Irish Studies in International Affairs*, "Irish Studies in International Affairs," Vol. 12 (2001), pp. 191–202.
Murphy G., *The Politics of Economic Realignment, Ireland 1948–1964*, Dissertation submitted for the degree of Ph.D. under the supervision of Professor Eunan O'Halpin, Dublin City University Business School Dublin City University, September 1996.
Murray CRG, O'Donoghue A., *Life after Brexit: Operationalising the Belfast/ Good Friday Agreement's Principle of Consent*, "Dublin University Law Journal," (2019), vol 42(1), pp. 147–189.
Murtagh T., *Hibernian Sans-Culottes? Dublin's Artisans and Radical Politics 1790–1798*, "La Révolution française," Number 11, 2016, pp. 1–19.
Musiał-Karg M., *Operations Brexit. British referendums of 1975 and 2016 on EU membership*, "Acta Politica Polonica," 2016, 37 (3), pp. 5–18.
Nelsson R., *The day Ireland became a republic – archive, April 1949*, "Guardian," 8 April 2020, online.

Neville A., *Ireland and Denmark in the EU*, "BRIEFING," European Union History Series, EPRS – European Parliamentary Research Service, January 2022, published online.
Neville Williams E., *The Eighteenth-Century Constitution, 1688–1815: Documents and Commentary* Cambridge University Press, 1965.
NI Assembly, *After the Agreement*, published online.
Nogacz A., *The IRA and Sinn Féin during the Troubles: Two Faces of the Same Organization*, British Columbia 2012.
Ó Clabaigh C., *The Church, 1050– 1460*, in: *The Cambridge History of Ireland*, vol. 1, pp. 355–385.
Ó Corráin D., *Ireland before the Normans*, Dublin 1972.
Ó Dochartaigh N., *Bounded by Violence: Institutionalizing Local Territories in the North of Ireland*, "Nationalism and Ethnic Politics," 19:1 (2013), pp. 119–139.
Ó Siochrú M., Ciardha E. (eds.), *The Plantation of Ulster: Ideology and Practice* (Studies in Early Modern Irish History), Manchester 2012.
O'Beirne Ranelagh J., *A Short History of Ireland*, Cambridge 2012.
O'Brien B., *A Short History of the IRA: From 1916 Onwards*, Dublin 2019.
O'Brien B., *The Life of Charles S. Parnell, Vol. I 1846–1891*, London 1898.
O'Brien E., *The Years of the French: The French Revolution as a Spatio-Temporal Event*, in: E. Maher and C. Maignant (eds.), *Peter Franco-Irish Connections in Space and Time: Peregrinations and Ruminations*, Oxford 2012.
O'Connell R. et al., *The Belfast/Good Friday Agreement and Transformative Change: Promise, Power and Solidarity*, "Israel Law Review" (2023), pp. 1–33.
O'Donnell R., *Ireland's Economic Transformation Industrial Policy, European Integration and Social Partnership*, published online.
O'Donnell R., *Robert Emmet and the Rising of 1803*, Dublin 2003.
Ohlmeyer J. et al, *Ireland: 1641: Contexts and reactions*, Manchester 2013.
O'Kane E., *Anglo – Irish Relations and the Northern Ireland Peace Process: From Exclusion to Inclusion*, "Contemporary British History," 18:1, 2004, pp. 78–99.
Ollerenshaw P., *Neutrality and Belligerence: Ireland, 1939–1945*, in: T. Bartlett, (ed.), *Cambridge History of Ireland, Volume 1V: From the 1880s to the Present*, Cambridge 2018, pp. 349–378.
O'Mahony J., *Ireland's EU Referendum Experience*, "Irish Political Studies," Vol. 24, No. 4, 429–446, December 2009, pp. 429–430.
O'Neill Sh., *Critical Theory and Ethno-National Conflict: Assessing Northern Ireland's Peace Process as a Model of Conflict Resolution*, "Irish Political Studies," 22:4, 2007, pp. 411–431.

Oppenheimer A. R., *IRA, The Bombs and the Bullets: A History of Deadly Ingenuity*, Dublin 2018.
O'Rourke K., *Burn everything British but their coal: the Anglo-Irish economic war of the 1930s*, "Journal of Economic History," 51.2 (1991), pp. 357–366.
Orpen G. H., *Ireland under the Normans, 1169–1333*, Dublin 1911.
O'Sullivan D. J., *The Irish Constabularies, 1822–1922: A Century of Policing in Ireland*, Brandon 1999.
Paseta S., *Northern Ireland and Second World War, an essay*, St. Hugh College, Oxford, published online.
Pawłowska A., *Mit niezawodności – brytyjski wywiad na terenie Irlandii w przededniu wojny o niepodległość* [The myth of reliability – British intelligence in Ireland in the eve of War of Independence], "Acta Universitatis Lodziensis. Folia Historica," Issue 111, 2022, pp. 143–160.
Perceval-Maxwell M., *The Scottish Migration to Ulster in the Reign of James I*, London 1973.
Perry P., *Modernizing Ireland's Economy*, "Finance & Development," March 1965, p. 70.
Petrakos G., Sotiriou A., *Grexit and Brexit: Incidents, accidents and wake-up calls on the bumpy road of European (dis)integration*, "European Urban and Regional Studies," 2021, Vol. 28(1), pp. 20–25.
Public Record Office of Northern Ireland, *Ireland 1900–1925: Crisis, War and Revolution A Resource for 'A' Level Students*, Belfast 2021, pp. 90–100.
Quinn D. B., *Henry VIII and Ireland, 1509–34*, "Irish Historical Studies," Vol. 12, No. 48 (Sep., 1961), pp. 318–344.
Ranger P., *The World in Paris and Ireland too: The French Diplomacy of Sinn Féin, 1919–1921*, "Etudes Irlandaises," number 36–2, February 2011, pp. 36–57.
Roberts H., *Sound Stupidity: The British Party System and the Northern Ireland Question*, "Government and Opposition," vol. 22, no. 4, Oct. 1987, pp. 315–355.
Robinson P., *The Plantation of Ulster: British Settlement in an Irish Landscape, 1600–1670*, Dublin 1984.
Roche R., *The Norman Invasion of Ireland*, online.
Roulston W. J., *Researching Scots-Irish Ancestors, The Essential Genealogical Guide to Early Modern Ulster, 1600–1800*, Belfast 2005.
Ryle Dwyer T., *De Valera: The Man & the Myths*, Dublin 1992, p. 372.

Schlesinger K., *Partie skrajnie prawicowe w Unii Europejskiej wobec integracji europejskiej w latach 1992–2004* [Far-right parties in the European Union and European integration in 1992–2004], Warszawa 2024, pp. 258–261.
Simmons & Simmons, *Brexit: The Transition Period. The Legal Consequences of Brexit and Their Impact on UK Businesses*, published online.
Smith B. (ed.), *Britain and Ireland, 900–1300: Insular Responses to Medieval European Change*, Cambridge 1999.
Smith B., *Disaster and Opportunity: 1320– 1450*, in B. Smith, T. Bartlett (eds.), *op. cit.*, Cambridge 2018, pp. 244–271.
Smith B., *The Bruce Invasion and County Louth*, 1315–18, "Journal of the County Louth Archaeological and Historical Society," Vol. 22, No. 1 (1989), pp. 7–15.
Sposato P., *The Perception of Anglo-Norman 'modernity' and the Conquest of Ireland*, "In Comitatus: A Journal of Medieval and Renaissance Studies," vol. 40, 2009, pp. 25–44.
Stevens C. J., *The Londonderry Plantation, 1609–1914: The History, Architecture and Planning of the Estates of the City of London and its Livery Companies in Ulster*, Chichester 1986.
Story J., *Brexit: A Certain Idea of Europe*, "politique étrangère," 2:2017, pp. 1–12.
Svendsen O., Ruy D., *The Windsor Framework Heralds a Breakthrough in EU-UK Relations*, "CSIS Policy Paper," 6th of March 2024, publish online.
Szymanek J., *Druga izba we współczesnym parlamencie. Analiza porównawcza na przykładzie europejskich państw unitarnych* [*The second chamber in the modern parliament. Comparative analysis on the example of European unitary states*], Warszawa 2005.
Tannam E., *British-Irish Relations in the Twenty-First Century: The Good Friday Agreement, Brexit, and the Totality of Relations*, Oxford 2024, pp. 1–27.
Tannam E., *The Future of UK-Irish Relations*, "European Journal of Legal Studies," 2019, Vol. 12, SI, pp. 275–304, Special Issue on 'The Brexit negotiations and the May government'; Published online: 29 October 2019.
Taylor P., *Brits. The War Against the IRA*, London 2005.
Thomson A., *Thomas Paine and the United Irishmen*, "Etudes irlandaises," Année 1991, no 16–1, pp. 109–119.
Toboła-Pertkiewicz P., *De Valera. Gigant polityki irlandzkiej i jego epoka* [*De Valera. The giant of Irish politics and his era*], Warszawa 2014.

Tonge J., *Northern Ireland: Conflict and Change*, New York 2002.
Townshend Ch. (review), *Patrick Pearse. The Triumph of Failure* by Ruth Dudley Edwards, "The English Historical Review," Vol. 95, No. 374, January 1980, pp. 168–170.
Tulejski T., *Quo vadis Britannia? Davida Hume'a rozważania nad angielską konstytucją* [*Quo vadis Britannia? David Hume's consideration on the English constitution*], "Przegląd Sejmowy" [*The Sejm Review*], nr 4(171)/2022, pp. 163–187.
Ullmann W., *A Short History of the Papacy in the Middle Age*, London 2002, pp. 142–172.
Veach C., 'Conquest and Conquerors,' in Brendan Smith (ed.), *Cambridge History of Ireland, Volume 1: Medieval Ireland, 650–1550*, Cambridge 2018, pp. 157–181.
Warntjes I., *Regnal succession in early medieval Ireland*, "Journal of Medieval History," vol. 30, 2004, pp. 377–410.
Watt J. A., *The Church in Medieval Ireland*, Dublin 1998.
Whelan I., The Bible War in Ireland: The Second "Reformation" and the Polarization of Protestant-Catholic Relations, 1800–1840, University of Wisconsin Press, Madison 2005.
White T. J., *The Impact of British Colonialism on Irish Catholicism and National Identity: Repression, Reemergence, and Divergence*, "Études irlandaises," 35–1, 2010, pp. 21–37.
Whitten L. C., *Brexit and Strand Three of the 1998 Agreement: The Three Faces of East-West*, "The Political Quarterly," Vol. 94, No. 1, January/March 2023, pp. 122–132.
Whitten L. C., *Post-Brexit dynamism: the dynamic regulatory alignment of Northern Ireland under the Protocol on Ireland/Northern Ireland*, "Northern Ireland Legal Quarterly," NI after Brexit, Vol. 73, No S2 (2022), pp. 37–64.
Wiepking R., *The Path to Peace: Conflict Theory and Northern Ireland's Troubles (1968–1998)*, San Francisco 2011, Master's Theses. 13, published online.

Index

Note: Page references followed by "n" indicates a single note number and "nn" indicates a range or series of note numbers on the cited page.

B

Studies in Politics, Security and Society

Edited by Stanisław Sulowski

VOL. 1 Robert Wiszniowski (ed.): Challenges to Representative Democracy. A European Perspective. 2015.

VOL. 2 Jarosław Szymanek: Theory of Political Representation. 2015.

VOL. 3 Alojzy Z. Nowak (ed.): Global Financial Turbulence in the Euro Area. Polish Perspective. 2015.

VOL. 4 Jolanta Itrich-Drabarek: The Civil Service in Poland. Theory and Experience. 2015.

VOL. 5 Agnieszka Rothert: Power of Imagination. Education, Innovations and Democracy. 2016.

VOL. 6 Zbysław Dobrowolski: Combating Corruption and Other Organizational Pathologies. 2017.

VOL. 7 Vito Breda: The Objectivity of Judicial Decisions. A Comparative Analysis of Nine Jurisdictions. 2017.

VOL. 8 Anna Sroka: Accountability and democracy in Poland and Spain. 2017.

VOL. 9 Anna Sroka / Fanny Castro-Rial Garrone / Rubén Darío Torres Kumbrián (eds.): Radicalism and Terrorism in the 21st Century. Implications for Security. 2017.

VOL. 10 Filip Pierzchalski: Political Leadership in Morphogenetic Perspective. 2017.

VOL. 11 Alina Petra Marinescu: The Discursive Dimension of Employee Engagement and Disengagement. Accounts of keeping and leaving jobs in present-day Bucharest organizations. 2017.

VOL. 12 Jacek Giedrojć: Competition, Coordination, Social Order. Responsible Business, Civil Society, and Government in an Open Society. 2017.

VOL. 13 Filip Ilkowski: Capitalist Imperialism in Contemporary Theoretical Frameworks. 2017.

VOL. 14 Leszek Leszczyński / Adam Szot (eds.): Discretionary Power of Public Administration. Its Scope and Control. 2017.

VOL. 15 Tadeusz Klementewicz: Understanding Politics. Theory, Procedures, Narratives. 2017.

VOL. 16 Tomasz Bichta: Political Systems of the Former Yugoslavia. 2018

VOL. 17 Miroslav Palárik / Alena Mikulášová / Martin Hetényi / Róbert Arpáš: The City and Region Against the Backdrop of Totalitarianism. 2018

VOL. 18 Jolanta Itrich-Drabarek / Stanisław Mazur / Justyna Wiśniewska-Grzelak (eds.): The Transformations of the Civil Service in Poland in Comparison with International Experience. 2018.

VOL. 19 Jerzy Juchnowski / R. Jan Sielezin / Ewa Maj: The Image of "White" and "Red" Russia in the Polish Political Thought of the 19th and 20th Century. Analogies and Parallels. 2018.

VOL. 20 Roman Kuźniar: Europe in the International Order. 2018.

VOL. 21 Piotr Jaroszyński: Europe - the Clash of Civilisations. 2018.

VOL. 22 Stanisław Filipowicz: Truth and the Will to Illusion. 2018.

VOL. 23 Andrzej Szeptycki: Contemporary Relations between Poland and Ukraine. The "Strategic Partnership" and the Limits Thereof. 2019.

VOL. 46 Stanisław Sulowski / Tomasz Słomka (eds.): The Political System of Poland. Tradition and Contemporaneity. 2022.

VOL. 47 Ewelina Kancik-Kołtun / Josef Smolík (eds.): New Political Parties in the Party Systems of the Czech Republic. 2022.

VOL. 48 Ewa Feder-Sempach: Economic Populism in British and American Political Discourse. A Comparative Analysis of Boris Johnson's and Donald Trump's Speeches. 2022.

VOL. 49 Katarzyna Kołodziejczyk (ed.): The EU Towards the Global South During the COVID19 Pandemic. 2022.

VOL. 50 Silvia Amato: Public Undertakings of Nuclear Waste Storage. The Role of the Government in the Dissemination of Public Knowledge. 2022.

VOL. 51 Agnieszka Cholewińska-Nielsen: Evolving Humanitarianism. The Work of the International Red Cross and Red Crescent Movement. 2022.

VOL. 52 Josef Smolik / Ewelina Kancik-Kołtun: New Political Parties in the Party System of Poland. 2023.

VOL. 53 Rafał Wiśniewski / Elżbieta Szyszlak / Radosław Zenderowski (eds.): Cultural Security. Theory – Selected Aspects – Case Studies. 2023.

VOL. 54 Filip Pierzchalski: Political Leadership: Structure – Consciousness – Emotions. 2023.

VOL. 55 Łukasz Zamęcki / Li-Jiuan Chen-Rabich (eds.): The Democratisation Process of Poland and Taiwan: Comparative Perspective. 2023.

VOL. 56 Marcin Gajek: Refusing to be Forgotten: Southern Conservatism and the Political Thought of M. E. Bradford. 2023.

VOL. 57 Sulowski Stanisław (ed.): Security Challenges at the Dawn of a New International Order. 2023.

VOL. 58 Alicja Z. Nowak / Kinga Anna Gajda (eds.): University and War in Ukraine. 2023.

VOL. 59 Bernard Wiśniewski / Paulina Polko (eds.): Contemporary Understanding of Security and Its Contexts. 2024.

VOL. 60 Aleksander Żołnierski / Dariusz Jaruga (eds.): Big Data. Post-truth and Disinformation in Politics and Economy during Times of Conflict. 2024.

VOL. 61 Mirosław Karwat / Marcin Tobiasz / Jacek Ziółkowski (eds.): Constituents of Political Theory (2). Selected Articles by the Warsaw School of Political Theory. 2025.

VOL. 62 Katarzyna Stachurska-Szczesiak: Sustainable Development. Theoretical Approach. 2025.

VOL. 63 Joanna Sanecka-Tyczyńska: Reason of State in Contemporary Polish Political Thought. 2025.

VOL. 64 Agnieszka Kampka / Wojciech Mincewicz (eds.): A Worrying Present and an Uncertain Future. Challenges for Security in Central and Eastern Europe Region. 2025.

VOL. 65 Robert Geisler / Tomasz Pawłuszko (eds.): Public Policy and Local Crises. Lessons from Poland and Central Europe. 2025.

VOL. 66 Kinga Anna Gajda (ed.): The Collapse of the Bipolar World and the New Identity in Eastern Europe and Its Sub-Regions. 2026.

VOL. 67 Szymon Bachrynowski: Ireland and the United Kingdom: A Century of Relations (1921–2021). 2026.

FSC
www.fsc.org
MIX
Papier | Fördert gute Waldnutzung
FSC® C083411

Kolibri 360 GmbH
Ferdinand-Jühlke-Straße 7
99095 Erfurt, Deutschland
produktsicherheit@kolibri360.de

Druck:
CPI Druckdienstleistungen GmbH
im Auftrag der
Kolibri 360 GmbH
Ferdinand-Jühlke-Str. 7
99095 Erfurt